NATIONAL DIRECTORY
for CATECHESIS

NATIONAL DIRECTORY
for CATECHESIS

UNITED STATES CONFERENCE OF CATHOLIC BISHOPS

United States Conference of Catholic Bishops
Washington, D.C.

The *National Directory for Catechesis* was developed by the Committee on Education and the Committee on Catechesis of the United States Conference of Catholic Bishops (USCCB). It was approved by the full body of U.S. Catholic bishops at its June 2003 General Meeting, received the subsequent *recognitio* of the Holy See, and has been authorized for publication by the undersigned.

Msgr. William P. Fay
General Secretary, USCCB

Contents

Abbreviations

AA — *Decree on the Apostolate of the Lay People (Apostolicam Actuositatem)*
AG — *Decree on the Church's Missionary Activity (Ad Gentes Divinitus)*
AN — *On Social Communications on the Twentieth Anniversary of "Communio et Progressio" (Aetatis Novae)*
CA — *On the Hundredth Anniversary of Rerum Novarum (Centesimus Annus)*
CCC — *Catechism of the Catholic Church*
CD — *Decree on the Pastoral Office of Bishops in the Church (Christus Dominus)*
CIC — *Code of Canon Law, Latin-English Edition, New English Translation*
CL — *The Vocation and Mission of the Lay Faithful in the Church and in the World (Christifideles Laici)*
CT — *On Catechesis in Our Time (Catechesi Tradendae)*
DD — *Keeping the Lord's Day Holy (Dies Domini)*
DI — *On the Unicity and Salvific Universality of Jesus Christ and the Church (Dominus Iesus)*
DS — *Enchiridio Symbolorum*
DV — *Dogmatic Constitution on Divine Revelation (Dei Verbum)*
EA — *The Church in America (Ecclesia in America)*
ECE — *Ex corde Ecclesiae*
EE — *On the Eucharist (Ecclesia de Eucharistia)*
EN — *On Evangelization in the Modern World (Evangelii Nuntiandi)*
EV — *The Gospel of Life (Evangelium Vitae)*
FC — *On the Family (Familiaris Consortio)*
FD — *On the Publication of the "Catechism of the Catholic Church" (Fidei Depositum)*
GDC — *General Directory for Catechesis*
GIRM — *General Instruction of the Roman Missal*
GS — *Pastoral Constitution on the Church in the Modern World (Gaudium et Spes)*
HV — *On the Regulation of Birth (Humanae Vitae)*
IM — *Decree on the Mass Media (Inter Mirifica)*
LG — *Dogmatic Constitution on the Church (Lumen Gentium)*
LM — *Apostolic Letter in Which the Latin Typical Edition of the "Catechism of the Catholic Church" Is Approved and Promulgated (Laetamur Magnopere)*
MusSacr — *Instruction on Music in the Liturgy (Musicam Sacram)*
NA — *Declaration on the Relation of the Church to Non-Christian Religions (Nostra Aetate)*
NPI — *National Parish Inventory*
OE — *Decree on the Catholic Eastern Churches (Orientalium Ecclesiarum)*
OHWB — *Our Hearts Were Burning Within Us: A Pastoral Plan for Adult Faith Formation in the United States*
OS — *Reserving Priestly Ordination to Men Alone (Ordinatio Sacerdotalis)*
PO — *Decree on the Ministry and Life of Priests (Presbyterorum Ordinis)*

PT   *Peace on Earth (Pacem in Terris)*
RCIA   *Rite of Christian Initiation of Adults*
RM   *On the Permanent Validity of the Church's Missionary Mandate*
        (Redemptoris Missio)
RP   *Reconciliation and Penance (Reconciliatio et Paenitentia)*
RV   *Renewing the Vision: A Framework for Catholic Youth Ministry*
SC   *Constitution on the Sacred Liturgy (Sacrosanctum Concilium)*
SRS   *On Social Concerns (Sollicitudo Rei Socialis)*
TMA   *On the Coming of the Third Millennium (Tertio Millennio Adveniente)*
UUS   *That They All May Be One (Ut Unum Sint)*
UR   *Decree on Ecumenism (Unitatis Redintegratio)*
VQA   *On the Twenty-Fifth Anniversary of the Constitution on the Sacred Liturgy*
        (Vicesimus Quintus Annus)
VS   *The Splendor of Truth (Veritatis Splendor)*

NATIONAL DIRECTORY
for CATECHESIS

Introduction

Go, therefore, and make disciples of all nations,
baptizing them in the name of the Father, and of the Son,
and of the holy Spirit, teaching them to observe all that
I have commanded you. And behold, I am with you
always, until the end of the age. (Mt 28:19-20)

1. A VISION FOR THE
NATIONAL DIRECTORY FOR CATECHESIS

Jesus Christ is the unique emissary of the Father, and the apostles are the emissaries of Jesus Christ. "As the Father has sent me, so I send you."[1] The ministry of the apostles continues the mission of Christ—from the Father and in the Holy Spirit for the salvation of all.

Christ first directs his apostles to go, to set out in all directions with a specific goal in their hearts: to proclaim his Gospel and bring people into communion with God. They are not to stay where they are, wondering what to do. This sense of movement, direction, and outward orientation to embrace all in God's universal plan of salvation in Christ is vital to the authenticity and success of the mission entrusted to them by Christ. Their mission is Christ's mission: urgent, determined, and led by the Holy Spirit.

The command of Jesus Christ to his apostles sets the course from the very beginning for the Church's fundamental mission to make disciples of all nations. The Lord's missionary mandate issues from the eternal love of the Holy Trinity. In God's eternal plan of salvation in Christ and through the Spirit, the Church is the universal sacrament of that salvation and as such is missionary by nature. Her missionary dynamism is urged on by the love of Christ[2] and led by the Holy Spirit.[3] "Because she believes in God's

---

1   Jn 20:21.
2   Cf. 2 Cor 5:14.
3   Cf. John Paul II, *On the Permanent Validity of the Church's Missionary Mandate* (*Redemptoris Missio*) (RM) (Washington, D.C.: United States Conference of Catholic Bishops [USCCB], 1990), no. 21.

universal plan of salvation, the Church must be missionary."[4] In obedience to the divine command, the apostles, their successors, and their disciples have responded through the ages by enthusiastically proclaiming
the Gospel message to the whole world. That fundamental mission is
always inseparable from the person of Jesus Christ.

Jesus Christ is the energizing center of evangelization and the heart of
catechesis. Christ, the first evangelizer, is himself the Good News who proclaims the Kingdom of God and accomplishes the salvation of all by his
redemptive suffering, death, and Resurrection. Catechesis unfolds the fullness of God's eternal plan entirely in the person of Jesus Christ. He is "the
way and the truth and the life."[5] Jesus Christ is at once the message, the
messenger, the purpose of the message, and the consummation of the message. Only he can lead us to the love of the Father in the Holy Spirit and
invite us to share the life of the Holy Trinity. The work of evangelization
and catechesis is always "through [Christ] . . . in one Spirit to the Father."[6]

The Lord's missionary command charges the apostles to baptize in
the name of the Father and of the Son and of the Holy Spirit. Thus his
missionary mandate is Trinitarian in nature. It was born in the Father's
heart; it was articulated in the Son's announcement of the Kingdom of
heaven on earth, present already in mystery in the Church; it is continually sanctified by the presence and guidance of the Holy Spirit. The ultimate purpose of this mission is to incorporate men and women into the
communion between the Father and the Son in their Spirit of love.[7]

According to the plan of the Father, the Church has as her origin the
mission of the Son and the Holy Spirit.[8] According to the divine plan of
redemption, the Father sends the Son. He created man and woman to
share his own divine life. That communion of God and humanity is
brought about in the Church.

Jesus Christ, the eternal Son of the Father, instituted the Church in
order to accomplish the Father's plan of salvation for all. Christ proclaimed

4   Catechism of the Catholic Church (CCC), 2nd. ed. (Washington, D.C.: USCCB-Libreria Editrice Vati-
     cana, 2000), no. 851.
5   Jn 14:6.
6   Eph 2:18.
7   Cf. RM, no. 23.
8   Cf. Second Vatican Council, Decree on the Church's Missionary Activity (Ad Gentes Divinitus) (AG), no.
     2, in Austin Flannery, Vatican Council II: Vol. 1: The Conciliar and Post Conciliar Documents (new rev. ed.)
     (Northport, N.Y.: Costello Publishing, 1996). All subsequent Vatican II references come from the Flan-
     nery edition, unless otherwise noted.

the Good News of the coming of the Kingdom of God for all to hear and respond. In fact he inaugurated the Kingdom in his person. The Church is "the kingdom of Christ already present in mystery."[9]

The Holy Spirit is the "principal agent for the accomplishment of this work in the human spirit and in the history of the world."[10] He leads the Church on her mission, following in the footsteps of her founder to bring glad tidings to the poor, liberty to captives, and sight to the blind—always unfolding the mystery of Christ in the mission of the Church.

It is Christ who gives the great commission to the apostles. He entrusts the continuation of his own mission to them. In fact, he prays that he may be in them as the Father is in him.[11] Christ is the center of salvation history and the end toward which human history is being drawn. The apostles are to announce the salvation won by Christ to all the world and are to gather the many nations into communion with him. This missionary mandate is "Christocentric" by its very nature. It origi-nates in him; it conveys the truth about him and reaches the end toward which he directs it. The Gospel message is precisely the Good News of Jesus Christ. It can be centered on no one other than Jesus Christ.

Christ's commission to his apostles involves teaching Christ and the teachings of Christ. In fulfilling their apostolic commission, the twelve are to transmit the teachings of Christ, the truth that he communicates—or to put it more precisely, the Truth that he is.[12] Like their Master, the apostles must declare, "My teaching is not my own but is from the one who sent me."[13] This is true not only because Christ gave them his teachings, but also because Christ gave them himself. Like St. Paul, they must confess, "I received from the Lord what I also handed on to you."[14] This is true not only because they did not conceive the teachings, but also because they must in turn preserve the teachings until the end of the age.

After Jesus completed the task given him by the Father and his phys-ical presence was taken from his apostles, he did not leave them orphans. Jesus sent his Spirit, and through his Spirit, Christ abides eternally within the Church and her apostolic mission to go, make disciples, baptize, and

---

9   Second Vatican Council, *Dogmatic Constitution on the Church (Lumen Gentium)* (LG), no. 3.
10   RM, no. 21.
11   Cf. Jn 17:23.
12   Cf. Jn 14:6.
13   Jn 7:16.
14   1 Cor 11:23.

teach. By communicating his Spirit, Christ mystically constitutes as his body the faithful gathered together from every nation.[15]

Jesus entrusted a divine mission to his apostles, and it will continue until the end of time. The Gospel that the apostles handed on is "the principle of all of [the Church's] life for all time."[16] Their office and ministry has permanence. For the Church, "time" is the time of the Risen Christ who promised to be with us always. The living presence of the Risen Christ in the Church anticipates the fulfillment of the Church as the Kingdom of God at "the end of the age." The Church herself is the living witness to the Risen Lord, for her life and activity are a constant testimonial that Jesus lives.

In obedience to the divine command, the apostles, their successors, and their disciples have responded through the ages by enthusiastically proclaiming the Gospel message to the whole world. That fundamental mission is always inseparable from the person of Jesus Christ.

Catechesis is the word used to describe this essential ministry of the Church through which the teachings of Christ have been passed on to believers throughout the ages. Pope John Paul II in the apostolic exhortation *Catechesi Tradendae* proposes the following description of the ministry of catechesis:

> Quite early on, the name *catechesis* was given to the totality of the Church's efforts to make disciples, to help men believe that Jesus is the Son of God so that believing they might have life in his name, and to educate and instruct them in this life, thus building up the body of Christ.[17]

> "Catechesis is an *education in the faith* of children, young people, and adult which includes especially the teaching of Christian doctrine imparted, generally speaking, in an organic and systematic way, with a view to initiating the hearers into the fullness of Christian life."[18]

---

15   Cf. LG, no. 7.
16   LG, no. 20.
17   CCC, no. 4; cf. John Paul II, *On Catechesis in Our Time* (Catechesi Tradendae) (CT) (Washington, D.C.: USCCB, 1979), nos. 1, 2.
18   CCC, no. 5, quoting CT, no. 18.

In the years since the Second Vatican Council, the ministry of cate-chesis has received renewed emphasis in the Church.

2. RENEWAL OF CATECHESIS

The renewal of catechesis called for by the Second Vatican Council resulted in the promulgation of the first *General Catechetical Directory* in 1971.[19] The years since its promulgation have been a remarkable period for the reorientation and promotion of catechesis in the universal Church. The publication for the Latin Church of the *Rite of Christian Initiation of Adults* in 1972 has proved especially useful for catechetical renewal. In his apostolic exhortation *On Evangelization in the Modern World* (*Evangelii Nuntiandi*), Pope Paul VI articulated an important principle for the renewal of catechesis when he described catechesis as a work of evangelization in the context of the mission of the Church.[20] Pope John Paul II further developed this concept in his apostolic exhortation *On Catechesis in Our Time* (*Catechesi Tradendae*), in which he described cate-chesis as a very remarkable moment "in the whole process of evangeliza-tion."[21] Throughout his pontificate, Pope John Paul II has vigorously con-tributed to the worldwide renewal of catechesis through his many encyclical letters, apostolic exhortations, and discourses.

Guided by these documents of the Magisterium and prompted by the 1979 *Sharing the Light of Faith: National Catechetical Directory for Catholics of the United States*, the renewal of catechesis in the United States has included the recovery of some of the evangelizing enthusiasm of the early Church, a revived interest in the writings and teachings of the Fathers of the Church, and the restoration of the catechumenate. The development of catechesis has been characterized by the generous dedication of bish-ops, pastors, catechetical leaders, and catechists. Many praiseworthy ini-tiatives and efforts have produced positive results in the catechetical instruction and formation of adults, youth, and children.

---

19 For a history of the development of the *General Catechetical Directory* (1971) see its Foreword. In *Sharing the Light of Faith: National Catechetical Directory for Catholics in the United States*, see nos. 2-7 for its history. For the *Catechism of the Catholic Church*, see John Paul II, apostolic constitution *Fidei Depositum*. For the development of the *General Directory for Catechesis*, see nos. 8-13.

20 Paul VI, *On Evangelization in the Modern World* (*Evangelii Nuntiandi*) (EN) (Washington, D.C.: USCCB, 1975), no. 44.

21 CT, no. 18.

Here in the United States, the publication of this *National Directory for Catechesis* expresses our continuing pastoral care for catechetical ministry. Since the 1979 publication of *Sharing the Light of Faith*, we bishops have devoted considerable attention to catechesis and have continued to develop an important catechetical heritage in the Catholic Church in the United States. The publication of more than a dozen documents, statements, and pastoral plans to support the catechetical mission of the Church in the United States bears witness to our commitment to proclaim the Gospel.[22] It is our earnest hope that this new *National Directory for Catechesis* will be received and carefully studied in the context of the pastoral needs of each diocese and parish in the United States.

3. SIGNS OF VITALITY IN CATECHETICAL MINISTRY IN THE UNITED STATES

Ample evidence from recent years shows remarkable vitality in the ministry of catechesis in the United States.

- Sacred Scripture and Sacred Tradition remain the foundation for the Church's ministry of the word. It continues to play an essential and indispensable role in catechesis. Sacred Scripture inspires, directs, and nourishes the Church's catechetical mission.
- Documents of the universal Church as well as those we have issued as a Conference have been well received and are providing the direction for catechesis in the United States. Many dioceses have used these documents to guide the development, evaluation, and revision of their catechetical programs. Authors, editors, and publishers of catechetical texts and resources have employed these documents to improve their materials. These documents have also prompted more serious study and research in the field of catechetics.

---

22   Among these documents are *Catholic Higher Education and the Pastoral Mission of the Church*; *A Vision of Evangelization*; *Empowered by the Spirit*; *Statement in Support of Catholic Elementary and Secondary Schools*; *Guidelines for Doctrinally Sound Catechetical Materials*; *The Teaching Ministry of the Diocesan Bishop*; *Go and Make Disciples: A National Plan and Strategy for Catholic Evangelization in the United States*; *Renewing the Vision*; *Statement in Support of Catechetical Ministry*; *Sharing Catholic Social Teaching*; and *Our Hearts Were Burning Within Us*.

- As Catholic bishops of the United States, both individually and collectively, we have increased and intensified our involvement in and oversight of catechesis. On the diocesan level, many of us have become more directly involved in supervising the catechetical ministry. On the national level, as the United States Conference of Catholic Bishops (USCCB), we have established a standing Committee on Catechesis and an Ad Hoc Committee to Oversee the Use of the *Catechism of the Catholic Church.*

- Serious efforts in catechetical planning continue to characterize both diocesan and parish initiatives. Many dioceses have developed comprehensive policies that govern the catechetical mission of the diocese. These policies often include curriculum, ecumenical, Catholic-Jewish, interreligious, and sacramental guidelines; personnel procedures; and catechist formation objectives. Many parishes have developed parent handbooks that set forth the goals of the parish catechetical programs. In addition, those responsible for planning diocesan and parish catechetical programs have become more aware of the needs of racial, ethnic, and cultural groups as well as the richness that their diversity and unique contributions add to the Church.

- The increasing diversity present in most local churches has provided rich opportunities. The multiple ethnic, racial, and cultural communities make possible a spirit that renews and sustains the life of the local church.

- The formation of catechists continues to be a high priority for most dioceses and parishes in the United States. Many dioceses directly provide a systematic program of training and formation for catechists. Others work closely with Catholic colleges, universities, and other institutes of higher education to offer programs of formation and certification for catechists and catechetical leaders. On the national level, the USCCB Commission on Certification and Accreditation has approved a series of standards for the certification of parish youth ministry and catechetical leaders and lay ecclesial leaders.

- Lay involvement in the catechetical ministry continues to increase. More lay people are assuming significant responsibility and exercising leadership in catechesis on the diocesan level. In parishes throughout the country, tens of thousands of lay faithful give themselves generously to the catechetical apostolate as cate-chetical program leaders. Moreover, hundreds of thousands serve as catechists in parish catechetical programs and Catholic schools.

- Clergy and religious continue to devote themselves enthusiasti-cally to catechesis. Programs for the continuing education of the clergy and religious have notably expanded to include support for their respective roles in catechesis. We strongly encourage par-ticipation in these programs. Deacons have made significant contributions to catechesis, especially in the areas of sacramen-tal preparation, homiletics, and social justice.

- The missionary character of catechesis is more evident now than it has been in the past. Catechesis that awakens an initial faith and encourages conversion to Christ in an increasingly secular culture is bearing positive results.

- The implementation of the *Rite of Christian Initiation of Adults* in many dioceses and parishes in the United States has emphasized the need for a catechesis based more directly on the baptismal catechumenate. In this context, catechesis aims to achieve a more integral formation of the person rather than merely to com-municate information. The restored catechumenate seeks to fos-ter a committed conversation through a systematic catechesis based upon a more thorough integration of Sacred Scripture and Sacred Tradition, through liturgical catechesis, proper pastoring, and insertion into the parish community. These four aspects lead people to a life of faith in Christ, hope in his promises, and char-ity toward those in need. This life of faith, hope, and charity is nourished through communion with Jesus in the Liturgy, above all in the Eucharist.

- Adult catechesis has become more prominent, and dioceses are paying much closer attention to the centrality of adult catechesis in their pastoral programming. Lifelong catechesis is absolutely necessary for the Christian formation of the faithful. An essential dimension of the lay vocation that is sometimes overlooked or neglected is the social mission of Christians in the world. Every believer is called to serve "the least of these," to "hunger and thirst for justice," to be a "peacemaker." This social mission of the Church belongs to all of us. It is an essential part of what it is to be a believer. Being a believer means that one lives a certain way—walking with the Lord, doing justice, loving kindness, living peaceably among all people. Adult catechesis ought to include opportunities to learn and reflect upon how one is called to live out the basic principles of Catholic social teaching in family life, workplace, community, and the world. More and more, adult catechesis is understood to be the chief form of catechesis and is given priority in catechetical planning.

- In recent years, the Church's catechetical leaders and catechists have shown a greater commitment to serving the needs of persons with physical, mental, emotional, and developmental disabilities. Many more dioceses now offer special catechetical programs for persons with special needs.

- The catechetical component in a comprehensive program of youth ministry has been strengthened. Youth ministry seeks to empower young people to live as disciples of Jesus Christ, to draw them into responsible participation in the life and mission of the Church, and to foster their personal and spiritual growth. The articulated goals for diocesan and parish youth ministry programs increasingly include knowledge of the core content of the Catholic faith through a comprehensive and substantive catechesis based on the *Catechism of the Catholic Church*.[23]

- Catholic schools continue their efforts to become more authentic communities of faith and centers of evangelization. Many Catholic schools have addressed a new challenge in clarifying their distinctive Catholic identity as they have welcomed large numbers of the poor and disadvantaged, many of whom come from other Christian traditions and other faiths. These schools provide a unique situation for Catholic evangelization and a privileged context for exercising the virtue of charity toward those of other religious communities as well as for strengthening Catholic identity in the presence of other religious beliefs.

---

23 Cf. also the standards outlined in USCCB, *Renewing the Vision: A Framework for Catholic Youth Ministry* (Washington, D.C.: USCCB, 1997).

- In recent years, catechesis in the United States has included a more substantive treatment of the Church's social justice doctrine. There has been a more effective integration of the Church's social teaching. We encourage continued effort in this endeavor.
- Catechetical resources, texts, materials, and aids continue to improve. Through our Ad Hoc Committee to Oversee the Use of the *Catechism of the Catholic Church*, we bishops have initiated a process by which catechetical texts are reviewed for their conformity to the *Catechism of the Catholic Church*, with the cooperative participation of the publishers of catechetical materials.
- There is a growing awareness that effective catechesis in the United States should use the latest communication technology. The media may become essential instruments for the proclamation of the Gospel in evangelization and catechesis. Significant strides have been made in understanding the influence of the media on the culture and cultures of the United States and in employing the various communication technologies to spread the Christian message and the Church's authentic teaching in ways that make sense in the contemporary world. Catechetical leaders and catechists continue to commit themselves to developing the skills necessary to use all available technological means to proclaim the Gospel message.

These signs of vitality in catechetical ministry in the United States give witness that we do indeed speak of the "Word of Life."[24]

4. CHALLENGES IN CATECHETICAL MINISTRY IN THE UNITED STATES

Alongside these signs of vitality we find some significant challenges. Many of these challenges parallel the signs of vitality just noted.

---

24   1 Jn 1:1.

A. Challenges to Catechesis from Social and Cultural Conditions

These challenges arise from several conditions:

- The pervasive secularism of our culture and the consequent struggle to live the Catholic faith in the home, as well as to establish a Catholic culture and identity visible in the workplace and community
- Religious indifference, religious ambiguity, and the growth of sects, cults, and New Age spirituality, all of which exist side by side with the desire of many for a return to the sacred and the transcendent
- The challenge in engaging adults in lifelong formation
- The challenge of inspiring commitment of young adults to the Church in light of their distinctive characteristics, attitudes, and spiritual concerns
- The significant number of Catholic children and young people who are not enrolled in any systematic catechetical program[25]
- The need to work toward a more collaborative vision for ministry on all levels
- The challenge of encouraging and developing lay leadership in the catechetical ministry
- The variety of needs related to diverse cultures

B. Challenges to Catechesis Regarding Doctrine

These challenges raise questions about the presentation of the complete and authentic content of the faith. They require those responsible for catechesis to give greater attention to providing catechesis that

---

25 Presently in the United States, 52 percent of all Catholic school-age children are enrolled in parish-based catechetical programs; and 16 percent of Catholic elementary school-age children are enrolled in Catholic schools. Perhaps 2 percent are being home-schooled, and the percentage of Catholic young people of high school age who receive no systematic catechesis is generally much higher. Cf. Bryan T. Froehle and Mary L. Gautier, *Catholicism USA: A Portrait of the Catholic Church in the United States* (Washington, D.C.: Center for Applied Research in the Apostolate [CARA], 2000), 63-86.

- Focuses on the mystery of the Holy Trinity, the central mystery of the Christian faith, and the Trinitarian structure of the Church's beliefs and teachings
- Emphasizes God's initiative in the world and human activity as response to that initiative
- Presents the fullness of the mystery of Christ, divine and human, and his centrality in salvation history
- Ensures the ecclesial nature and context of catechesis with proper emphasis on Tradition—the living and authentic transmission of the entirety of the Word of God in the Church
- Teaches that God's revealed law, as grounded in the natural law and as taught by the Church, is the source of Christian morality and the formation of conscience
- Provides an adequate development of the interrelationship of the Magisterium with Sacred Scripture and Tradition and presents the ecclesial context of Catholic beliefs and magisterial teachings; the Magisterium is the living, teaching authority of the Church that includes the pope and the bishops in union with the pope
- Presents a distinctively Christian understanding of the nature of the human person: containing the fundamental notions that human persons are by nature religious, that the desire for God is written in the human heart, and that the human person is a unity of soul and body and is not reducible to the merely material or the merely spiritual
- Presents a more adequate understanding of grace and original sin
- Presents the sacraments within the context of the Paschal Mystery and as the means by which we share in the new life of Christ through the outpouring of the Holy Spirit
- Integrates the liturgical rites and symbols, liturgical celebrations, and the liturgical year into the catechetical process
- Brings about a deeper understanding of other churches, ecclesial communities, and non-Christian religions in their particular contexts and the relationships of the Catholic Church with each of them
- Gives greater attention to the social teachings of the Church

C. Challenges in the Ministry of Catechesis

There are also many challenges to the ministry of catechesis in the United States.

For many Catholics, there is a gap between their faith and their everyday life and an inadequate connection between their religious beliefs and their moral choices. The U.S. culture at times excludes or marginalizes both the individual and institutional religious values of Catholics. Catechesis needs to present the Christian life as a response to Christ's invitation to follow him—in one's personal life and family, the parish, and the wider human community.

The widening gap between the rich and the poor presents a difficult problem for catechesis. For some Catholics, their world is characterized by growing prosperity. For others, it is characterized by pervasive poverty. Both of these factors influence their ability to receive and proclaim the Gospel message and their ability to live a Christian life. If catechesis is to make a significant impact on the culture and affect the everyday life of Catholics, it must consistently put the needs of the poor and the vulnerable first. It must offer criteria by which economically poor Catholics can reconcile the fact of their poverty with the demands of the Gospel. It must also offer criteria by which affluent Catholics can reconcile the fact of their wealth with those same demands. Both the disadvantaged and the affluent must come to know through catechesis that the ultimate goal of the Christian life is communion with God, not power, riches, and influence.

The frantic pace of life caused by economic and social expectations leads to serious time constraints for many people's participation in catechetical programs and in the life of the Church. Since so much time is programmed for other activities, there is often little or no time left for participation in Church-related activities. The way people, including Catholic people, choose to live their lives today simply does not allow them the same free time that they once had. Family and other social commitments are often arranged so that attendance at Mass or participation in catechetical programs becomes very difficult.

If the message of Jesus Christ is to take root, catechesis must incorporate the fact that parents are likely to cultivate independent thinking and problem-solving skills in their children, so that their children are more likely to succeed economically. Consequently, young people today are also more critically-minded in their learning styles than ever before, and they develop those skills at earlier ages. This does not mean that they automatically reject everything they learn, but it does mean that they will be very likely to reject some of what they learn, or to refuse to integrate it in their lives, if it is not taught in ways that make sense to them emotionally, spiritually, and intellectually.

Catholic young people, like their counterparts in other faith traditions, have emerged as principal consumers of a developing popular culture, a culture that emphasizes a level of materialism and permissiveness designed to sell products and entertainment to the greatest number as efficiently as possible. This popular culture has deeply influenced considerations of right and wrong and often has increasingly come to obscure authentic human culpability associated with making choices. The movies, television shows, interactive video games, and websites that promote popular culture often use images that display value-free judgments of right and wrong founded only on expediency or utilitarianism. Much of the advertising that is aimed at young people seeks to glamorize a popular culture that has no reference to Christian values. These powerful and attractive messages not only ignore or devalue any religious aspirations, morals, or values that young people might have, but often contradict the Gospel message.

The consumerism and materialism that dominate the culture of the United States present extremely demanding challenges for catechesis because they are often seen as primary values or even ends in themselves. Catechesis has to find ways to help people break the "buy, use, buy again, use again" cycle and yet relate these forms of everyday decision making to the integration of Gospel values in their lives. Catechesis must make it clear that the person of Jesus Christ offers a realistic alternative to immediate gratification and the satisfaction of personal needs.

The information revolution, including the Internet, media in all its forms, and social communications in general, presents major challenges for catechesis. Most people today, but especially young people, expect learning experiences to be entertaining and tend to judge the effectiveness of those experiences on the superficial level of how entertaining they are rather than how humanly enriching or authentic they are. Young people are taught both by the excitement generated by technology and by the effervescence of popular culture to reject something if it bores them—and often the only things that do not bore them are those that seduce or titillate.

Catechesis has to investigate new possibilities offered by the existence of the new technologies and imagine whole new models and systems if the Gospel message is to penetrate the culture, make sense to the next generation of Catholics, and bring about a response of faith. Catechesis needs to find more sophisticated ways to employ these new technologies in linking the extensive personnel and material resources of the Church in order to bring others to know Christ, his message, and his way of life.

5. PURPOSE OF THE *DIRECTORY*

We bishops hope this *National Directory for Catechesis* will be a source of inspiration for catechesis in the dioceses and parishes of the United States and an important reference point for the formation of catechists and the preparation of catechetical resources. It has three basic purposes that are aimed at the orientation and general planning of catechetical activity in this country:

1. To provide those fundamental theological and pastoral principles drawn from the Church's Magisterium and apply them to the pastoral activity of catechesis
2. To offer guidelines for the application of those fundamental theological and pastoral principles in this country in order to continue a renewal of catechesis
3. To set forth the nature, purpose, object, tasks, basic content, and various methodologies of catechesis

6. AUDIENCE AND USE

The *National Directory for Catechesis* is intended primarily for those who have responsibility for catechesis in the dioceses, parishes, and schools in the United States. These include, in accord with their competence, bishops, diocesan staff with catechetical responsibility, priests, deacons, seminarians, religious women and men, parish catechetical leaders, catechists, Catholic school principals and teachers, campus ministers, members of diocesan and parish educational/catechetical boards and committees, and parents and guardians exercising their responsibilities as the primary educators of their children. It may also be helpful for youth ministers and those who teach catechetics and related disciplines in institutions of higher education and catechetical institutes. This directory will be especially useful in the formation of those preparing for ordination to the diaconate and priesthood, in the continuing formation of deacons and priests, and in the preparation and continuing formation of catechetical leaders and catechists. This directory should also be a fundamental point of reference for authors, editors, and publishers of catechetical texts and other catechetical resources. Because some with specialized catechetical interests may concentrate their study of this document on individual chapters that express their needs or concerns, readers of the whole document will find some repetition of directives. We hope that this *National Directory for Catechesis* will be read in its entirety in order to promote future study, deepen research in the field of catechesis, and lead to a continuing and deepening renewal of catechesis in the United States.

7. AUTHORITY

The *National Directory for Catechesis* is an official document of the United States Conference of Catholic Bishops.[26] It has been reviewed and approved by the Congregation for the Clergy according to the norms established in the *General Directory for Catechesis* and the apostolic constitution *Pastor Bonus*.

It should be noted, however, that not all parts of this document are of equal importance or theological authority. Some content provides the teaching of the Church; some provides pastoral directives. The teaching of the Church is to be interpreted in light of the guidance of the Magisterium. The pastoral directives are prudential judgments, applications, or guidelines that may continue to evolve; consequently, they have less inherent authority.

Because the Church will continue to provide guidance and direction for the renewal of catechesis and because the cultural context for catechesis in the United States will continue to change, this document will be reviewed periodically for updating and improvement.

8. CONCLUSION

Christ's command to his apostles has resounded through the ages, calling men and women of every race and nation in every time and place to join

---

26　This document was developed on behalf of the United States Conference of Catholic Bishops as a project initially of the Bishops' Committee on Education; toward the end of the project, responsibility was transferred to the new Bishops' Committee on Catechesis. Both committees were aided in the task by an Editorial Oversight Board, appointed in 2000 by the Committee on Education.

him in announcing the coming of the God's kingdom of love, justice, and peace with clarity, enthusiasm, and resolve. Christ himself inaugurates that kingdom in his own person and leads us to share in the life of the Holy Trinity.

Day after day, Jesus sat teaching in the Temple.[27] The apostles, his disciples, and even his enemies called him "teacher": "Teacher, I will follow you wherever you go";[28] "Teacher, what must I do to inherit eternal life?";[29] "Teacher, we wish to see a sign from you."[30] Nicodemus confessed to Jesus, "We know that you are a teacher who has come from God."[31] Christ taught individuals, small groups, and great crowds. He taught from hillsides and boats, in towns and synagogues, on the mountains and the seashores, on Sabbaths and feasts, early in the morning and in the dark of night. He taught with authority.[32]

Christ is the unique Teacher because his teaching is not merely a collection of abstract truths but the Truth itself, "the communication of the living mystery of God."[33] In fact, Christ is the "one teacher,"[34] whose message is identical with himself. His words do not merely express the word of God; he *is* the Word of God. Who he is and what he says form an integral harmony, a singular union in the firstborn of the Father, the only-begotten Son of God, the Word made flesh. After he washed the feet of his apostles, he said to them, "You call me 'teacher' and 'master,' and rightly so, for indeed I am."[35] This unique Teacher pledged to be with his Church until the end of the age. Together with his Father, Christ sent his Spirit to usher in the Kingdom of God. It was already present in Christ and his Church, though not yet fulfilled. The mission of Christ and the Holy Spirit is brought to completion in the Church, which is the Body of Christ and the Temple of the Holy Spirit.

This divine mission that Jesus entrusted to his Church will continue until the end of time. It is the sacrament, the sign in this world of the eternal communion of Father, Son, and Holy Spirit. Christ's pledge is a source

---

27 Cf. Mt 26:55.
28 Mt 8:19.
29 Lk 10:25.
30 Mt 12:38.
31 Jn 3:2.
32 Cf. Mk 1:22.
33 CT, no. 7.
34 CT, no. 6.
35 Jn 13:13.

of great hope for the whole Church, for all her members share in this mission, though in various ways. But his pledge also reminds all the members that the fruitfulness of the mission depends entirely on their vital union with Jesus Christ.

The Holy Spirit has given all those responsible for catechesis in the Church a vocation and a mission to sanctity. The Spirit also guides them in the development of a spirituality proper to their specific roles in catechesis. The spirituality of those involved in the catechetical ministry centers on an encounter with Christ. It is rooted in the living Word of God. It fosters an abiding hope that all should come to the knowledge of the truth of Christ and accept salvation from him. It expresses itself in a sincere love for the Church in imitation of Christ. It seeks interior growth in the peace and joy of Christ. It embraces the Paschal Mystery, enters into the apostolic mission of Christ, and is enriched by a deep devotion to the Mother of God. The challenge to all those involved in catechesis is to bear each of these marks within their hearts and souls.

CHAPTER 1

Proclaiming the Gospel in the United States

Now there were devout Jews from every nation under heaven staying in Jerusalem. At this sound, they gathered in a large crowd, but they were confused because each one heard them speaking in his own language. They were astounded, and in amazement they asked, "Are not all these people who are speaking Galileans? Then how does each of us hear them in his own native language?" (Acts 2:5-8)

9. INTRODUCTION

The sound of the strong, driving wind signaled the descent of the Holy Spirit at Pentecost. It drew the disciples and foreign-born Jews from all over the world together in a diverse assembly that foreshadowed the gathering of all nations at the end of time. The power of the Holy Spirit transformed the disciples' native dialect so that the same Word of God, Jesus Christ, could be understood in the languages and cultures of all peoples throughout the earth. In this dramatic encounter of the divine with the human, the Holy Spirit launched the Church on her mission of evangelization. In the Holy Spirit, always the primary agent of evangelization, the eternal and transcendent Word of God continually penetrates the hearts and minds of men and women in every time and in every place.

This chapter presents some of the cultural and religious factors that affect catechesis in the United States in 2003. Catechists proclaim the Gospel so that it may take root in those being catechized and may foster their conversion to the person and message of Jesus Christ. The circumstances in which the catechetical process takes place condition both the reception of the Gospel and the response to it. This chapter briefly

- Describes the culture and cultures in the United States
- Offers a profile of Catholics
- Describes catechesis
- Presents the situation of family and home in the United States

10. GENERAL CHARACTERISTICS OF U.S. CULTURE

A. Freedom

The Declaration of Independence makes the historic assertion "We hold these truths to be self-evident, that all men are created equal, that they are endowed by their Creator with certain inalienable rights, that among these are life, liberty, and the pursuit of happiness."[36] These words illuminate the founding principles of the United States. The rights that they affirm come from God. They do not derive from kings or presidents, decrees or edicts, charters or laws. The democracy of the United States of America is founded on these rights; and over the more than two centuries of this nation's existence, the right to freedom has embedded itself most deeply in our psyche.

In our own day, this right to liberty is sometimes in danger of becoming distorted into a right detached from responsibilities and expressing itself in an unconditional right to individual freedom of choice and an exaggerated right to privacy. This strong emphasis on the individual, individual freedom, and individual rights, without a corresponding emphasis on the natural law endowed by their Creator, has also generated a multiplicity of cultural and belief systems, which include various religious traditions and many expressions of community life. Such individualism and pluralism pose challenges for social cohesion in the United States.

U.S. society reflects the diversity of the individuals whom it comprises, each of whom has the inalienable right to liberty. This pluralism shows itself in religious freedom, ethnic and cultural diversity, and the

---

36 Declaration of Independence, par. 2.

expression of a wide variety of social and moral choices. It is also a contributing factor to the privatization of religion and a growing sense of moral relativism in the United States.

B. Religious Freedom

Many people migrated to these shores to escape religious persecution and to search for religious liberty. From the foundation of the republic, the general right to liberty included the specific right to freedom of religion, which according to Catholic teaching is a fundamental natural right. The commitment of the founders to freedom was so resolute that the U.S. Constitution, in the Bill of Rights, articulates a vision for the United States that includes the freedom of religion: "Congress shall make no law which establishes religion or prohibits the free exercise thereof."[37] The founders' emphasis on individual freedom shows itself today in a cultural commitment to religious liberty. Religious tolerance is a hallmark of the American experiment. Generations of Christians, Jews, Muslims, Buddhists, and followers of many other religious groups have all found a home in the United States along with the Native American religious believers who preceded them.

The strong heritage of individualism can also incline U.S. citizens to treat religious beliefs and values as private concerns that have no place in public life. While religion must always remain separate from government in the American constitutional system, religion must never be separated from society. The Church teaches that Catholics are to "embrace their citizenship not merely as a duty and privilege, but as an opportunity to participate [more fully] in building the culture of life."[38] "In the Catholic tradition, responsible citizenship is an [important private and public] virtue; participation in the political process is a moral obligation."[39] Moreover, the constitutional separation of religion from government means that government must refrain from establishing a single religion as the religion of the state or from preferring one religion over another—and must, at the same time, protect the free exercise of religion in all the states. In recent years, some institutions of higher education and the

---

37 Constitution of the United States, Bill of Rights, First Amendment.
38 USCCB, *Living the Gospel of Life: A Challenge to American Catholics* (Washington, D.C.: USCCB, 1998), no. 34.
39 USCCB, *Faithful Citizenship: Civic Responsibility for a New Millennium* (Washington, D.C.: USCCB, 1999), 9.

media have promoted a movement away from neutrality toward religion and contributed to a growing hostility toward religion in general and Catholicism in particular. This has even led to the enactment of laws legitimizing such policies. Although the right to freedom of religion has suffered and continues to suffer some severe challenges, this principle of religious freedom, as articulated in the Bill of Rights, still inspires the people of the United States to the common good.

C. Economic Freedom

Individual responsibility, equality of opportunity, and the free enterprise system dominate the economic structure of the United States. Some people who originally migrated to this nation envisioned a land of political freedom, economic opportunity, and personal religious freedom. They found a vast land with open fields, fertile soil, and a great expanse of natural resources. Through the years millions of immigrants have found productive work that has enabled them to broaden their freedoms, improve the quality of their lives, and contribute to the building of a great nation. As a result, the culture of the United States values economic freedom. There is general agreement in the United States that all individuals should have equal access to economic and social opportunities in a free-market setting. Still, however, a wide gap separates the poor from the rich, and greed can and does corrupt some of our economic institutions. "Every economic decision and institution must be judged in light of whether it protects or undermines the dignity of the human person . . . what it does *for* and *to* people and . . . how it permits all to *participate* in it."[40] All people have a right to life and to secure the basic necessities of life (e.g., food, clothing, shelter, education, health care, safe environment, economic security).

D. Pragmatism

Another mark of the culture of the United States is pragmatism. A strongly individualist, philosophical utilitarianism permeates U.S. culture, showing itself in a preoccupation with practical knowledge rather than intellectual knowledge. Many people in the United States think readily in

---

40   USCCB, *Tenth Anniversary Edition of "Economic Justice for All: Pastoral Letter on Catholic Social Teaching and the U.S. Economy"* (Washington, D.C.: USCCB, 1997), no. 13.

terms of personal or corporate utility but may be less inclined to think in the abstract. This practical orientation makes U.S. culture open to a wide variety of new ideas and possibilities but susceptible to utilitarian purposes. An individualist consumer culture can encourage a selfishness expressed in the attitude "What's in it for me?"

E. Interest in Science and Technology

This preoccupation with practicality has led to remarkable developments in science and technology. The people of the United States now possess an unprecedented power either to achieve immense good on behalf of the human race or to bring about unconscionable evil. Science and technology have provided the tools to rid the world of some of its most vexing problems—such as hunger, many diseases, or the inequitable distribution of the world's goods—as well as the tools to deny human dignity, violate authentic human freedom, and even cause the mass destruction of human life. Developments in science and technology are so rapid that often the means to do something is discovered before the impact is given adequate consideration. In all areas of scientific and technological development, the fundamental concerns are not simply what we can do, but what we ought to do. The basic criterion should not be simply what a particular technological development accomplishes for the human person and for the human community, but rather, what its implications are for the well-being of the human person and for the human community.

Significant new advances, especially in biotechnology and information technology, present opportunities in which the human family can genuinely advance. But they present new moral dilemmas as well.

Decisions regarding abortion, infanticide, the care of persons with disabilities, the infirm or aged, behavior control through surgery or drug therapy, genetic engineering, and population control—even the very definitions of life and death—need to be determined based on the inherent value of each human life. Since every person is made in God's image, every attack on innocent human beings is morally unjustifiable. This principle is especially important in a society that seems to place few if any limits on an individual's freedom of choice.

The revolution in information technology provides the Church with unprecedented new ways to proclaim the Gospel in the United States. The Word of God that, through the power of the Holy Spirit on Pentecost, was able to be understood by people of many different languages can now, in a new way, invite people of all languages and cultures to know Christ and follow him. The rapid developments of newer, faster, and more efficient means of communication require the Church to evaluate these developments in light of the Gospel. The communications media have now become a fundamental arena in which Christ's message must be conveyed to the whole world. "Today the media affect our lives more than ever."[41] In order to be faithful to her mission, the Church should employ all modern means of communications technology as effectively as possible to bring others to Christ.

F. Globalization

The rapid globalization of communication, transportation, and markets has drawn the world together. Economic development throughout the world has led to higher standards of living for almost everyone as compared to previous eras in human history. Nevertheless, within the context of globalization of economies, some rich nations have become richer and some poor nations have become poorer, widening the gap that already existed between peoples and nations.

The message of Jesus Christ calls us to global responsibility and solidarity. "Beyond differences of language, race, ethnicity, gender, culture, and nation, we are one human family."[42] We must genuinely reach out to defend and enhance the dignity of the poor and the vulnerable here in the United States and around the world. We must protect human life and care for God's creation as we advance authentic human freedom and foster human rights and solidarity. We are our brothers' and sisters' keepers, for God's love knows no boundaries or borders.

Catholics in the United States bear special responsibilities and have extraordinary opportunities to enhance global solidarity. We are members of a universal Church that transcends national boundaries and whose mission is to make disciples of all the nations and proclaim the Gospel to the ends of the earth. We are also citizens of a rich and powerful nation with

---

41   USCCB, *Renewing the Mind of the Media: Statement on Overcoming the Exploitation of Sex and Violence in Communications* (Washington, D.C.: USCCB, 1998), 2; Second Vatican Council, *Decree on the Mass Media (Inter Mirifica)* (IM), no. 11.

42   USCCB, *Called to Global Solidarity: International Challenges for U.S. Parishes* (Washington, D.C.: USCCB, 1997), 3.

massive influence beyond our borders. We must ensure that unlicensed free enterprise does not further impoverish the poor. More than any other nation on earth, we are responsible for cultural and economic globalization. Catholics in the United States have often shown commitment and generosity to bring about a more just world. We consistently demonstrate our concern for the poor and the oppressed through our humanitarian efforts. But so much more must be done in this new age of global communications and economic interdependence "to preserve the unity of the spirit through the bond of peace: one body and one Spirit . . . one Lord, one faith, one baptism; one God and Father of all, who is over all and through all and in all."[43]

G. Mobility

The culture of the United States continues to be shaped by the presence of immigrants. One in ten persons in the United States today was born in another country, a proportion that has increased rapidly over the past decade. More than ever in the United States, "community" is less rooted in a geographical or neighborhood context. Instead, community life takes place in affinity groups of those with like interests or of those who associate at work, at school, or in other environments, such as over the Internet or via infrequent face-to-face meetings.

Transportation and communications technology, combined with the tradition of mobility, have made geographic boundaries less important than ever. This situation affects parishes since they are communities of faith, and communities of faith are likewise less connected by geography than ever. Research suggests that as many as one in five Catholics regularly attend Mass at a parish that is not the one closest to their home.[44] This can affect catechesis, since often those interested in religious education for themselves or their children will tend to look for parishes where they can form a strong sense of community rather than simply find the one closest to them. As a general practice, however, most Catholics participate in the life of their territorial parish.

---

43   Eph 4:3-6.
44   Cf. CARA, Catholic Poll 2002.

11. DIVERSITY IN U.S. CULTURE

A. Cultural Diversity

Nearly every race, ethnic, and cultural group on earth is represented in the population of the United States. Consequently, significant cultural differences exist between and among these diverse racial, ethnic, and cultural groups.

Today, 12 percent of the United States population consists of African Americans; 13 percent are Hispanics/Latinos,[45] 4 percent Asians, 1 percent Native Americans, and 70 percent people of European or Middle Eastern descent. Growth patterns vary in these groups due to different age structures, immigration patterns, and reproductive practices. According to U.S. census projections, by 2025 the Hispanic/Latino population will grow by 71 percent, the Asian population by 78 percent, and the African American population by 26 percent. Those of Anglo or white, European, and Middle Eastern descent will grow by 6 percent.[46]

B. Religious Diversity

The United States has long been a refuge for those fleeing religious persecution; consequently, every major world religion is represented in the population of the United States. Today, survey results show that Catholics represent about 23 percent of the population of the United States. Ten different Orthodox Churches represent less than 1 percent of the population, and more than six hundred non-Catholic Christian religious bodies together represent about 52 percent of the U.S. population. Jews make

---

45   USCCB, *Encuentro and Mission: A Renewed Pastoral Framework for Hispanic Ministry* (Washington, D.C.: USCCB, 2002), note 5: "The term 'Hispanic' was used during the 1970 Census and was adopted by the church leadership of the time to help define a people with a common identity, vision, and mission. It has been integral to the *memoria histórica* of Hispanic ministry since 1970 and continues to be integral to the pastoral efforts of the entire Church today. In recent years, the term 'Latino' has become widely used by church and community leaders, particularly in urban areas. It is a self-identifying term that has emerged from the community and is embraced by the Church. Even though this population is labeled 'Hispanic,' however, it is essential for understanding and for effective working relationships to recognize that the people come from different countries and come with special identities. The binding forces are the faith tradition, language, and values."

46   Cf. U.S. Census Bureau National Population Projections, 2003 and 2025, http://www.census.gov/population/www/projections/natsum-T5.html (accessed August 29, 2003).

up more than 1 percent of the U.S. population and represent three major traditions. Finally, about 23 percent of the adult population of the United States either identifies with religious bodies outside the Judeo-Christian tradition (3 percent), say that they are not affiliated with any religious body (14 percent), or decline to answer survey questions about their religious affiliation (6 percent).[47]

The United States enjoys a rich community life that has been sustained by an emphasis on pluralism and individual freedom. Because of the emphasis on individual freedom of choice, religious life in the United States is experienced in the context of individuals' freely associating with individuals of other religious beliefs. Dynamics associated with the freedom of association and religious pluralism in general, along with the lack of entanglement of any religious organization with the national government, are the factors typically used to explain the considerable religious vitality of the United States. In the United States, almost one of every two people attend a worship service on a regular basis.

C. Diversity Within the Catholic Church

1. Ethnic Diversity

Just as all races, ethnicities, and cultures in the world are represented in the population of the United States, so too do they find a home within the Catholic Church. Each group brings its own language, history, customs, rituals, and traditions "for building up the body of Christ."[48] Since persons can only achieve their full humanity by means of culture, the Catholic Church in the United States embraces the rich cultural pluralism of all the faithful, encourages the distinctive identity of each cultural group, and urges mutual enrichment. At the same time, the Catholic Church promotes a unity of faith within the multicultural diversity of the people.

---

47   Cf. Barry Kosim, Egon Mayer, and Ariela Keysar, *American Religious Identification Survey* (New York: The Graduate Center of the City of New York, 2001), 12. Cf. also David B. Barret, George T. Kurian, and Todd M. Johnson, *World Christian Encyclopedia* (Oxford: Oxford University Press, 2001), 789. Barrett et al. cite 610 Protestant denominations existing in America in the year 2000. Additionally, they list more than 4,000 Christian religious bodies—mostly very small groups, but also a few large membership organizations such as the Church of Jesus Christ of Latter-Day Saints and Church of Christ, Scientist— that are not classified as "Protestant."

48   Eph 4:12.

While the influence of Hispanic/Latino Catholics within the Church has been substantial even before the founding of the nation, their increasing numbers and their growing presence in the United States today have a significant impact on the inculturation of the faith in the United States and the continuing formation of a new People of God.

"The historical roots of Black America and those of Catholic America are intimately intertwined."[49] The experience of slavery has profoundly shaped the lives and culture of African American Catholics. Evangelization has been woven into their story since their arrival in this country, and elements of their culture continue to enrich and enhance the Church in the United States.

The European colonization of the Americas was often harsh and painful for the indigenous peoples. These peoples were more often than not displaced from homelands, subjected to the ravages of war and disease, and ultimately relegated to living on reservations made up of lands that no one else wanted. Nevertheless, Native Americans responded generously to God's gift of the Christian faith, and his word took root in their cultures. Due to the Church's pastoral care and evangelizing presence among the Native peoples, the proportion of Native Americans who are Catholics is often higher than other ethnic groups.

Many new immigrants come from Latin America and the Caribbean, Asia and the Pacific Islands, the Middle East, Africa, and Eastern Europe.[50] The Church has a unique opportunity to call these recent immigrants to "conversion, communion and solidarity."[51] The diversity of ethnicity, education, and social status challenges the Church to integrate the new immigrants in ways that both respect their diverse cultures and experiences of Church and enrich both the immigrants and the Church. The Church of the twenty-first century in the United States will be a Church of many cultures, languages, and traditions—yet one in faith.

49   Black Bishops of the United States, *What We Have Seen and Heard* (Cincinnati: St. Anthony Messenger Press, 1984), 17.

50   Cf. USCCB, *Welcoming the Stranger Among Us: Unity in Diversity* (Washington, D.C.: USCCB, 2000), 1.

51   John Paul II, *The Church in America (Ecclesia in America)* (EA) (Washington, D.C.: USCCB, 1999), no. 3.

2. Autonomous Churches

The Eastern Catholic Churches,[52] which are autonomous Churches, follow either the Byzantine, Antiochian, Chaldean, Armenian, Coptic, or Alexandrian traditions. Those with established hierarchies in the United States are the Melkites, Ukrainians, Ruthenians, and Romanians of the Byzantine tradition; the Syriacs and Maronites of the Antiochian tradition; the Chaldeans and Syro-Malabars of the Chaldean tradition; and those of the Armenian tradition.

The Latin Church in the West and the Eastern Catholic Churches together compose the one Catholic Church. Since the first century, the Churches of East and West have developed diverse traditions with distinctive theological emphases, liturgies, and forms of spirituality, all faithful expressions of the teaching of Christ. The Latin and Eastern Churches, in communion with the Bishop of Rome as supreme head of the universal Church, are a visible sign to the world of the unity of the Church of Christ. At the same time, each particular Church has its own identity and traditions; each governs itself according to its own proper procedures.[53] "The universal Church needs the witness which the particular Churches can give one another; for no one theological or liturgical tradition can exhaust the richness of Christ's message and His love."[54] In its fostering of the expression of all the traditions that make up the universal Church, the Church's unity is clearly not based on a particular language, rite, spiritual tradition, or theological school, but rather upon the one cornerstone, Jesus Christ.[55]

In the midst of this diversity, "the Church has constantly confessed this one faith, received from the one Lord, transmitted by one Baptism, and grounded in the conviction that all people have only one God and Father."[56]

---

52   Cf. USCCB, *Eastern Catholics in the United States of America* (Washington, DC: USCCB, 1999).

53   Cf. Second Vatican Council, *Decree on the Catholic Eastern Churches* (*Orientalium Ecclesiarum*) (OE), no. 5.

54   USCCB, *Sharing the Light of Faith: National Catechetical Directory for Catholics of the United States* (Washington, D.C.: USCCB, 1977), no. 73. Hereafter cited as *National Catechetical Directory*.

55   Cf. Pt 2:4-8.

56   CCC, no. 172.

D. Regional Diversity

Considerable regional diversity characterizes the United States.

The Northeast of the United States, comprising the nine states from Maine in the north to Pennsylvania and New Jersey in the south, is more industrialized and urbanized than any of the other three major regions of the United States. The mainline Protestant traditions have historically been predominant in this region, which contains large numbers of Catholics.[57] In general, the cultural climate in the Northeast tends to separate religion from other areas of life more than in the Midwest or South. Its ethnic mix has long been a diverse combination of European populations from northern, central, eastern, and southern Europe. New population groups entering in the latter half of the twentieth century included blacks from the southern United States and Hispanics/Latinos primarily from Puerto Rico, the Dominican Republic, and Mexico.[58] As U.S. citizens, Puerto Ricans were able to emigrate freely to the mainland at a time when legal restrictions significantly reduced immigration to the large port cities of the Northeast that had historically been main points of entry. Asian immigrants have also settled in the Northeast during the latter half of the twentieth century—including more recent waves of Vietnamese immigration to Massachusetts, Pennsylvania, and New York.[59]

The South, comprising the sixteen states south of the Ohio River and east of the Mississippi, plus Texas, Oklahoma, Arkansas, and Louisiana, as well as the District of Columbia, has a rapidly developing economy and a somewhat younger population base than that of the Northeast.[60] Historically, the ethnic mix of the South has primarily consisted of blacks, descended from Africans who worked as slaves on the plantations of pre-Civil War times, and whites, descended from the largely English-origin plantation owners, the French, the Scotch-Irish who settled on small farms in the back country and mountainous areas, and those who came from Mexico. This region is now the site of rapidly growing Hispanic/Latino immigration and large numbers of internal U.S. migrants, particularly from the Northeast

---

57   Cf. Edwin S. Gaustad and Philip L. Barlow, *The New Historical Atlas of Religion in America* (Oxford: Oxford University Press, 2001), 321-323.

58   Cf. Frank Hobbs and Nicole Stoops, *Demographic Trends in the Twentieth Century* (Washington D.C.: U.S. Census Bureau, 2002), 83-87.

59   Cf. *Demographic Trends in the Twentieth Century*, 83. Cf. also U.S. Department of Commerce, *We the Americans: Asians* (Washington, D.C.: U.S. Department of Commerce, 1993), 2-3.

60   Cf. *Demographic Trends in the Twentieth Century*, 60.

and Midwest. Asian immigrants, particularly from Vietnam, have also settled in Texas, Florida, Virginia, Georgia, and Louisiana.[61] Evangelical Protestant faiths and religious bodies play a special role in Southern culture, and religion occupies a more public place than in the Northeast. Except for southern Louisiana, Florida, and parts of Texas, Catholics remain a decided minority amidst the evangelical Protestant majority of the South.

The Midwest consists of the twelve states that are north of Oklahoma, Arkansas, and the other southern border states, are west of Pennsylvania, and are east of Montana. It combines the distinctive features of rural life and small-town culture, particularly in the Plains states, with large cities and major metropolitan areas, especially around the Great Lakes region. Since the late nineteenth century, its ethnic mix has included a strong presence, in its rural areas, of both Protestant and Catholic groups from Northern Europe. Metropolitan areas also have a strong presence of African Americans as well as Eastern and Southern European-descended populations. Recent years have seen dramatic increases in the presence of Hispanics/Latinos from Mexico and elsewhere in Latin America in the small towns of the Great Plains as well as in the urban centers. Predominant Protestant denominations include Lutherans and Methodists. Cultural features share aspects of the more secular Northeast and the more socially conservative and evangelical Protestant South.

The West comprises the thirteen Rocky Mountain and Pacific states. The percentage of those who indicate some affiliation with organized religion, particularly traditional Protestant denominations, is lowest here.[62] The population in this region has always included Hispanics/Latinos— indeed, much of this region was a part of Mexico, and, just as in the case of Texas, many Hispanics/Latinos can trace their roots to ancestors who lived here before the United States annexed these lands in the 1840s. Along with the Hispanics/Latinos whose ancestors have been here a long time are many newly arrived Mexican migrants and immigrants. The population has also long included Asians, who are present here in much greater numbers than in other regions in the United States. These areas also include more recent incoming concentrations of Vietnamese, Laotian, and Hmong immigrants in the metropolitan areas of northern and southern California.[63]

---

61   Cf. *Demographic Trends in the Twentieth Century*, 83; *We the Americans: Asians*, 2-3. Cf. also U.S. Census 2000.

62   Cf. *The New Historical Atlas of Religion in America*, 352.

63   Cf. *Demographic Trends in the Twentieth Century*, 83. Cf. also *We the Americans: Asians*, 2-3; cf. U.S. Census 2000.

Anti-Catholicism is a distinct reality in the Pacific Northwest. The Northwest has the lowest percentage of churched people in the nation, with 33 percent listing a religious denomination. Of those listing a denomination, more than one-third are Roman Catholic.

Finally, the residents of Alaska and Hawaii, many of whom are of Native American, Asian, and Polynesian descent, further enrich the diversity of life in these United States.

12. PROFILE OF CATHOLICS IN THE UNITED STATES

A. Demographics

While a complete description of Catholicism in the United States is not possible, salient elements of the picture can be provided.

The Catholic population of the United States now numbers more than 62 million and continues to grow.[64] Catholics are better educated and more affluent than they were before the Second Vatican Council. The Catholic population in the United States is generally comparable, in racial and ethnic distribution, to the population of the United States as a whole, with a slightly smaller proportion of African Americans and a larger proportion of Hispanics/Latinos. The Catholic population of the United States is more ethnically diverse than a similarly sized Catholic population in any other country in the world.[65]

Significant differences in attitude between generations, combined with the shifts in church life associated with the experience of the Second Vatican Council, provide another crucial key to understanding the diversity of church life and practice. For example, in polls conducted in 2001 and 2002, older Catholics were more likely than younger Catholics to report being satisfied with the parish where they attend Mass and with how the Church meets their spiritual needs.[66]

---

64 Cf. Eileen W. Linder (Ed.), *Yearbook of American and Canadian Churches* (Nashville: Abingdon Press, 2002), 9, 11-12. Cf. also *The Official Catholic Directory* (New Providence, N.J.: P. J. Kenedy & Sons, 2002).

65 Cf. *Catholicism USA*, 4-19.

66 Cf. CARA, Catholic Poll 2001, 2002.

B. Pastoral Life

Catholic pastoral settings have changed dramatically over the past few decades. As Catholics have grown in number, so have the number of diocesan churches that serve them under the leadership of a diocesan or eparchial bishop. Eparchies are the equivalents of dioceses in the Eastern Churches. The United States now has sixteen eparchies of the Eastern Churches (serving the Maronite, Chaldean, Malabar, and Byzantine Churches, including Melkites, Romanians, Ruthenians, Ukrainians, and Syrians) and one exarchate (for Armenian Catholics). Combined, they minister to nearly half a million Eastern Catholics. In addition, 179 dioceses of the Latin Church now minister to more than 62 million Catholics.[67]

While the number of Catholics has increased, the number of parishes without full-time resident pastors also has increased: from 4 percent of all parishes in 1980 to 15 percent of all parishes in 2001.[68] Pastors' ministering in two or three parish communities is a reality; these demanding settings require great commitment so that appropriate catechetical oversight is provided. Catholic parish schools have declined in number, from 9,700 in 1950 to 7,500 in 2001.[69] As fewer Catholic young people are enrolled in Catholic schools, the number of Catholic young people in parish-based catechetical programs has increased dramatically. One-quarter fewer students attend Catholic schools today than did in 1950, but more than four times as many students participate in parish catechetical programs.[70]

Parish life has increased in scale and complexity over the past few decades. The number of parishes has grown, and the average number of Catholics per parish has increased. Only about 25 percent of Catholic parishes in the United States have fewer than 430 registered parishioners. About 22 percent of all parishes in the United States celebrate Mass in languages other than English at least once a month; in the vast majority of these, the second language is Spanish. About one third of all parishes minister to more than one ethnic group. Finally, about one third of all parishes in the United States are located in rural areas.[71]

---

67   Cf. *The Official Catholic Directory* (2002).

68   Cf. *The Official Catholic Directory* (years noted).

69   Cf. *Catholicism USA*, 68. Cf. *The Official Catholic Directory* (2002).

70   Cf. *Catholicism USA*, 76.

71   Cf. CARA, *Special Report: National Parish Inventory* (NPI) (Washington, DC: Center for Applied Research in the Apostolate, 2000).

C. Personnel

The past thirty years have seen remarkable changes in the number of people who exercise ministry in the Catholic Church. The number of diocesan priests and priests in religious communities has not kept pace with growth in the Catholic population. Since the peak years of the mid-1960s, the numbers of both women and men religious have declined by half, and the average age of the remaining religious is more than sixty-three years.

Lay ecclesial ministers constitute the most notable increase in church personnel over the past thirty years. While the need to provide adequate formation for all the laity involved in ecclesial ministry is an ongoing challenge, this increased lay involvement has still been a blessing for the Church and is a hopeful sign for the future. Some have developed professional skills through graduate degree and ministry formation programs with specializations in catechetics, Liturgy, and pastoral ministry. They exercise valuable leadership in these areas. Many more serve as catechists, catechumenate team members, liturgical ministers, youth ministers, social justice advocates, pastoral ministers, parish council and committee members, ecumenical representatives, and so on. The number of permanent deacons has also increased dramatically over the past few years. And, in a truly remarkable development, many Catholic young people now spend a year or two after college graduation as volunteers in programs sponsored by religious communities or other church entities. In light of Christ's missionary command, the challenge to the ordinary lay Catholic is to become still more active in the Church's mission to evangelize the culture and to assume more responsibility for proclaiming the Gospel in their daily lives.

13. FAMILY AND HOME IN THE UNITED STATES

While the speed of social change in the United States over the past thirty years has accelerated considerably, family life continues to be the cornerstone of social life in the United States. Churches, other religious communities, and dedicated groups are working together to support families and to encourage public policy that strengthens the role of the family in society.

We see significant signs of hope for today's families.

- Across the nation is a growing movement to strengthen and support family life. Men and women are sharing the responsibilities of parenting, and fathers' and mothers' roles have become more flexible.

- Many service institutions are showing a renewed interest in family life and in how to provide their services in ways that support families' own responsibilities.
- Some political leaders seem to be moving toward a consensus belief that family concerns should be at the front and center of the public policy-making process,[72] even as others seek to redefine the family.

Other changes in society present both opportunities and risks for many families. Even the basic definitions of "marriage" and "family" are being challenged.

- While Catholics tend to marry at older ages and divorce at somewhat lower rates than the U.S. population as a whole, these statistics are gradually changing toward the general culture's practice. Especially significant is the large increase in the percentage of Catholics who have divorced or separated in recent years, despite Christ's teaching on the indissolubility of marriage. While the divorce rate has declined slightly, still almost half of all U.S. marriages will end in divorce; about one third of marriages between two Catholics end in divorce. An increasing number of children are not living with both natural parents. About half the children born today are expected to experience their parents' divorce by the time they reach age eighteen. A growing number of children will experience multiple divorces and family breakups, and most research on the consequences of divorce indicates a negative impact on children.
- It is still true that Catholics do not remarry as often as the rest of society; but there is increasing convergence of attitudes between younger Catholics and non-Catholics. The difference in attitude and behavior between Catholics and non-Catholics in marriage and family life is disappearing.[73]

---

72   Cf. USCCB Committee on Marriage and Family, *A Family Perspective on Church and Society* (Washington, D.C.: USCCB, 1998), 1.

73   Cf. USCCB Secretariat for Family, Laity, Women, and Youth, *The Changing American Family: Is There a Difference?* (Washington, D.C.: USCCB, 1995), 8.

- Traditional nuclear families—that is, those with a mother, father, and at least one child under age eighteen living at home—are on the decline. Today, traditional nuclear families make up a notably smaller percentage of all types of families with children living at home than in previous decades.

- In more than half the families with school-age children, both parents work outside the home. In addition, over half of mothers with children under age six, and three quarters of those with school-age children, are employed outside the home.[74]

- More persons of both sexes choose to remain single.

- Almost half the couples who come for marriage preparation in the Catholic Church are living together, in contradiction to church teaching on marriage and human sexuality. "This cohabitation is a pervasive and growing phenomenon with a negative impact on the role of marriage as the foundation of the family. . . . [It] is a major factor in the declining centrality of marriage in family structure."[75]

- The average number of children born per household in the United States has been steadily declining.

- In 1980, 82 percent of all families with children under age eighteen had two parents living at home; in 2000, only 76 percent of families had two parents living at home.[76] Meanwhile, the number of single-parent households is increasing, and almost half of single parents have never been married.[77]

- The number of Americans raising their grandchildren is growing.

- Adequate income is a major problem for single-parent families, most of which are headed by mothers with little or no financial or emotional support from the children's fathers.[78] One quarter of all births occur outside of marriage. Paternity is never established for a large majority of these children.[79] About two thirds of mothers are trying to raise their children essentially alone and are working

74   Cf. A Family Perspective on Church and Society, 2.

75   USCCB Committee on Marriage and Family, Marriage Preparation and Cohabiting Couples (Washington, D.C.: USCCB, 1999), 6, http://www.usccb.org/laity/marriage/cohabitating.htm (accessed on June 12, 2003).

76   Cf. Demographic Trends in the Twentieth Century, A-49.

77   Cf. A Family Perspective on Church and Society, 4.

78   Cf. A Family Perspective on Church and Society, 4.

79   Cf. A Family Perspective on Church and Society, 4.

outside the home. The number of children in nursery schools and day-care centers continues to grow. The number of children who stay home alone after school also continues to rise. Another issue is the high rate of Catholics who do not marry Catholics. The Church needs to provide special guidance to help these couples raise their children as Catholic Christians.

The following trends indicate an erosion of some fundamental values. Often, these trends underlie the social changes listed above.

- Respect for the dignity and value of every human life is challenged by the social acceptance of abortion, the move toward physician-assisted suicide, and a contraceptive mentality.
- The essential bond between husband and wife is challenged by an increasing individualistic attitude of the spouses in relation to each other.
- The natural authority of parents in relationship to children is challenged by the sense of self-sufficiency and autonomy that children develop at increasingly earlier ages.
- The transmission of traditional values within the family is challenged by the increasing growth and persuasion of popular culture as well as by the mobility factor for migrant families.

"At the root of these negative phenomena there frequently lies a corruption of the idea and the experience of freedom, conceived not as a capacity for realizing the truth of God's plan for marriage and the family, but as an autonomous power of self-affirmation, often against others, for one's own selfish well-being."[80]

The Catholic Church in the United States offers a hopeful alternative to the erosion of these fundamental societal values. The Church has a distinctly Christian vision of marriage and family that is rooted in natural law and to which Sacred Scripture and Tradition testify. The relationship of loving communion that exists between and among the persons of the Trinity forms the model for Christian family life. The family constitutes a special

---

80   John Paul II, *On the Family (Familiaris Consortio)* (FC) (Washington, D.C.: USCCB, 1982), no. 6.

revelation and realization of ecclesial communion, and for this reason it can and should be called the "domestic church" "by participating in the life and mission of the church."[81]

14. CONCLUSION

This overview has presented some contemporary cultural and religious factors that influence catechesis in the United States. These factors are like the many languages of the visitors to Jerusalem on that first Pentecost. Each different language presented a potential obstacle to hearing the word of God proclaimed by the apostles; but the Holy Spirit, who makes present "the unique Revelation brought by Christ to humanity,"[82] made the same message accessible to all in their particular circumstances. The Church and her catechists must continually meditate upon and grow in understanding the Pentecost experience in order to express in every language and culture "the inscrutable riches of Christ."[83] If catechesis is to be effective, all those responsible for it must monitor the rapid changes in social and cultural trends. The catechist must be able to introduce the real person of Jesus Christ to the real persons of this time and place in history.

In the process of boldly proclaiming the Gospel to this culture and the discrete cultures within it, the Church holds fast to the fact that, through the mystery of the incarnation, people of all cultures are capable of receiving the Gospel; and through the Gospel, people of all cultures can experience conversion to Jesus Christ and commit to following his way in order to be in communion with the universal Church. Since catechesis always occurs within a social and cultural context, catechists must carefully consider both the integrity of the Christian message they announce and the particular circumstances in which they announce it. They do this within the community of the Church and with the firm confidence that the one Teacher and the first Evangelizer will be with them "until the end of the age."[84] This theme will be developed in greater detail in the next chapter.

---

81   FC, no. 49.
82   Pope John Paul II, *On the Coming of the Third Millennium (Tertio Millennio Adveniente)* (TMA) (Washington, D.C.: USCCB, 1994), no. 44.
83   Eph 3:8.
84   Mt 28:20.

CHAPTER 2

Catechesis Within the Church's Mission of Evangelization

Go into the whole world and proclaim the
gospel to every creature. (Mk 16:15)

---

15. INTRODUCTION

Christ commissioned his apostles to "go into the whole world and proclaim the gospel to every creature."[85] As a result they "went forth and preached everywhere, while the Lord worked with them and confirmed the word through accompanying signs."[86] Christ taught his apostles what he received from the Father: "What I heard from him I tell the world."[87] The apostles, in turn, were to echo this divine word faithfully and completely. This "echo" of the Word of God is catechesis.[88]

Christ calls all the faithful to proclaim the Good News everywhere in the world and to hand his message on to successive generations by professing, living, and celebrating the faith in Liturgy and prayer. Evangelization and catechesis are among the principal means by which the Church hands on the faith. "Evangelizing is in fact the grace and vocation proper to the Church, her deepest identity. She exists in order to evangelize."[89] Catechesis is an indispensable stage in the rich, complex, and dynamic reality of

---

85   Mk 16:15.
86   Mk 16:20.
87   Jn 8:26.
88   Cf. Acts 18:25; Rom 2:18; Gal 6:6.
89   EN, no. 14

evangelization. It is a remarkable moment "in the whole process of evangelization."[90] Other elements of evangelization include ecumenical collaboration among Christians and the promotion of their unity, since "the sign of unity among all Christians [is] the way and instrument of evangelization."[91]

This chapter describes the proper role of catechesis within the Church's mission of evangelization. Catechesis begins with the primacy of Revelation, presents the Church's fundamental mission of evangelization, shows how catechesis is set within the context of evangelization, and identifies the source and sources of catechesis. The chapter then sets forth the purposes and tasks of catechesis and concludes by describing the dynamic relationship between the Gospel message and culture.

16. REVELATION

A. God's Self-Disclosure in Salvation History

"It pleased God, in his goodness and wisdom, to reveal himself and to make known the mystery of his will."[92] The divine will is that we should come to the Father through Christ, the Word made flesh, and, in the Holy Spirit, become sharers in the divine nature (*theosis*). Divine Revelation, then, is the supernatural manifestation of the inner life of God: Father, Son, and Holy Spirit. God's desire to communicate himself to us is entirely his own initiative. God's self-revelation aims to bring about our participation in the life of the Blessed Trinity, something so wondrous that it is impossible for us even to imagine.

From the beginning, God has made known the inexhaustible mystery of his love in order to give us a share in his own divine life. In doing so, God summons a response in faith from his people. So unimaginable is God's gift of himself that our response can only be self-surrender, the obedience of faith. God reveals himself to us gradually and in stages, drawing us ever closer in order to prepare us to welcome the culmination of God's self-revelation in the person and mission of the incarnate Word, Jesus Christ. The pattern of this Revelation unfolds through "deeds and words, which are intrinsically [connected:] . . . the works performed by God in

---

90   CT, no. 18.
91   EN, no. 77.
92   Second Vatican Council, *Dogmatic Constitution on Divine Revelation (Dei Verbum)* (DV), no. 2.

the history of salvation show forth and bear out the doctrine and realities signified by the words; the words, for their part, proclaim the works, and bring to light the mystery they contain."[93]

God first revealed himself through creation and continually provides evidence of himself in the created order. God sustains and directs creation toward its fulfillment in Jesus Christ. God revealed himself in a special way through the history of Israel.[94] He created our first parents in communion with him. After their fall, he revealed his loving plan for redemption through covenants with Noah and Abraham. In the time of the patriarchs, Isaac, Jacob, and Joseph, he formed Israel as his people so that they would know him to be the one, true God. God freed the Israelites from slavery in Egypt, established the covenant of Mount Sinai, and, through Moses, gave them his law. He spoke to his people through judges, priests, and prophets and continued to shape his people in hope for the promised Savior. God made a covenant with King David and promised that through David's offspring, he would establish his kingdom for ever.[95] We see this covenant promise fulfilled in Mary, the virgin mother of God's only-begotten Son. She was a unique vessel of God's Revelation, obediently bringing forth his Word in human flesh in order to establish his kingdom for ever.

God revealed himself fully in Jesus Christ, the Son of God made man. Jesus is the "mediator and the sum total of Revelation."[96] In Christ, God has said everything in one, perfect, transcendent Word. Jesus Christ "completed and perfected Revelation. . . . He did this by the total fact of his presence and self-manifestation—by words and works, signs and miracles, but above all by his death and glorious resurrection from the dead, and finally by sending the Spirit of truth."[97] There will be no new public revelation until Christ returns in glory at the end of time.

The Spirit of truth continues to reveal God in the world and, especially, in the Church. The Holy Spirit inspired the sacred authors to preserve the message of salvation in writing and to ensure the authentic interpretation of the word of God contained in Sacred Scripture through the Magisterium. The Magisterium is the teaching authority of the

---

93   DV, no. 2.
94   Cf. Pontifical Biblical Commission, *The Jewish People and Their Scriptures in the Christian Bible* (Vatican City: Libreria Editrice Vaticana, 2002), Section II, 19-65.
95   Cf. 2 Sm 7:13.
96   DV, no. 2.
97   DV, no. 4.

Church that consists of the pope and bishops in union with the pope. Through the Holy Spirit, the Risen Christ is alive in those who believe, helping them to understand their experiences in the light of faith.

B. The Transmission of Revelation

God's Revelation is intended for all humanity because God "wills everyone to be saved and to come to knowledge of the truth."[98] To fulfill this divine plan, Jesus Christ founded the Church on the apostles, filled them with the Holy Spirit, and sent them to preach the Gospel to the whole world. This apostolic commission has been the life of the Church since her foundation. The Church has preserved the integrity and entirety of the Gospel since Christ entrusted it to her. The Gospel has been the source of her inspiration, the object of her contemplation, the subject of her proclamation, and the reason for her missionary activity. "The integral conservation of Revelation, the word of God contained in Tradition and Scripture, as well as its continuous transmission, are guaranteed in their authenticity"[99] by the Holy Spirit.

Through Tradition, "the Church, in her doctrine, life and worship, perpetuates and transmits to every generation all that she herself is, all that she believes."[100] Handing on Divine Revelation to future generations of believers is a principal work of the Church under the guidance of the Holy Spirit. Christ commanded the apostles to preach the Gospel, which he himself proclaimed, and which he fulfilled in his own person. They did so through their own preaching, their example, and the institutions they established. They also communicated what they had seen and heard in writing, under the inspiration of the Holy Spirit. These sacred books held the message of salvation that Christ entrusted to them and that they were to safeguard until the end of time. "In order that the full and living Gospel might always be preserved in the church the apostles left bishops as their successors. They gave them 'their own position of teaching authority.'"[101]

---

98   1 Tm 2:4.
99   Congregation for the Clergy, *General Directory for Catechesis* (GDC) (Washington, D.C.: USCCB, 1998), no. 44.
100   DV, no. 8.
101   DV, no. 7

By the power of the Holy Spirit, Christ must be proclaimed to every person and to all nations in every age so that God's Revelation may reach the ends of the earth. "God, who spoke in the past, continues to converse with the spouse of his beloved Son [the Church]. And the Holy Spirit, through whom the living voice of the Gospel rings out in the Church—and through her in the world—leads believers to the full truth, and makes the Word of Christ dwell in them in all its richness."[102]

God's self-revelation given through his only Son in the Holy Spirit remains living and active in the Church. Sacred Tradition and Sacred Scripture together are the Deposit of Faith, which is guarded and protected by the Magisterium because it was given to us by Christ and cannot change. The transmission of that Revelation, in its integrity, is entrusted, by Divine Commission, to the Magisterium, to the Successor of St. Peter and the Successors of the Apostles. In a harmonious collaboration with the Magisterium in the Church's mission of evangelization, all the members of the People of God, priests, deacons, men and women religious, and the lay faithful, hand on the faith by proclaiming the Good News of salvation in Jesus Christ and communicating God's gift of his own divine life in the sacraments.

C. Faith

From the beginning, God has made known the inexhaustible mystery of his love in order to give us a share of his own divine life. In doing so, God summons a response in faith from his people, a response that itself is a gift. So unimaginable is God's gift of himself that our response can only be self-surrender, the obedience of faith,[103] of which Mary is the perfect embodiment.

Human beings are unique in creation because they alone can offer God a response of faith to his initiative of love. The response of faith has two integral dimensions: the faith *by which* one believes and the faith *which* one believes. Faith is a supernatural virtue. Faith is one's personal adherence to God who reveals himself; at the same time, faith is the free assent of one's intellect and will to the whole Truth that God has revealed.[104] The faith *by which* one believes is itself a gift from God. It is

---

102   DV, no. 8.
103   Cf. Rom 16:26.
104   Cf. CCC, no. 150.

God's grace that moves and assists the individual to believe. It is the interior help of the Holy Spirit that moves the heart and converts it to God.[105] The faith *which* one believes is also God's gift. It consists of the content of Divine Revelation. Faith, then, is the human response to a personal God, who has revealed himself, and to the Truth that God has revealed through the Catholic Church.

17. EVANGELIZATION AND THE MINISTRY OF THE WORD

A. The New Evangelization

Pope John Paul II has summoned the Church to undertake the new evangelization of the world and has invited peoples everywhere to open wide the doors to Christ. "I sense," he said, "that the moment has come to commit all of the Church's energies to a new evangelization and to the mission *ad gentes*.[106] No believer in Christ, no institution of the Church can avoid this supreme duty: to proclaim Christ to all peoples."[107] The Good News of Jesus Christ must be carried forth to every person and every nation so that it may penetrate the heart of every person and renew the human race. We carry forward this task of proclaiming the Gospel with our fellow Christians, where possible. Such common witness is an integral dimension of our mission to evangelize.[108] An ardent longing to invite others to encounter Jesus is the spark that starts the evangelizing mission to which the whole Church is called. The Church can spare no effort in leading all humanity to Christ because in Christ all humanity discovers the deepest truths about itself.

To evangelize individuals is not sufficient. The Gospel is intended for every people and nation; it finds a home in every culture. Those who proclaim the Christian message must know and love the culture and the people to whom they bring the message in order for it to be able to transform the culture and the people and make them new in Christ. "The new

---

105   Cf. DV, no. 5.
106   "*Ad gentes*" means "to the nations," meaning that this mission is to everyone in the world.
107   RM, no. 3.
108   Cf. John Paul II, *That They All May Be One* (*Ut Unum Sint*) (UUS) (Washington, D.C.: USCCB, 1995), nos. 89-90.109

evangelization calls for a clearly conceived, serious and well organized effort to evangelize culture."[109] The dynamism inherent in the new evangelization demands both the inculturation of the Gospel and the transformation of the culture by the Gospel.

In summary, the new evangelization is primarily the "clear and unequivocal proclamation of the person of Jesus Christ, that is, the preaching of his name, his teaching, his life, his promises and the Kingdom which he has gained for us by his Paschal Mystery."[110] It involves the active participation of every Christian in the proclamation and demonstration that the Christian faith is the only fully valid response to the problems and hopes that life poses to every person and society.[111] The new evangelization is directed to the Church herself: to the baptized who were never effectively evangelized before, to those who have never made a personal commitment to Christ and the Gospel, to those formed by the values of the secularized culture, to those who have lost a sense of faith, and to those who are alienated. It is also directed to all human cultures so that they might be open to the Gospel and live in harmony with Christian values.[112] The new evangelization is aimed at personal transformation through the development of a personal relationship with God, participation in sacramental worship, the development of a mature ethical and social conscience, ongoing catechesis, and a deepening integration of faith into all areas of life.

The purpose of this evangelization is to bring about faith and conversion to Christ. Faith involves a profound change of mind and heart, a change of life, a "*metanoia.*"[113] Such a change can only arise from deep within the interior of one's being, where one faces the truly important questions about human life. Such a change, engendered by the action of the Holy Spirit, shows itself in the transformation of one's life. One begins to live "in Christ" and is able to confess with St. Paul, "Yet I live, no longer I, but Christ lives in me."[114]

---

109   EA, no. 70.

110   EA, no. 66.

111   Cf. Pope John Paul II, *The Vocation and Mission of the Lay Faithful in the Church and in the World* (*Christifideles Laici*) (CL) (Washington, D.C.: USCCB, 1988), no. 34.

112   Cf. Pope John Paul II, Opening Address at Santo Domingo, 1992, no. 22.

113   EN, no. 10.

114   Gal 2:20.

B. Conversion

"The Christian faith is, above all, conversion to Jesus Christ."[115] It is the fruit of God's grace and the free response to the prompting of the Holy Spirit. It arises from the depths of the human person and involves such a profound transformation of heart and mind that it causes the believer to change radically both internally and externally. The Blessed Virgin Mary's perfect response to the grace of the Holy Spirit represents the primordial conversion to Christ and the "purest realization of faith."[116]

For the Christian, this *metanoia* reorients all aspects of the person's life to Christ. This conversion is the acceptance of a personal relationship with Christ, a sincere adherence to him, and a willingness to conform one's life to his. Conversion to Christ involves making a genuine commitment to him and a personal decision to follow him as his disciple. Through this discipleship the believer is united to the community of disciples and appropriates the faith of the Church. The faith of the Church "is a gift destined to grow in the hearts of believers."[117]

The process of conversion involves understanding who Christ is in order to change and follow him more closely. Conversion begins with an openness to the initial proclamation of the Gospel and a sincere desire to listen for its resonance within. This search arouses in those coming to Christ a desire to know him more personally and to know more about him. This knowledge of the person, message, and mission of Christ enables the believer to "make it into a living, explicit and fruitful confession of faith."[118] This profession of faith forms the foundation for the continuing journey under the guidance of the Holy Spirit. It is nourished by the sacraments, prayer, and the practice of charity "until we all attain to the unity of faith and knowledge of the Son of God . . . to the extent of the full stature of Christ."[119] "This is crucial: we must be converted—and we must continue to be converted! We must let the Holy Spirit change our lives! We must respond to Jesus Christ."[120]

---

115 GDC, no. 53; Cf. Catholic Church and Lutheran World Federation, *Joint Declaration on the Doctrine of Justification* (1999), no. 16, http://www.vatican.va/roman_curia/pontifical_councils/chrstuni/documents/rc_pc_chrstuni_doc_31101999_cath-luth-joint-declaration_en.html (accessed on August 29, 2003).

116 CCC, no. 149.

117 GDC, no. 56.

118 GDC, no. 82.

119 Eph 4:13.

120 USCCB, *Go and Make Disciples: A National Plan and Strategy for Catholic Evangelization in the United States (Tenth Anniversary Ed.)* (Washington, D.C.: USCCB, 2002), no. 14.

C. The Process of Evangelization

The Church's evangelizing activity consists of several essential elements: proclaiming Christ, preaching Christ, bearing witness to Christ, teaching Christ, and celebrating Christ's sacraments.[121]

Evangelization aims at both the interior change of individuals and the external change of societies. It is the totality of the Church's efforts to bring "the Good News into all the strata of humanity, and through its influence transforming humanity from within and making it new."[122] The essential elements of evangelization are distributed throughout a complex process of stages or moments.[123] These stages include the following: missionary activity directed toward non-believers or those who live in religious indifference, the initial proclamation of the Gospel, initial catechetical activity for those who choose the Gospel or need to complete or modify their initiation, and pastoral activity directed toward those of mature Christian faith.[124]

The ministry of the word is a fundamental element of evangelization through all its stages because it involves the proclamation of Jesus Christ, the eternal Word of God. "There is no true evangelization if the name, the teaching, the life, the promises, the Kingdom and the mystery of Jesus of Nazareth, the Son of God, are not proclaimed."[125]

The word of God nourishes both evangelizers and those who are being evangelized so that each one may continue to grow in his or her Christian life. From apostolic times the Church has exercised the ministry of the word in a variety of forms and functions that are closely linked in practice. First, the listeners are prepared for the first proclamation of the Gospel, or *pre-evangelization*. Pre-evangelization ordinarily builds on basic human needs, such as security, love, or acceptance, and shows how those basic human needs include a desire for God and his word.

Then comes the initial announcement of the Gospel, or *missionary preaching*. This form of the ministry of the word is directed toward non-believers, those who have chosen not to believe, those who follow other religions, and the children of Christians. In our age it may also be addressed to those who may have been baptized but have little or no awareness of their Baptism and who consequently live on the margins of Christian life.

---

121   Cf. EN, no. 17.
122   EN, no. 18.
123   Cf. CT, no. 18.
124   Cf. AG, no. 6.
125   EN, no. 22.

Initiatory catechesis follows for catechumens, those who are coming to the Catholic faith from another Christian tradition, Catholics who need to complete their initiation, children, and the young. The function of initiatory catechesis is to introduce the life of faith, the Liturgy, and the charity of the People of God to those being initiated.[126]

Mystagogical or *post-baptismal catechesis* is the form of the ministry of the word in which the implications for living a sacramental life are drawn out. The function of mystagogical catechesis is to lead the baptized deeper into the Christian life, celebration of the sacraments, prayer life of the Church, and her missionary activity.

Permanent or *continuing catechesis* involves the systematic presentation of the truths of the faith and the practice of Christian living. The function of permanent catechesis is to nourish the faith of believers throughout their lives.

While all Liturgy has a catechetical dimension, liturgical catechesis is most explicit in the form of the homily received during the celebration of the sacraments. As such, liturgical catechesis within the context of a sacred action is an integral part of that action.[127] Its function is "the immediate preparation for reception of the different sacraments, the celebration of sacramentals and above all of the participation of the faithful in the Eucharist, as a primary means of education in the faith."[128] Liturgical catechesis also includes reflection upon the ritual celebration.

Theological catechesis is the "systematic treatment and the scientific investigation of the truths of faith."[129] It has a distinctly theological function: namely, to help Christians understand the faith by engaging in a dialogue with "philosophical forms of thought, various forms of humanism, and the human sciences."[130]

D. The Context of Evangelization

Evangelization in the United States occurs within diverse and rapidly changing social, religious, and cultural contexts. Some have never

---

126 Cf. AG, no. 14.

127 Cf. Second Vatican Council, *Constitution on the Sacred Liturgy* (*Sacrosanctum Concilium*) (SC), no. 35.

128 GDC, no. 51.

129 Sacred Congregation for the Clergy, *General Catechetical Directory* (1971), no. 17, http://www.vatican.va/roman_curia/congregations/cclergy/documents/rc_con_cclergy_doc_11041971_gcat_en.html (accessed on March 15, 2005).

130 GDC, no. 51.

encountered Christ and have never been baptized. They are in need of the initial announcement of the Gospel and the first call to conversion. Some have been baptized but were never formed in the faith after their childhood. Some have lost their faith, have drifted away from the Church because of one issue or another, and now live their lives at a considerable distance from Christ and the Gospel. Some feel alienated from the Church because of the way they perceive the Church or her teaching. Although many of them may say they are Catholic, they no longer worship with the community; and thereby they deprive themselves of the gifts of God's Word and the sacraments of the Church.[131] An enthusiastic re-evangelization or new evangelization and a basic catechesis are needed. On the other hand, some of the baptized remain fervent in their faith and vibrant in their Christian living. They know Christ and his Gospel and have committed themselves to the Church's universal mission. A permanent catechesis centered around continual conversion "makes evangelizers of those who have been evangelized."[132]

These diverse and rapidly changing social, religious, and cultural contexts and the Church's evangelical and catechetical responses to them coexist in the same communities in many parts of the United States. The boundaries between and among the diverse social, religious, and cultural contexts are not clearly definable. In addition, the initial announcement of the Gospel and a basic catechesis, the new evangelization and an initiatory catechesis, and a more permanent catechesis are stages not entirely distinct from one another as dimensions of the Church's mission of evangelization. Catechesis in the United States receives from evangelization a missionary dynamic that encourages us to continue to evangelize the culture, affirming what is compatible and challenging what is not.

E. Pastoral Directives for Evangelization

In light of the social, cultural, and religious context of life in the United States, it is possible to suggest several pastoral directives to revitalize the Church's response to Pope John Paul II's call for a new evangelization. Dioceses and parishes are encouraged to study, reflect on, and adopt the goals of Go and Make Disciples: A National Plan and Strategy for Catholic

---

131 Cf. Go and Make Disciples, no. 39.
132 GDC, no. 58.

Evangelization in the United States and integrate them into their respective missions. All dioceses and parishes, in the efforts and resources they focus on the new evangelization, should pursue the following fundamental objectives:

1. To foster in the heart of every believer an experience of personal conversion to Jesus Christ that leads to a personal renewal and greater participation in the Christian life in the Church, the Mystical Body of Christ

2. To encourage a greater knowledge of the Holy Scriptures and Sacred Tradition of the Church

3. To focus their efforts and resources on the conversion and renewal of every parish, especially through the implementation of the Rite of Christian Initiation of Adults

4. To rededicate themselves to a liturgical renewal that develops a greater appreciation for the presence and power of Christ in the word of God and the sacraments of the Church, especially the Eucharist, and a stronger commitment to celebrating the Eucharist each Sunday

5. To make the evangelical and social justice dimensions of the Sunday Eucharist more explicit

6. To call their people to a more effective integration of daily prayer in their lives, especially the ancient practice of praying the Psalms and the Church's Liturgy of the Hours, contemplation of the mysteries of the life of Christ through the Rosary, and a greater reverence of the Eucharist through adoration of the Blessed Sacrament

7. To ensure that all Catholic institutions, especially parishes, are accessible and welcoming to all

(Other pastoral directives related to particular aspects of evangelization and catechesis will be outlined in subsequent chapters.)

These pastoral directives for evangelization give catechesis in the United States a missionary dynamic that encourages us to continue to evangelize the culture, affirming what is compatible and challenging what is not:

Seeing both the ideals and the faults of our nation, we Catholics need to recognize how much our Catholic faith, for all it has received from American culture, still has to offer to our nation.

On the level of truth, we have a profound and consistent moral teaching based on the dignity and destiny of every person created by God. On the practical level, we have the witness of American Catholics serving those most in need, educationally, socially, materially, and spiritually.[133]

The ministry of catechesis, as an essential moment in the Church's mission of evangelization,[134] is a fundamental ecclesial service for the realization of the missionary mandate of Jesus here in the United States.

18. SOURCE AND SOURCES OF CATECHESIS

The source of catechesis is found in the word of God revealed by Jesus Christ. "Catechesis will always draw its content from the living source of the word of God transmitted in Tradition and the Scriptures, for 'sacred Tradition and sacred Scripture make up a single sacred deposit of the word of God, which is entrusted to the Church.'"[135] Together they make the mystery of Christ present and fruitful in the Church.

Sacred Scripture "is the speech of God as it is put down in writing under the breath of the Holy Spirit."[136] Sacred Tradition "transmits in its entirety the Word of God which has been entrusted to the apostles by Christ the Lord and the Holy Spirit. It transmits it to the successors of the apostles so that, enlightened by the Spirit of truth, they may faithfully preserve, expound and spread it abroad by their preaching."[137]

To refer to the word of God in Sacred Scripture and Sacred Tradition as the principal source of catechesis means, on the one hand, that catechesis must be primarily based on the thought, spirit, and perspective of the Old and New Testaments. On the other, it means that the biblical texts from which catechesis proceeds must be read from within the Church's two-thousand-year experience of faith and life.

The Church, guided by the Holy Spirit in every age, must interpret the word of God. The Church performs this function authoritatively through

---

133   *Go and Make Disciples*, no. 59.
134   GDC, no. 63, citing CT, no. 18.
135   CT, no. 27.
136   DV, no. 9
137   DV, no. 9.

her living, teaching office, the Magisterium. The Magisterium ensures the Church's fidelity to the teaching of the apostles in matters of faith and morals. "The task of giving an authentic interpretation of the Word of God, whether in its written form or in the form of Tradition, has been entrusted to the living teaching office of the Church alone. Its authority in this matter is exercised in the name of Jesus Christ."[138] The Magisterium is the servant of the word of God. "It teaches only what has been handed on to it. At the divine command and with the help of the Holy Spirit, it listens to this devotedly, guards it with dedication and expounds it faithfully. All that it proposes for belief as being divinely revealed is drawn from this single deposit of faith."[139] Thus, the word of God, contained and transmitted in Sacred Scripture and Sacred Tradition and interpreted by the Magisterium, is the principal source of catechesis.

Catechesis has secondary sources as well. Catechesis is nourished when the word of God is more deeply understood and developed by the people exercising their faith under the guidance of the Magisterium. It is enlivened in the celebration of the Liturgy. Catechesis draws on theology as it seeks the fuller understanding of the Gospel message. Catechesis is enriched when the word of God shines forth in the life of the Church, especially in the lives of the saints and in the Christian witness of the faithful. And it is made more fruitful when the word of God is known from those genuine moral values that, by divine providence, are found in human society.

19. NATURE AND PURPOSE OF CATECHESIS: INITIATORY AND ONGOING

A. Nature and Purpose of Catechesis

"Catechesis is that particular form of the ministry of the word which matures initial conversion to make it into a living, explicit and fruitful confession of faith."[140]

Catechesis aims to bring about in the believer an ever more mature faith in Jesus Christ, a deeper knowledge and love of his person and message, and a firm commitment to follow him. In many situations, however,

---

138   DV, no. 10.
139   DV, no. 10.
140   GDC, no. 82.

catechesis must also be concerned with arousing initial faith and sustaining the gradual conversion to complete adherence to Jesus Christ for those who are on the threshold of faith. With God's grace, catechesis develops initial faith, nourishes the Christian life, and continually unfolds the mystery of Christ until the believer willingly becomes his disciple.

> To put it more precisely: within the whole process of evangelization, the aim of catechesis is to be the teaching and maturation stage, that is to say, the period in which the Christian, having accepted by faith the person of Jesus Christ as the one Lord and having given him complete adherence by sincere conversion of heart, endeavors to know better this Jesus to whom he has entrusted himself: to know his "mystery," the Kingdom of God proclaimed by him, the requirements and promises contained in his Gospel message, and the paths that he has laid down for any one who wishes to follow him.[141]

B. The Object of Catechesis

The object of catechesis is communion with Jesus Christ. Catechesis leads people to enter the mystery of Christ, to encounter him, and to discover themselves and the meaning of their lives in him. "At the heart of catechesis we find, in essence, a Person, the Person of Jesus of Nazareth, 'the only Son from the Father . . . full of grace and truth,'[142] who suffered and died for us and who now after rising, is living with us forever.'"[143] For in Christ the whole of God's eternal plan is revealed, a plan that begins with the Father's generation of his only Son and reaches its fulfillment in him. Christ is the living center of catechesis, who draws all persons to his Father through the Holy Spirit. "The definitive aim of catechesis is to put people not only in touch but in communion, in intimacy, with Jesus Christ: only he can lead us to the love of the Father in the Spirit and make us share in the life of the Holy Trinity."[144] St. Paul declared, "For to me life is Christ."[145]

---

141   CT, no. 20.
142   Jn 1:14.
143   CT, no. 5.
144   CT, no. 5.
145   Phil 1:21.

Jesus Christ himself is always the first and last point of reference in catechesis because he is "the way and the truth and the life."[146]

C. Catechesis and the Church

"Catechesis is an essentially ecclesial act"—an action of the Church:

> The true subject of catechesis is the Church which, continuing
> the mission of Jesus the Master and, therefore animated by the
> Holy Spirit, is sent to be the teacher of the faith. The Church imi-
> tates the Mother of the Lord in treasuring the Gospel in her heart.
> She proclaims it, celebrates it, lives it, and she transmits it in cat-
> echesis to all those who have decided to follow Jesus Christ. This
> transmission of the Gospel is a living act of ecclesial tradition.[147]

Thus, catechesis is a pivotal dimension of the Church's pastoral activity
and a significant element in all the Church does to hand on the faith.
Every means that the Church employs in her overall mission to go and
make disciples has a catechetical aspect. Catechesis gives form to the missionary preaching that is intended to arouse the first signs of faith. It
shapes the initial proclamation of the Gospel. Catechesis assists the early
examination of reasons for belief. It communicates the essential elements
in the experience of Christian living. It prepares for the celebration of the
sacraments. It facilitates integration into the ecclesial community. It urges
apostolic activity and missionary witness. It instills a zeal for the unity of
Christians and prepares one for the ecumenical understanding and mission of the Church. "Catechesis is intimately bound up with the whole of
the Church's life. Not only her geographical extension and numerical
increase but even more her inner growth and correspondence with God's
plan depend essentially on catechesis."[148]

The Church is the historical realization of God's gift of communion in
Christ. As such she is the origin, *locus*, and goal of catechesis. Catechesis
springs from the Church. "The profession of faith received by the Church
(*traditio*), which germinates and grows during the catechetical process, is

---

146   Jn 14:6.
147   GDC, no. 78.
148   CT, no. 13.

given back (*redditio*), enriched by the values of different cultures."[149] The Church depends on an effective catechesis to be faithful to Christ's command to proclaim the Gospel. "The Christian community is in herself living catechesis."[150]

The Church is a natural environment for catechesis. She provides the primary setting for the proclamation of the Gospel, the point of welcome for those who seek to know the Lord, the place where men and women are invited to conversion and discipleship, the environment for the celebration of the sacraments, and the motivation for apostolic witness in the world.

The Church is also the goal of catechesis. Catechesis aims to build up the Body of Christ, the Church. "The more the Church, whether on the local or the universal level, gives catechesis priority over other works and undertakings the results of which would be more spectacular, the more she finds in catechesis a strengthening of her internal life as a community of believers and of her external activity as a missionary Church."[151]

D. Initiatory Catechesis

Within the Church's mission of evangelization, catechesis promotes and matures initial conversion, educates persons in the faith, and incorporates them into the life of the Christian community. Today, however, catechesis must often take the form of the primary proclamation of the Gospel because many who present themselves for catechesis have not yet experienced conversion to Jesus Christ. Some level of conversion is necessary, however, if catechesis is to be able to fulfill its proper task of education in the faith.[152]

In some situations initial catechesis precedes Baptism, while in others it follows Baptism; but in all situations, catechesis serves initiation. In seeking to foster the initial faith of the catechumen in the person of Jesus Christ, catechesis leads to a genuine profession of faith. This profession of faith is the goal of catechesis and an inherent element in the sacraments of initiation. It forms the link between the catechesis and the sacraments

---

149 GDC, no. 78.
150 GDC, no. 141.
151 CT, no. 15.
152 Cf. International Commission on English in the Liturgy (ICEL) and USCCB Bishops' Committee on the Liturgy, *Rite of Christian Initiation of Adults* (RCIA) (Washington, D.C.: USCCB, 1988), no. 9.

of initiation, especially Baptism. The aim of catechetical activity is to encourage a living, explicit and fruitful profession of faith.[153]

Initiatory catechesis "should be of a kind that while presenting Catholic teaching in its entirety also enlightens faith, directs the heart toward God, fosters participation in the liturgy, inspires apostolic activity, and nurtures a life completely in accord with the spirit of Christ."[154] Such initiatory catechesis is a

> comprehensive and systematic formation in the faith [that] . . . includes more than instruction: it is an apprenticeship of the entire Christian life, it is a 'complete Christian initiation,' which promotes an authentic following of Christ, focused on his Person; it implies education in knowledge of the faith and in the life of faith, in such a manner that the entire person, at his deepest lev-els, feels enriched by the word of God.[155]

It is "a basic and essential formation, centered on what constitutes the nucleus of Christian experience, the most fundamental certainties of the faith and the most essential evangelical values."[156] Initiatory catechesis cultivates the roots of faith, nurtures a distinctively Christian spiritual life, and prepares the person to be nourished at the table of the Eucharist and in the ordinary life of the Christian community.

Initiatory catechesis incorporates those preparing for the sacraments of initiation into the Christian community that knows, lives, celebrates, and bears witness to the faith. The richness of this initiatory catechesis should serve to inspire other forms of catechesis.[157]

E. Ongoing Catechesis

Catechesis for those who have received the sacraments of initiation goes beyond that which was provided by initiatory catechesis. It serves the continuing conversion and ongoing formation of those who have been

---

153   Cf. Second Vatican Council, *Decree on the Pastoral Office of Bishops in the Church* (*Christus Dominus*) (CD), no. 14.
154   RCIA, no. 78.
155   GDC, no. 67.
156   GDC, no. 67.
157   GDC, no. 68.

initiated into the faith. Such continuing conversion and ongoing formation are the responsibility of the whole Catholic community and occur most fruitfully within the community. Ongoing catechesis fosters the growth of a more mature faith in the members of the community. It aims to make each person's faith "living, explicit and active, . . . enlightened by doctrine."[158] While catechesis seeks to enrich the faith life of people at every stage of their development, every form of catechesis is oriented in some way to the catechesis of adults who are capable of a full response to God's word.[159] Ongoing catechesis is "a lifelong process for the individual and a constant and concerted pastoral activity of the Christian community."[160] The most effective forms of this lifelong catechesis involve the study and praying of Sacred Scripture, a systematic catechesis that gradually leads people deeper into their relationship with Jesus because they grow in their understanding of who he is and what he has done for us, liturgical and sacramental catechesis, initiatives of spiritual formation, and thorough examination of the Church's social teachings.

20. TASKS OF CATECHESIS

Jesus formed his disciples by making known to them the various dimensions of the Kingdom of God. He entrusted to them "the mysteries of the kingdom of heaven";[161] he taught them how to pray;[162] he opened his "meek and humble heart" to them;[163] and he sent them "ahead of him in pairs to every town and place he intended to visit."[164] The fundamental task of catechesis is to achieve this same objective: the formation of disciples of Jesus Christ. Jesus instructed his disciples; he prayed with them; he showed them how to live; and he gave them his mission.

Christ's method of formation was accomplished by diverse yet interrelated tasks. His example is the most fruitful inspiration for effective catechesis today because it is integral to formation in the Christian faith. Catechesis must attend to each of these different dimensions of faith;

---

158   CD, no. 14.
159   Cf. *General Catechetical Directory*, no. 20.
160   *National Catechetical Directory*, no. 32.
161   Mt 13:11.
162   Cf. Lk 11:2.
163   Mt 11:29.
164   Lk 10:1.

each becomes a distinct yet complementary task. Faith must be known, celebrated, lived, and expressed in prayer. So catechesis comprises six fundamental tasks, each of which is related to an aspect of faith in Christ. All efforts in evangelization and catechesis should incorporate these tasks.

1. *Catechesis promotes knowledge of the faith.* The initial proclamation of the Gospel introduces the hearers to Christ for the first time and invites conversion to him. By the action of the Holy Spirit, such an encounter engenders in the hearers a desire to know about Christ, his life, and the content of his message. Catechesis responds to this desire by giving the believers a knowledge of the content of God's self-revelation, which is found in Sacred Scripture and Sacred Tradition, and by introducing them to the meaning of the Creed. Creeds and doctrinal formulas that state the Church's belief are expressions of the Church's living tradition, which from the time of the apostles has developed "in the Church with the help of the Holy Spirit."[165]

2. *Catechesis promotes a knowledge of the meaning of the Liturgy and the sacraments.* Since Christ is present in the sacraments,[166] the believer comes to know Christ in the liturgical celebrations of the Church and is drawn into communion with him. Christ's saving action in the Paschal Mystery is celebrated in the sacraments, especially the Eucharist, where the closest communion with Jesus on earth is possible as Catholics are able to receive his living Flesh and his Precious Blood in Holy Communion. Catechesis should promote "an active, conscious genuine participation in the liturgy of the Church, not merely by explaining the meaning of the ceremonies, but also by forming the minds of the faithful for prayer, for thanksgiving, for repentance, for praying with confidence, for a community spirit, and for understanding correctly the meaning of the creeds."[167] Sacramental catechesis prepares for the initial celebration of the sacraments and provides enrichment following their reception.

---

165   DV, no. 8.
166   Cf. SC, no. 7.
167   *General Catechetical Directory*, no. 25.

3. *Catechesis promotes moral formation in Jesus Christ.* Jesus' moral teaching is an integral part of his message. Catechesis must transmit both the content of Christ's moral teachings as well as their implications for Christian living. Moral catechesis aims to conform the believer to Christ—to bring about personal transformation and conversion. It should encourage the faithful to give witness—both in their private lives and in the public arena—to Christ's teaching in everyday life. Such testimony demonstrates the social consequences of the demands of the Gospel.[168]

4. *Catechesis teaches the Christian how to pray with Christ.* Conversion to Christ and communion with him lead the faithful to adopt his disposition of prayer and reflection. Jesus' entire life, death, and Resurrection were an offering to his Father. His prayer was always directed toward his Father. Catechesis should invite the believer to join Christ in the Our Father. Prayer should be the ordinary environment for all catechesis so that the knowledge and practice of the Christian life may be understood and celebrated in its proper context.

5. *Catechesis prepares the Christian to live in community and to participate actively in the life and mission of the Church.* Jesus said to his disciples, "Love one another. As I have loved you. . . ."[169] This command provides the basis for the disciples' life in community. Catechesis encourages an apprenticeship in Christian living that is based on Christ's teachings about community life. It should encourage a spirit of simplicity and humility, a special concern for the poor, particular care for the alienated, a sense of fraternal correction, common prayer, mutual forgiveness, and a fraternal love that embraces all these attitudes. Catechesis encourages the disciples of Jesus to make their daily conduct a shining and convincing testimony to the Gospel.[170] "He also distributes special graces among the faithful of every rank. By these gifts he makes them fit and ready to undertake various tasks and offices for the renewal and building up of the Church, as it is written, 'the manifestation

---

168 Cf. CT, nos. 29ff.
169 Jn 13:34.
170 Cf. CL, nos. 34, 51.

of the Spirit is given to everyone for profit' (1 Cor 12:7)."[171] Preparation for community life has an ecumenical dimension as well: "In developing this community sense, catechesis takes special note of the ecumenical dimension and encourages fraternal attitudes toward members of other Christian churches and ecclesial communities."[172] It should always provide a clear exposition of all that the Church teaches and at the same time should foster a "true desire for unity"[173] and inculcate a zeal for the promotion of unity among Christians. Catechesis will have an ecumenical dimension as it prepares the faithful to live in contact with persons of other Christian traditions, "affirming their Catholic identity while respecting the faith of others."[174]

6. *Catechesis promotes a missionary spirit that prepares the faithful to be present as Christians in society.* "The 'world' thus becomes the place and the means for the lay faithful to fulfill their Christian vocation."[175] Catechesis seeks to help the disciples of Christ to be present in society precisely as believing Christians who are able and willing to bear witness to their faith in words and deeds. In fostering this spirit of evangelization, catechesis nourishes the evangelical attitudes of Jesus Christ in the faithful: to be poor in spirit, to be compassionate, to be meek, to hear the cry of injustice, to be merciful, to be pure of heart, to make peace, and to accept rejection and persecution.[176] Catechesis recognizes that other religious traditions reflect the "seeds of the Word"[177] that can constitute a true "preparation for the Gospel."[178] It encourages adherents of the world's religions to share what they hold in common, never minimizing the real differences between and among them. "Dialogue is not in opposition to the mission *ad gentes*."[179]

---

171   LG, no. 12.
172   GDC, no. 86.
173   CT, no. 32.
174   CT, no. 32.
175   CL, no. 15.
176   Cf. Mt 5:3-11.
177   AG, no. 11.
178   LG, no. 16.
179   RM, no. 55. Cf. Second Vatican Council, *Declaration on the Relation of the Church to Non-Christian Religions (Nostra Aetate)* (NA).

These six tasks of catechesis constitute a unified whole by which cat-echesis seeks to achieve its objective: the formation of disciples of Jesus Christ. All these tasks are necessary in order to attain the full develop-ment of the Christian faith. Each task, from its own perspective, realizes the object of catechesis, and all the tasks are interdependent. Knowledge of the Christian faith, for example, leads to celebrating it in the sacramen-tal Liturgy. Participation in the sacramental life encourages moral trans-formation in Christ. Christian moral living leads to prayer, enhances com-munity life, and encourages a missionary spirit. To accomplish these tasks, catechesis depends on the "transmission of the Gospel message and expe-rience of the Christian life."[180] "It is very important that catechesis retain the richness of these various aspects in such a way that one aspect is not separated from the rest to the detriment of others."[181]

21. INCULTURATION OF THE GOSPEL MESSAGE

A. The Mystery of the Incarnation: Model of Evangelization

Jesus Christ, the incarnate Word of God, conceived in the womb of the Virgin Mary by the Holy Spirit, became man—a particular man in space and time and within a specific culture. In the mystery of his incarnation, Jesus Christ is the human face of God and the divine face of humanity.[182] The incarnation of the only Son of God is the original inculturation of God's word. The mystery of the incarnation is also the model of all evan-gelization by the Church. Every culture needs to be transformed by Gospel values because the Gospel always demands a conversion of atti-tudes and practices wherever it is preached. Cultures must often be puri-fied and restored in Christ.

B. The Evangelization of Culture

Just as "the Word became flesh / and made his dwelling among us,"[183] so too the Good News, the word of God proclaimed to the nations, must

---

180   GDC, no. 87
181   *General Catechetical Directory*, no. 31.
182   Cf. EA, no. 67.
183   Jn 1:14.

take root in the life situation of the hearers of the word. Inculturation is precisely the insertion of the Gospel message into cultures. Inculturation is a requirement for evangelization, a path toward full evangelization. It is the process by which "catechesis 'takes flesh' in the various cultures."[184]

"The new evangelization calls for a clearly conceived, serious and well organized effort to evangelize culture."[185] The inculturation of the faith is a complex and deliberate process. It "needs to take place gradually, in such a way that it really is an expression of the community's Christian experience."[186] "It is not simply an external adaptation designed to make the Christian message more attractive or superficially decorative."[187]

C. The Process of Inculturation

The inculturation of the Gospel occurs within a dynamic process that has several interactive elements. Inculturation involves listening to the culture of the people for an echo of the word of God. It involves the discernment of the presence of authentic Gospel values or openness to authentic Gospel values in the culture. This discernment is governed by two basic principles: "compatibility with the Gospel and communion with the universal Church."[188] It involves, when necessary, the purification of the elements in the culture that may be hostile or adverse to the Gospel. And it involves an invitation to conversion.

> True inculturation occurs when the gospel penetrates the heart of cultural experience and shows how Christ gives new meaning to authentic human values. However, the Church must never allow herself to be absorbed by any culture, since not all cultural expressions are in conformity with the gospel. The Church retains the indispensable duty of testing and evaluating cultural expressions in the light of her understanding of revealed truth. Cultures, like individual human beings and societies, need to be purified by the blood of Christ.[189]

---

184   CT, no. 53.
185   EA, no. 70.
186   RM, no. 54.
187   GDC, no. 109.
188   RM, no. 54.
189   USCCB, *To the Ends of the Earth: A Pastoral Statement on World Mission* (Washington, D.C.: USCCB, 1986), no. 44.

The inculturation of the Gospel message is an urgent mission for the dioceses in the United States because it correlates faith and life. It seeks to dispose the people of the United States, who live in a multicultural and pluralistic society, to receive Jesus Christ in every dimension of their life. The process of inculturation must involve the people to whom the Gospel is addressed, so that they can receive the faith and reflect it. It touches them on the personal, cultural, economic, and political levels so that they can live a holy life in total union with God the Father, through the action of the Holy Spirit. "It is necessary to inculturate preaching in such a way that the Gospel is proclaimed in the language and in the culture of its hearers."[190]

In the inculturation of the faith, catechesis has several specific tasks:

- To discover the seeds of the Gospel that may be present in the culture
- To know and respect the essential elements and basic expressions of the culture of the persons to whom it is addressed
- To recognize that the Gospel message is both transcendent and immanent—it is not bound by the limitations of any single human culture, yet it has a cultural dimension, that in which Jesus of Nazareth lived
- To proclaim the transforming and regenerating force that the Gospel works in every culture
- To promote a new enthusiasm for the Gospel in accordance with evangelized culture
- To use the language and culture of the people as a foundation to express the common faith of the Church
- To maintain the integral content of faith and avoid obscuring the content of the Christian message by adaptations that would compromise or diminish the deposit of faith

Within the ecclesial community, the catechist is an important instrument of inculturation. The catechist has encountered Christ, has been converted by Christ, follows Christ, and shares in Christ's life and mission. The catechist also possesses a living social conscience and is well rooted in the cultural environment. Thus, the catechist needs to be alert to all these tasks that incarnate the Gospel in a particular culture and

190 EA, no. 70.

likewise introduce the culture into the life of the Church. At the same time, the faithful have a right to receive the whole deposit of faith; catechists "must take diligent care faithfully to present the entire treasure of the Christian message."[191]

Effective catechesis presents the authentic Gospel message, "the words of eternal life."[192] The genuine deposit of faith given by Christ to his apostles and preserved by them for more than two thousand years must be faithfully handed on to future generations of Christians.

> Evangelization loses much of its force and effectiveness if it does not take into consideration the actual people to whom it is addressed, if it does not use their language, their signs and symbols, if it does not answer the questions they ask, and if it does not have an impact on their concrete life. But on the other hand, evangelization risks losing its power and disappearing altogether if one empties or adulterates its content under the pretext of translating it.[193]

The evangelization of culture through the communication of the complete and authentic Gospel message, and the inculturation of that message through a profound dialogue between it and the language, customs, and practices of a people, constitute what Pope Paul VI termed the "drama of our time."[194]

D. Inculturation and the Media

Especially in the United States, "the very evangelization of modern culture depends to a great extent on the influence of the media."[195] In fact, the mass media are so influential that they have a culture of their own, which has its own language, customs, and values. Heralds of the Gospel must enter the world of the mass media, learn as much as possible about that culture, evangelize that culture, and determine how best to employ the media to serve the Christian message.

---

191   *General Catechetical Directory*, no. 38, cited in GDC, no. 112.
192   Jn 6:68.
193   EN, no. 63.
194   EN, no. 20.
195   RM, no. 37.

If the new evangelization of the mass media is going to be effective, however, the Church must deepen her understanding of the culture in which the communications media are so consequential and learn how to make proper use of the media to proclaim Christ's message. Pastoral ministers need to be trained as specialists in communications technology; state-of-the-art production centers need to be set up; communication networks need to be developed; and the faithful need to learn how to be more discriminating in their use of the media, especially in their homes. "Using the media correctly and competently can lead to a genuine inculturation of the Gospel."[196]

22. CONCLUSION

Evangelization is so central to the life of the Church that, should she neglect her sacred responsibility of bringing the Good News of Jesus Christ to all of humanity, she would be faithful neither to the mission entrusted to her by her Lord nor to her identity as mother and teacher. As it is, through the power of the Holy Spirit, the Church's ministry of evangelization animates her life. The pastoral and missionary activity that constitute the Church's resolute commitment to evangelize comprises certain elements that have distinctly catechetical aspects: the initial proclamation of the Gospel that awakens faith, the examination of reasons for belief, the celebration of the sacraments, the experience of Christian living and integration into the ecclesial community, and apostolic witness. The Church's mission of evangelization is permeated by catechesis. While catechesis and evangelization cannot be simply identified with one another, "there is no separation or opposition between catechesis and evangelization. . . . Instead, they have close links whereby they integrate and complement each other."[197]

Catechesis is so central to the Church's mission of evangelization that, if evangelization were to fail to integrate catechesis, initial faith aroused by the original proclamation of the Gospel would not mature, education in the faith through a deeper knowledge of the person and message of Jesus Christ would not transpire, and discipleship in Christ

---

196   EA, no. 72.
197   CT, no. 18.

through genuine apostolic witness would not be fostered. Catechesis nurtures the seed of faith sown by the Holy Spirit through the initial proclamation of the Gospel. It gives growth to the gift of faith given in Baptism and elaborates the meaning of the sacraments. Catechesis develops a deeper understanding of the mystery of Christ, encourages more profound incorporation into the Church, and nourishes Christian living. It encourages discipleship in Christ and instructs in Christian prayer. Just as the mission of evangelization enlivens the Church's pastoral and missionary activity, catechesis makes concrete her mission of evangelization. It constitutes the "good news" that Christ commissioned his apostles to spread throughout the whole world and announce to every person.[198] This good news, which is the faith of the Church, will be presented in Chapter 3.

---

198   Cf. Mk 16:15.

CHAPTER 3

This Is Our Faith; This Is the Faith of the Church

For I handed on to you as of first importance what I also received: that Christ died for our sins in accordance with the scriptures; that he was buried; that he was raised on the third day in accordance with the scriptures; that he appeared to Cephas, then to the Twelve. (1 Cor 15:3-5)

23. INTRODUCTION

In expressing and handing on the faith that Jesus entrusted to them before he ascended to his Father, the apostles made use of brief summaries by which all could come to know the fundamental content of Christian belief and preaching. These initial creedal statements synthesized the Christian faith and became the original catechetical reference points for the apostolic Church. They were the first professions of faith; they were intended especially for candidates for Baptism; and they have preserved the substance of the Christian message for people of all the nations for more than two thousand years.

Since the *Catechism of the Catholic Church* is a catechesis of the Creed, this chapter presents a brief introduction to it in order to facilitate its better understanding and use in the catechetical ministry. This chapter also provides the criteria for the authentic presentation of the Christian message in the United States at this time in history.

24. THE SYMPHONY OF THE FAITH

A. Normative Instruments of Catechesis

Sacred Scripture, the *Catechism of the Catholic Church*, the *General Directory for Catechesis*, and this *National Directory for Catechesis* are distinct yet complementary instruments that serve the Church's catechetical activity. The *General Directory for Catechesis* provides "the basic principles of pastoral theology taken from the Magisterium of the Church, and in a special way from the Second Vatican Council, by which pastoral action in the ministry of the word can be more fittingly directed and governed."[199] This *National Directory for Catechesis* contains the general guidelines for catechesis in the United States and has been prepared by the United States Conference of Catholic Bishops. *Our Hearts Were Burning Within Us* gives a plan and strategies for development of an effective ministry of adult faith formation in parish life.

B. Sacred Scripture

Sacred Scripture, the word of God written under the inspiration of the Holy Spirit, has the preeminent position in the life of the Catholic Church and especially in the ministry of evangelization and catechesis. The earliest forms of Christian catechesis made regular use of the Old Testament and the personal witness of the apostles and disciples that would become the New Testament. Much of the catechesis of the patristic period took the form of commentary on the word of God contained in Sacred Scripture. Through all the ages of the Church, the study of Sacred Scripture has been the cornerstone of catechesis. The Second Vatican Council advised that catechesis, as one form of the ministry of the word, should be nurtured and should thrive in holiness through the word of the Scripture.[200] Catechesis should take Sacred Scripture as its inspiration, its fundamental curriculum, and its end because it strengthens faith, nourishes the soul, and nurtures the spiritual life. "Scripture provides the starting point, foundation, and norm of catechetical teaching."[201] Catechesis

---

199 GDC, no. 120.
200 Cf. DV, no. 12.
201 Pontifical Biblical Commission, *The Interpretation of the Bible in the Church* (Washington, D.C.: USCCB, 1994), 39.

should assume the thought and perspective of Sacred Scripture and make frequent direct use of the biblical texts themselves. "The presentation of the Gospels should be done in such a way as to elicit an encounter with Christ, who provides the key to the whole biblical revelation and communicates the call of God that summons each one to respond."[202]

C. The *Catechism of the Catholic Church*

The *Catechism of the Catholic Church* is an act of the Magisterium promulgated by Pope John Paul II by virtue of his apostolic authority.[203] It is "a statement of the Church's faith and of catholic doctrine, attested to or illumined by Sacred Scripture, the Apostolic Tradition, and the Church's Magisterium."[204] It "aims at presenting an organic synthesis of the essential and fundamental contents of Catholic doctrine, as regards both faith and morals, in the light of the Second Vatican Council and the whole of the Church's Tradition."[205] The *Catechism of the Catholic Church* is a valid and legitimate instrument for ecclesial communion; it is a sure norm for teaching the faith and an authentic reference text for teaching Catholic doctrine and particularly for preparing local catechisms. However, the *Catechism* is not just an authentic reference text; it is a beautiful collection of the truths of the Catholic faith, following in the footsteps of the early Church. The foundation of the *Catechism* is Sacred Scripture, and it includes writings of the Fathers, doctors, and saints of the Church. It is not intended to replace local catechisms, but rather to encourage the preparation of new local catechisms that take into account particular cultures and preserve the unity of faith and fidelity to Catholic doctrine.[206]

This *National Directory for Catechesis*, as far as the content of the Christian message is concerned, presumes and refers to the *Catechism of the Catholic Church*. The following exposition of the *Catechism of the Catholic Church* seeks not to summarize its content but instead to facilitate its better understanding and use in the catechetical ministry in the United States.

---

202   *The Interpretation of the Bible in the Church*, 39.

203   Cf. John Paul II, *On the Publication of the "Catechism of the Catholic Church" (Fidei Depositum)* (FD), no. 3. In CCC.

204   FD, no. 3.

205   CCC, no. 11.

206   Cf. FD, no. 3.

Pope John Paul II has called the *Catechism of the Catholic Church* "the 'symphony' of the faith"[207] because it is the result of the collaboration of the whole Episcopate of the Catholic Church throughout the world and because it expresses the harmony of their confession of the faith.

The *Catechism of the Catholic Church* is structured around four fundamental dimensions of the Christian life: (1) the profession of faith, (2) the celebration of the Liturgy, (3) Christian moral life, and (4) prayer. These four parts correspond to the essential aspects of the Christian mystery: (1) belief in the Triune God and his saving plan in Jesus Christ, (2) celebration of Christ's saving actions in the sacramental life, (3) living life in Christ, and (4) expression of the Christian faith in prayer. This structure in turn derives from the profound unity of the Christian life.

> The Church professes this mystery [of the faith] in the Apostles' Creed (*Part One*) and celebrates it in the sacramental liturgy (*Part Two*), so that the life of the faithful may be conformed to Christ in the Holy Spirit to the glory of God the Father (*Part Three*). This mystery, then, requires that the faithful believe in it, that they celebrate it, and that they live from it in a vital and personal relationship with the living and true God. This relationship is prayer (*Part Four*).[208]

The *Catechism of the Catholic Church* is the doctrinal point of reference for education in the basic tasks of catechesis.[209] However, it does not impose a predetermined format for the presentation of doctrine.

The inspiration of the *Catechism of the Catholic Church* derives from the person of Jesus Christ as he reveals the mystery of the Holy Trinity and the mystery of the human person. Through Jesus Christ, we come to know God and his divine plan for our salvation, we come to know ourselves and our destiny, and we come to know how to live. These are the four golden threads of the *Catechism*: the Blessed Trinity; Jesus as God and Man; the Paschal Mystery of Jesus' passion, death, Resurrection, and Ascension into heaven attaining our salvation; the dignity of the human person.

As the central mystery of the Catholic faith, the mystery of the Triune God animates and orders the presentation of the Christian message

---

207 FD, no. 1.
208 CCC, no. 2558.
209 See Chapter 2 of this *Directory*.

in the *Catechism of the Catholic Church*. The profession of faith is precisely a confession of faith in the Holy Trinity. It is divided into the fundamental doctrinal formulations that state Christian belief in the Father, the Son, and the Holy Spirit. It presents the sacraments and the Liturgy as the "work of the Holy Trinity."[210] It presents the Christian life as directed by the Trinity: "Everyone who follows Christ does so because the Father draws him and the Spirit moves him."[211] The profession of faith presents the prayer of the believer as "a communion with the Holy Trinity."[212]

The mystery of the human person is woven throughout the *Catechism of the Catholic Church* as well. Every human person longs to know God. "'Believing' is a human act, conscious and free, corresponding to the dignity of the human person."[213] The celebration of the Christian mystery in the Church's Liturgy and sacraments expresses the faith in words and signs that make sense to the human person. "It is with and through their own human culture, assumed and transfigured by Christ, that the multitude of God's children has access to the Father, in order to glorify him in the one Spirit."[214] In seeking to conform their lives to Christ, Christians are called to lead a life "worthy of the gospel of Christ."[215] "The vocation of humanity is to show forth the image of God and to be transformed into the image of the Father's only Son."[216] By deliberate actions, the human person "does, or does not, conform to the good promised by God and attested by moral conscience."[217] Christian prayer is "the life of the new heart. It ought to animate us at every moment."[218]

The *Catechism of the Catholic Church* is a catechism for the universal Church. As a catechism, it is "*an organic presentation* of the Catholic faith in its entirety."[219] It is universal in scope because it presents the "events and fundamental salvific truths which express the faith common to the People of God and which constitute the indispensable basic reference for

---

210   CCC, no. 1077.
211   CCC, no. 259.
212   CCC, no. 2655.
213   CCC, no. 180.
214   CCC, no. 1204.
215   Phil 1:27.
216   CCC, no. 1877.
217   CCC, no. 1700.
218   CCC, no. 2697.
219   CCC, no. 18.

catechesis."[220] It seeks "to link the wondrous unity of the Christian mystery with the varied needs and conditions of those to whom this message is addressed."[221] However,

> by design, this *Catechism* does not set out to provide the adaptation of doctrinal presentations and catechetical methods required by the differences of culture, age, spiritual maturity, and social and ecclesial condition among all those to whom it is addressed. Such indispensable adaptations are the responsibility of particular catechisms and, even more, of those who instruct the faithful.[222]

The *Catechism of the Catholic Church* presents and preserves the deposit of faith. The deposit of faith is the heritage of faith contained in Sacred Scripture and Tradition and handed on in the Church from the time of the apostles—a heritage from which the Magisterium draws all that it proposes for belief as being divinely revealed. "Catechesis will find in this genuine, systematic presentation of the faith and of Catholic doctrine a totally reliable way to present, with renewed fervor, each and every part of the Christian message to the people of our time. This text will provide every catechist with sound help for communicating the one, perennial deposit of faith within the local Church."[223]

Sacred Scripture has a preeminent position in catechesis because Sacred Scripture "present[s] God's own Word in unalterable form" and "make[s] the voice of the holy Spirit resound again and again in the words of the prophets and apostles."[224] The *Catechism of the Catholic Church* is intended to complement Sacred Scripture. Together with Sacred Tradition, Sacred Scripture constitutes the supreme rule of faith.

In practice, this means that catechesis must be permeated with biblical and evangelical thought, spirit, and attitudes through constant use of and reference to the word of God. The *Catechism of the Catholic Church* is not superior to the word of God but is, rather, at its service. Each nourishes the

---

220 GDC, no. 124.
221 John Paul II, *Apostolic Letter in Which the Latin Typical Edition of the "Catechism of the Catholic Church" Is Approved and Promulgated* (*Laetamur Magnopere*) (LM) (1997), xv. In CCC.
222 CCC, no. 24.
223 LM, p. xv.
224 DV, no. 21.

ministry of catechesis: "Both Sacred Scripture and the *Catechism of the Catholic Church* must inform biblical as well as doctrinal catechesis so that they become true vehicles of the content of God's word."[225]

In addition, the *Catechism of the Catholic Church* retrieves several important aspects of the catechetical tradition of the Church Fathers, who placed a high priority on the baptismal catechumenate in the life of the local churches. They emphasized the gradual and progressive movement of Christian initiation and formation through a series of stages and rituals. This was acknowledged when the Fathers of the Second Vatican Council called for the restoration of the adult catechumenate largely as it was celebrated and preserved in the patristic tradition.[226]

25. CRITERIA FOR THE AUTHENTIC PRESENTATION OF THE CHRISTIAN MESSAGE

The word of God contained in Sacred Scripture and Sacred Tradition is the single source of the fundamental criteria for the presentation of the Christian message. The presentation of the Christian message

- Centers on Jesus Christ
- Introduces the Trinitarian dimension of the Gospel message
- Proclaims the Good News of salvation and liberation
- Comes from and leads to the Church
- Has a historical character
- Seeks inculturation and preserves the integrity and purity of the message
- Offers the comprehensive message of the Gospel and respects its inherent hierarchy of truths
- Communicates the profound dignity of the human person
- Fosters a common language of the faith

A. The Christian Message, Centered on Christ

The Christian message concentrates on the person of Jesus Christ. Above all, catechesis must transmit this centrality of Christ in the Gospel message.

---

225   GDC, no. 128.
226   Cf. SC, no. 64.

Catechesis that is centered on Christ presents Christ first and presents everything else with reference to him,[227] for he is the center of the Gospel message. "At the heart of catechesis we find, in essence, a Person, the Person of Jesus of Nazareth, 'the only Son from the Father . . . full of grace and truth.'"[228]

Catechesis that is centered on Christ presents Christ as "the center of the history of salvation."[229] He came "in the fullness of time."[230] As the definitive Revelation of God, he is the point in salvation history toward which the created order proceeds from the beginning of time and the final event toward which it converges. "Jesus Christ is the same yesterday, today, and forever."[231] He is "the key, the center and the purpose of the whole of man's history."[232]

Christ-centered catechesis presents the Gospel message as the word of God written down by human authors under the inspiration of the Holy Spirit.[233] It transmits "the teaching of Jesus Christ, the Truth that he communicates or, to put it more precisely, the Truth that he is."[234]

Because the Gospels narrate the life of Jesus and the mystery of our redemption after Christ and the Reign of God that he proclaimed, catechesis will also be centered on Christ if the Gospels occupy a pivotal place within it. They "are our principal source for the life and teaching of the Incarnate Word, our Savior."[235] They transmit the life, message, and saving actions of Jesus Christ and express the teaching that was proposed to the first Christian communities. Catechesis must be centered in the Gospels, because "Jesus Christ is their center."[236]

In presenting catechesis that is centered on Christ, dioceses and parishes should

---

227   Cf. CT, no. 6.
228   CT, no. 5.
229   *General Catechetical Directory*, no. 41.
230   Eph 1:10.
231   Heb 13:8.
232   Second Vatican Council, *Pastoral Constitution on the Church in the Modern World (Gaudium et Spes)* (GS), no. 10.
233   CCC, nos. 105-106.
234   CT, no. 6.
235   DV, no. 18.
236   CCC, no. 139.

- Explicitly and consistently proclaim the name, teaching, promises, and mystery of Jesus Christ, as well as his announcement of the coming of the Reign of God
- Develop, through effective preaching, teaching, adult faith formation, and catechist formation programs, the personal relationship that Christ has initiated with each of his disciples
- Promote conversion to Jesus Christ and communion with him through the sacraments, especially the Holy Eucharist
- Teach, in a way that can be understood by specific cultures, that Christ is the ultimate meaning and purpose of history; and provide programs that help all who catechize to present the teachings of Christ "about God, man, happiness, the moral life, death, etc. without in any way changing his thought"[237]
- Help all who catechize to understand that, like Jesus, their teaching is not their own but, rather, comes from God[238]

B. The Trinitarian Character of the Christian Message

The Christian message is inherently Trinitarian because its source is the incarnate Word of the Father, Jesus Christ, who speaks to the world through his Holy Spirit.[239] Anointed by the Holy Spirit, Jesus' life is constantly oriented to the Father. He teaches in communion with the Father and the Holy Spirit. He leads us to the mystery of God in himself: Father, Son, and Holy Spirit. The Christian life and the Christian message are radically Trinitarian.

In presenting catechesis that is Trinitarian in nature, dioceses and parishes should help all who catechize to

- Understand that their presentation of the Gospel message must always proceed "through Christ, to the Father, in the Holy Spirit"[240] and "lead to [a] confession of faith in God, Father, Son and Holy Spirit"[241]

---

237 GDC, no. 98.
238 Cf. Jn 7:16.
239 The witness of the Eastern Catholic Churches to the explicitly Trinitarian character of Christian theology, liturgy, and spirituality has been a fruitful source of inspiration for the whole Church.
240 *General Catechetical Directory*, no. 41.
241 GDC, no. 99.

- Present God's plan of loving kindness, which was conceived by the Father, was fulfilled in the Son, and is directed by the Holy Spirit in the life of the Church
- Understand that the primary subject of catechesis is the mystery of the Holy Trinity, "the central mystery of Christian faith and life"[242]
- Present the fact that the innermost being of God, in whose image all are made, is a communion of love with vital implications for Christian living
- Draw out the moral implications for Christians who are called to be a people gathered in the unity of the Father, Son, and Holy Spirit

C. The Christian Message That Proclaims the Good News of Salvation and Liberation from Sin

The Christian message proclaims the gift of salvation in Jesus Christ. Jesus' announcement of the Kingdom of God marks a new and definitive intervention by God "with a transforming power equal and even superior to his creation of the world."[243] Christ's proclamation of salvation is the "center of his Good News."[244]

The Good News of the Kingdom of God, which proclaims salvation, includes a message of liberation for all, but especially for the poor. Jesus addressed his announcement of the kingdom principally to the frail, the vulnerable, the disabled, and the poor—not only the economically poor, but the culturally and religiously poor as well.[245] The Beatitudes proclaim the liberation that the kingdom brings. It is not merely a liberation from all the forms of injustice that oppress people; it is especially a liberation from sin.

Liberation from sin is the fundamental form of freedom from which all liberation emerges. Christ's message of liberation brought "glad tidings to the poor." He was sent "to proclaim liberty to captives / and recovery of sight to the blind, / to let the oppressed go free, / and to proclaim a year acceptable to the Lord,"[246] precisely so that the oppressed might be open to the action of the Holy Spirit in their lives.

---

242   CCC, no. 234.
243   GDC, no. 101.
244   EN, no. 9.
245   Cf. John Paul II, *On the Hundredth Anniversary of Rerum Novarum* (*Centesimus Annus*) (CA) (Washington, D.C.: USCCB, 1991), no. 57.
246   Lk 4:18-19.

In presenting catechesis that proclaims the Good News of salvation, dioceses and parishes should transmit the fundamental message of the Kingdom of God by emphasizing several basic points that Jesus made throughout his preaching:

1. God is a loving Father who abides with his people.
2. With the coming of the kingdom, God offers us salvation, frees us from sin, brings us into communion with him and all humanity, and promises eternal salvation.
3. The Kingdom of God is one of justice, love, and peace, in the light of which we shall be judged.
4. The Kingdom of God is inaugurated in the person of Jesus Christ;[247] it is in mystery present now on the earth and will be perfected when the Lord returns.
5. The Church, the community of disciples, "is, on earth, the seed and the beginning of that kingdom"[248] and "is effectively and concretely at the service of the Kingdom."[249]
6. The Church offers a foretaste of the world to come, and human life is a journey back to God.

Catechesis helps the Christian faithful to integrate Christ's message of liberation in several important ways. It first situates his message of liberation within the "specifically religious objective of evangelization."[250] Therefore, dioceses and parishes should help the Christian faithful to integrate Christ's message of liberation by

- Situating his message of liberation within the "specifically religious finality of evangelization"[251]
- Ensuring that the message of liberation "cannot be contained in the simple and restricted dimension of economics, politics, social or cultural life"[252]

---

247 Cf. LG, no. 3.
248 LG, no. 5.
249 RM, no. 20.
250 EN, no. 32.
251 EN, no. 32.
252 EN, no. 33.

- Presenting Christian social morality as a demand of the Gospel's message of liberation and a consequence of the great commandment of love
- Arousing "a love of preference for the poor"[253] in those being catechized
- Emphasizing that "what is already due in justice is not to be offered as a gift of charity"[254]

D. The Ecclesial Character of the Christian Message

Catechesis has a distinctly ecclesial character because the Christian community transmits the Gospel essentially as it has received it, understands it, celebrates it, lives it and communicates it.[255] Apostles received the Gospel message directly from Christ under the action of the Holy Spirit and preached it to the first Christian communities. Martyrs bore witness to it by their blood. Saints have lived it deeply. Fathers and Doctors of the Church have taught it wisely. Bishops have carefully preserved it with zeal and love and interpreted it authentically. Missionaries have proclaimed it courageously. Theologians have helped others understand it.[256] The People of God have applied it more fully in their daily lives. All continue these efforts today.

Although the community of the disciples of Jesus Christ is spread throughout the world, the Gospel message that binds them together is one; it is the same faith that is transmitted in many different languages and through many cultures. The Church has constantly and consistently confessed this: "one Lord, one faith, one baptism; one God and Father of all, who is over all and through all and in all."[257]

"Catechesis originates in the Church's confession of faith and leads to the profession of faith of the catechumen and those to be catechized."[258] In presenting catechesis, dioceses and parishes should ensure that catechesis

---

253   John Paul II, *On Social Concern* (*Sollicitudo Rei Socialis*) (SRS) (Washington, D.C.: USCCB, 1988), no. 42.
254   Second Vatican Council, *Decree on the Apostolate of the Lay People* (*Apostolicam Actuositatem*) (AA), no. 8.
255   Cf. CCC, no. 2558.
256   Cf. GDC, no. 105.
257   Eph 4:5-6.
258   GDC, no. 105.

- Transmits the one faith to all peoples
- Introduces catechumens and those to be catechized to the unity of the profession of faith
- Nourishes the unity of the Body of Christ

E. The Historical Character of the Christian Message

The Gospel message of salvation in Jesus Christ has a distinctly historical character. Jesus Christ is a historical figure who preached the Good News of the coming of the Kingdom of God in time. The Incarnation, passion, death, and Resurrection of Christ are real historical events. Jesus Christ poured out his Holy Spirit and established the Church on Pentecost, thereby ushering in a new era of salvation history: the age of the Church. During this era, Christ is revealing the work of salvation in the life of the Church "until he comes" again.[259]

While the Church transcends history, she is also part of it. For her part, the Church remembers the saving events of the past and makes them known in every age. These events constitute the "constant 'memory'" of the Church.[260] Christ lives now and acts now in and with his Church. His gift to the Church, the Holy Spirit, continues to "renew the face of the earth"[261] as the Church awaits the return of her Lord and Savior.

In presenting the historical character of the Christian message, dioceses and parishes should ensure that catechesis

- Proclaims the words and deeds of God throughout history
- Presents salvation history as it is set forth in Sacred Scripture through
    1. The various stages of Revelation in the Old Testament
    2. The fulfillment of Revelation in the life and teaching of Jesus
    3. The history of the Church whose responsibility it is to transmit Revelation to future generations
- Helps to interpret the meaning of the events of salvation history for the present age in light of Revelation

---

259 1 Cor 11:26.
260 GDC, no. 107.
261 Ps 104:30.

- Situates the sacraments within the history of salvation and helps those being catechized to "re-read and re-live the great events of salvation history in the 'today' of [the Church's] liturgy"[262]
- Helps those being catechized to understand the mystery at work in the historical events of salvation: the mystery of the Son of God at work in his humanity, the mystery of salvation at work in the history of the Church, and the evidence of God's presence at work in the signs of the times[263]
- Contributes to a healing of memories, to the reevaluation of past animosities and stereotypes among Christians, and to the interpretation of the past in a new way in the light of ecumenical developments

F. The Inculturation of the Christian Message

The inculturation of the Gospel is also a key criterion for the pastoral presentation of the Christian message because the Good News of Jesus Christ is intended for people of all cultures. It is not a superficial adaptation designed to make the Gospel more pleasing to its hearers. It is, rather, a process that brings the transforming power of the Gospel to touch persons in their hearts and cultures at their deepest levels.

In presenting catechesis that is both an inculturation of the Christian message and a careful preservation of the authenticity of that message, dioceses and parishes are encouraged to

- Present the same Gospel message that was given by Jesus Christ in its integrity and purity, avoiding any division, subtraction, or distortion of it
- Look to the Church as the principal agent of inculturation and involve persons of various cultures in planning the catechetical mission
- Gather information on the diverse cultural makeup of the community
- Develop and use culturally appropriate catechetical methods, tools, texts, and resources

---

262 CCC, no. 1095.
263 Cf. GDC, no. 108.

- Cultivate catechetical leadership that reflects the cultural diversity of the locality
- Prepare catechists in their native language and cultural situations
- Rely on catechists who not only have "a profound religious sense [but] also possess a living social conscience and [are] well rooted in [their] cultural environment"[264]
- Ensure that catechesis is grounded in the cultural environment in which it is presented
- Respond to the various requirements of diverse cultures
- Ensure that catechesis employs popular devotions and the distinctive symbols of faith common to various cultural groups
- Ensure that catechetical initiatives work toward making the catechumenate and catechetical formation programs into centers of inculturation that employ, with proper discernment, the language, symbols, and values of the catechumens and those being catechized
- Enable those being catechized to become more able to explain the faith to others in the culture in which they live and to be able to give "reason for [their] hope"[265]

G. The Comprehensive Hierarchical Character of the Christian Message

The "organic hierarchical character"[266] of the Christian message is another vital criterion for the presentation of the Gospel. The harmony and coherence of the Christian message require that the different truths of the faith be organized around a center, the mystery of the Most Holy Trinity: "the source of all the other mysteries of faith, the light that enlightens them."[267]

"In Catholic doctrine there exists an order or 'hierarchy' of truths, since they vary in their relation to the foundation of the Christian faith."[268] The existence of a hierarchy of truths does not provide the grounds for ignoring or eliminating some truths of the faith. Neither should such a hierarchy be confused with the assignment of degrees of

---

264 GDC, no. 110.
265 1 Pt 3:15.
266 CT, no. 31.
267 CCC, no. 234.
268 Second Vatican Council, *Decree on Ecumenism (Unitatis Redintegratio)* (UR), no. 11.

certainty to the individual truths of the faith: "This hierarchy does not mean that some truths pertain to faith itself less than others, but rather that some truths are based on others as of a higher priority, and are illumined by them."[269]

All levels of catechesis should carefully consider the hierarchy of truths in the presentation of the Christian message. All aspects and dimensions of the Christian message are related to these principle truths. In presenting the comprehensive hierarchical character of the Christian message, dioceses and parishes should ensure that catechesis presents

- The Christian message, organized around its central truths: "the mystery of God the Father, the Son, and the Holy Spirit, Creator of all things; the mystery of Christ the incarnate Word, who was born of the Virgin Mary, and who suffered, died, and rose for our salvation; the mystery of the Holy Spirit, who is present in the Church, sanctifying it and guiding it until the glorious coming of Christ, our Savior and Judge; and the mystery of the Church, which is Christ's Mystical Body, in which the Virgin Mary holds the preeminent place"[270]
- Baptism as the foundational sacrament of Christian life, which celebrates the saving action of Christ's life, death, and Resurrection; which grafts us onto the vine that is Christ; and which gives us a share in his mission to realize the Reign of God
- The history of salvation, organized in reference to Jesus Christ, the "center of the history of salvation"[271]
- The Apostles' Creed as "a synthesis of and a key to reading all of the Church's doctrine, which is hierarchically ordered around it"[272]
- The sacraments as "an organic whole in which each particular sacrament has its own vital place"[273]
- The Eucharist as the "Sacrament of sacraments," to which all the other sacraments are ordered as to their end[274]

---

269   *General Catechetical Directory*, no. 43.
270   *General Catechetical Directory*, no. 43.
271   *General Catechetical Directory*, no. 41.
272   GDC, no. 115.
273   CCC, no. 1211.
274   Cf. CCC, no. 1211.

- The double commandment of love of God and neighbor as the centerpiece of Jesus' moral teaching, summing up the Decalogue and lived in the spirit of the Beatitudes—"the whole law and the prophets depend on these two commandments"[275]
- The Our Father as the synthesis of prayer contained in Sacred Scripture and in the life of the Church[276]

H. The Communication of Profound Meaning for the Human Person

Another criterion for the presentation of the Christian message is that it must convey a profoundly meaningful message for the human person. Jesus Christ is "the image of the invisible God, / the firstborn of all creation."[277] In the mystery of his incarnation, Christ has united himself to every human being. He is the perfect man who reveals to all human beings their own true nature and their eternal destiny in communion with God. If we seek to know ourselves and the meaning of our lives, we should look to Christ, for "he worked with human hands, he thought with a human mind. He acted with a human will, and with a human heart he loved."[278]

In presenting catechesis that communicates profound meaning for the human person, dioceses and parishes should ensure

- That catechesis not only reveals God's identity but, in doing so, reveals the deepest truths about human beings: that we are made in God's image, that we are religious beings by nature, that the desire for God is written on our hearts, that God never ceases to draw us to himself, and that we are made to live in communion with him
- That catechesis is concerned with the ultimate meaning of life and its deepest questions
- That catechesis examines the more significant experiences of life in light of the Gospel

---

275   Mt 22:40.
276   Cf. GDC, no. 115.
277   Col 1:15.
278   GS, no. 22.

- That the initial proclamation of the Gospel is done with an awareness of human nature and shows how the Gospel fully satisfies the aspirations of the human heart[279]
- That biblical catechesis helps to interpret human experiences in the light of the experiences of the people of Israel and of Jesus Christ and his Church
- That doctrinal catechesis, based on the Creed, shows how the great themes of the faith are sources of life and enlightenment for human beings
- That moral catechesis is a "*catechesis of the beatitudes*, for the way of Christ is summed up in the beatitudes, the only path that leads to the eternal beatitude for which the human heart longs"[280]
- That liturgical catechesis explains the signs and symbols of the sacred rites corresponding to human experiences[281]
- That ecumenical catechesis helps all the faithful who are called upon to make a personal commitment toward promoting increasing communion with other Christians[282]
- That catechesis seeks to dispose people "to hope in the future life that is the consummation of the whole history of salvation"[283]

I. The Promotion of a Common Language of Faith in Transmitting the Christian Message

The final criterion for the presentation of the Christian message is that it should foster a common language of the faith so that it may be proclaimed, celebrated, lived, and prayed in words familiar to all the faithful. "We do not believe in formulas, but in those realities they express, which faith allows us to touch."[284] But as Catholics we do rely on the formulations of the faith to express and probe the meanings of the mysteries that the formulas attempt to describe. We also need familiar formulations of the faith in order to hand it on to future generations of believers. The

---

279 Cf. AG, no. 8.
280 CCC, no. 1697.
281 Cf. GDC, no. 117.
282 Cf. UUS, no. 8.
283 Col 1:23.
284 CCC, no. 170.

Church has guarded the words of the Lord since he spoke them and since apostolic times has preserved the formulations of the faith.

In presenting catechesis that fosters a common language of the faith, dioceses and parishes should ensure that catechesis

- Respects and values "the language proper to the message, especially biblical language, as well as the historical-traditional language of the Church (*creed, liturgy*) and doctrinal language (*dogmatic formulations*)"[285]
- Uses the technical language of the faith while also demonstrating the contemporary relevance of the traditional formulas for communicating the faith
- Enters into dialogue with the particular people to whom the Christian message is being presented
- Avoids terminology that would alter the substance of faith
- Employs language suited to today's children, young people, and adults in general, as well as to many other categories of people: for example, students, intellectuals and scientists, those who are illiterate, and persons with disabilities[286]

26. CONCLUSION

The sacred duty and the joy of each succeeding generation of Christian believers has been to hand on the deposit of faith that was first entrusted to the apostles by Christ himself. We have received this gift, the deposit of faith—we have not conceived it. It is the heritage of the whole Church. It is our privilege and our responsibility to preserve the memory of Christ's words and the words themselves and to teach future generations of believers to carry out all that Christ commanded his apostles.

Sound catechesis, however, involves more than the presentation of the content of Christ's message according to the criteria outlined above. The effective presentation of the content of the Christian faith also depends on the methodology employed in the transmission of the Good News. That methodology is the subject of the next chapter.

---

285   Cf. GDC, no. 208.
286   Cf. CT, no. 59.

CHAPTER 4

Divine and Human Methodology

For just as from the heavens
the rain and snow come down
And do not return there
till they have watered the earth,
making it fertile and fruitful,
Giving seed to him who sows
and bread to him who eats,
So shall my word be
that goes forth from my mouth;
It shall not return to me void,
but shall do my will,
achieving the end for which I sent it.
(Is 55:10-11)

27. INTRODUCTION

God's word has mighty power; it effects the purpose for which it is intended. More than a message, it is an event that inspires, even compels, action. Christ's missionary command was just such an event. It impelled the apostles to carry God's word to the ends of the earth. God infused humanity with the grace of his Holy Spirit in order to bring forth the divine fruit of conversion to Christ and confession of faith—so powerful is the word of God in accomplishing his will.

God's word continues to achieve its end through the human word. "The communication of the faith in catechesis is an event of grace, realized in the encounter of the word of God with the experience of the person."[287] Catechesis must express the word of God faithfully in the languages, signs, and cultures of those to whom it is directed. It should convey the whole word of God, as interpreted by the Church, in ways that can be easily understood. Just as God used a methodology to disclose his loving plan of salvation and prepare his people for the coming of his Son, so too does the Church employ a methodology that corresponds closely to God's original process of Revelation. This methodology for proclaiming the same Christian message to people in a variety of particular circumstances and conditions includes many different yet complementary means. All forms of the Church's methodology, however, are rooted in Christ.

This chapter describes God's self-revelation in Christ and through the Spirit as the norm for all catechetical methodology. It also addresses the human elements of catechetical methodology and the impact of communications technology on the proclamation of the Gospel.

28. GOD'S OWN METHODOLOGY

God's Revelation is the self-disclosure of the loving communion of Father, Son, and Holy Spirit in which he makes known the mystery of his divine plan. Since the ultimate purpose of his plan is human salvation,[288] God's own methodology engages persons and communities in light of their circumstances and their capacity to accept and interpret Revelation. God's self-communication is realized gradually through his actions and his words. It is most fully achieved in the Word made flesh, Jesus Christ. The history of this self-revelation itself documents the method by which God transmits the content of Revelation as contained in Sacred Scripture and Tradition. This is the pedagogy of God. It is the source and model of the pedagogy of the faith.[289]

---

287   GDC, no. 150.
288   GDC, no. 139.
289   Cf. DV, no. 15.

A. The Pedagogy of God

God is Father, Son, and Holy Spirit: one God in three divine persons. The inner life of the Trinity and the actions of the divine persons are undivided and inseparable. Who God is and what he does form a unity of divine life and activity. The work of Revelation is the common work of the three divine persons. Each person of the Trinity, however, shows forth what is proper to him within the one divine nature. Therefore, the Church confesses "one God and Father from whom all things are, and one Lord Jesus Christ, through whom all things are, and one Holy Spirit in whom all things are."[290] These properties of the divine persons within the Trinity are reflected in the pedagogy of God.

1. The Father

The Father made himself known in creation and in his eternal Word, Jesus Christ. Through the mystery of the incarnation, Jesus revealed God as Father and Creator: the eternal Father of his only-begotten Son and the Creator of all that exists. Out of nothing and through his eternal Word and Spirit, the Father created all things, and all creation is good. By his Word, who is his perfect image from all eternity, his "Son," the Father upholds and sustains the whole creation; he both transcends his creation and is present within it.

The Father bestowed his word on generation after generation of believers until in the fullness of time he communicated his one unsurpassable Word in the person of Jesus Christ. He made a covenant with his people that bound him to them and them to him in an everlasting pledge of love, liberating them from the bondage of slavery and sin. He transformed events in the life of his people into encounters with himself. He formed his people through victory and defeat, reward and punishment, happiness and sorrow, forgiveness and suffering. God the Father gave the Law to Moses as a means of leading the Chosen People to his son, Jesus. The moral law that derives from it "can be defined as fatherly instruction."[291] He showed himself throughout the history of Israel in many manifestations, "in which the cloud of the Holy Spirit both revealed him and concealed him in its shadow."[292]

---

290 Council of Constantinople II, no. 421. In Henricus Denziger and Adolfus Schönmetzer, eds., *Enchiridio Symbolorum* (DS) (Freiburg: Herder), 1300-1301.

291 CCC, no. 1950.

292 CCC, no. 707.

2. Jesus Christ

The redemptive mission of Jesus Christ continued the pedagogy of God in the history of salvation. Jesus Christ is the preeminent model for the communication of the faith and the formation of believers in the faith because he became truly human while remaining truly God. God's eternal Word became flesh to help us know God's love, to save us, to be our model of holiness, and to have us "share in the divine nature."[293] In the mystery of his incarnation, Christ joins divinity with humanity in teaching the faith and forming disciples.

Christ's relationship with his disciples also reveals God's own methodology as the model for all catechetical methods. In a sign of basic human affirmation, Jesus chose his apostles; they did not choose him.[294] He established a bond of friendship with them that was the context for his teaching. "I have called you friends," he said, "because I have told you everything I have heard from my Father."[295] He engaged them in lively conversations by asking them probing questions: "Who do people say that I am?"[296] He gave them hope: when they saw him coming toward them on the water, he said, "Take courage, it is I, do not be afraid!"[297] After he taught the crowds, he explained the meaning of his teaching to his disciples "in private."[298] Jesus said to them, "Knowledge of the mysteries of the kingdom of heaven has been granted to you. . . ."[299] He taught them to pray.[300] He sent them out as his apprentices on mission;[301] he instructed them, "Whoever wishes to come after me must deny himself, take up his cross, and follow me."[302] To sustain them on their mission, Jesus promised to send them the Spirit of Truth, who would lead the Apostles to all Truth.[303]

Christ's methodology was multi-dimensional. It included his words, his signs, and the wonders he worked. He reached out to the poor, to sinners, and to those on the margins of society. He proclaimed insistently the

---

293   2 Pt 1:4.
294   Cf. Jn 15:16.
295   Jn 15:15.
296   Mk 8:27.
297   Mk 6:50.
298   Mk 4:34.
299   Mt 13:11.
300   Cf. Lk 11:1-2.
301   Cf. Lk 10:1-20.
302   Mk 8:34
303   Cf. Mt 10:20; Jn 16:13.

coming of the Kingdom of God, the forgiveness of sins, and reconciliation with the Father. Especially in his parables, Christ invited his listeners to a whole new manner of life sustained by faith in God, encouraged by hope in the kingdom, and animated by love for God and neighbor. He used every resource at his disposal to accomplish his redemptive mission. "The whole of Christ's life was a continual teaching: his silences, his miracles, his gestures, his prayer, his love for people, his special affection for the little and the poor, his acceptance of the total sacrifice on the Cross for the redemption of the world, and his Resurrection are the actualization of his word and the fulfillment of revelation."[304]

3. The Holy Spirit

The action of the Holy Spirit in the Church continues the pedagogy of God. The Holy Spirit unfolds the divine plan of salvation within the Church. With Christ, the Holy Spirit animates the Church and directs her mission. The Holy Spirit makes the Paschal Mystery of Christ present in the human mind to accept Christ, converts the human heart to love Christ, and encourages the human person to follow Christ. Thus, the Holy Spirit makes new life in Christ possible for the believers. "The Holy Spirit, the artisan of God's works, is the master of prayer."[305] The Holy Spirit draws all humanity to Christ and, through Christ, into communion with the Trinity.

4. The Church

Under the guidance of the Holy Spirit, the Church continues God's own methodology in a living catechesis. "From her very beginnings the Church, which 'in Christ, is in the nature of a Sacrament,' has lived her mission as a visible and actual continuation of the pedagogy of the Father and of the Son."[306] The Church constantly seeks to discover the most fruitful way to announce the Good News and looks first to the method used by God. The Church's proclamation of the Gospel has been both progressive and patient, as was her Master's, respecting the freedom of individuals and taking into consideration their "slowness to believe."[307] In

---

304 CT, no. 9.
305 CCC, no. 741.
306 GDC, no. 141.
307 EA, no. 29.

the lives and teachings of the martyrs and saints, in the treasury of her teaching, in the witness of catechists, and in various examples of Christian life, the Church has reflected God's own methodology for communicating the faith. Those who wish to become disciples of Jesus today will pass through the same process of discovery and commitment.

B. Catechesis and Divine Methodology

"Catechesis, as communication of divine Revelation, is radically inspired by the pedagogy of God, as displayed in Christ and in the Church."[308] It conveys God's loving plan of salvation in the person of Jesus Christ. It emphasizes God's initiative in this plan, his attentive disclosure of it, and his respect for individual liberty. It recognizes the dignity of the human person within this profound dialogue with God and the continual need for conversion. Catechesis acknowledges the gradual nature of God's self-revelation, the profound mystery of the growth of God's word in a person, and the need for adaptation to different persons and cultures. It keeps Christ, the incarnate Word of God, ever at its center in order to bring humanity to God and God to humanity. It constantly draws inspiration from the Holy Spirit, who unfolds the mystery of Christ in the Church.

The methods employed by catechesis aim to harmonize the personal adherence of the believer to God, on the one hand, and to the content of the Christian message, on the other. Catechesis attends to the development of all the dimensions of the faith: as it is known, as it is celebrated, as it is lived, and as it is prayed. It seeks to bring about a conversion to Christ that leads to a profession of faith in the Triune God and to a genuine personal surrender to him. It helps believers to become disciples and to discern the vocation to which God is calling them.

God's own methodology inspires a plurality of methods in contemporary catechesis. The method or methods chosen, however, must ultimately be determined by a law that is fundamental for the whole of the Church's life. Catechetical methodology must exhibit a twofold fidelity. On the one hand, it must be faithful to God and to his Revelation; on the other, it must respect the liberty and promote the active participation of those being catechized. From the beginning of time, God has adapted his message to earthly conditions[309] so that we might be able to receive it.

---

308   GDC, no. 143.
309   Cf. DV, no. 13.

"This implies for catechesis the never ending task of finding a language capable of communicating the word of God and the creed of the Church, which is its development, in the various circumstances of those who hear it."[310] In this light, genuine catechesis employs methodology that

- Emphasizes God's loving initiative and the person's free response
- Accepts the progressive nature of Revelation, the transcendence and mysterious nature of the word of God, and the word's adaptation to different persons and cultures
- Recognizes the centrality of Jesus Christ
- Values the community experience of faith
- Is rooted in interpersonal relations and makes its own the process of dialogue
- Utilizes signs, which link words and deeds, teaching and experience
- Draws its power of truth, and its task to bear witness to the truth, from the Holy Spirit[311]

As the believer progresses on the journey toward the Father in the footsteps of Christ under the guidance of the Holy Spirit, catechesis should deepen the believer's understanding of the mystery of Christ. A strengthening of faith, in turn, leads to a change of heart (conversion) in order to be more committed and follow Christ more closely.[312] Catechesis should promote a synthesis of the faith by which we have been taught to believe and the faith which we enact in our everyday lives. It develops all dimensions of faith: knowledge, liturgical celebration, Christian living, and prayer. It challenges persons to abandon themselves completely and freely to God. It helps individuals to discern the vocation to which the Lord calls them. In short, catechesis "carries out [the] complete work of initiation, education and teaching."[313]

29. ELEMENTS OF HUMAN METHODOLOGY

In the transmission of the faith, the Church does not rely on any single human method. Rather, she uses God's own methodology as the paradigm

---

310 GDC, no. 146.
311 Cf. GDC, no. 143.
312 Cf. CT, no. 20.
313 GDC, no. 144.

and, with that divine pedagogy as the reference point, chooses diverse methods that are in accord with the Gospel. "Although certain norms or criteria apply to all catechesis, they do not determine a fixed methodology."[314] A variety of methods is required in order to ensure that the Gospel is proclaimed "to all the nations." "The variety in the methods used is a sign of life and a resource."[315]

The situation of those to whom catechesis is addressed is not a peripheral concern in the proclamation of the Gospel—rather, it is integral to its successful transmission. "The age and the intellectual development of Christians, their degree of ecclesial and spiritual maturity and many other personal circumstances"[316] must be carefully considered in choosing the appropriate methodologies. A diversity of methods in catechesis does not detract from its primary objective—evangelization and conversion to Jesus Christ—nor does it dilute the unity of faith. "Perfect fidelity to Catholic doctrine is compatible with a rich diversity of presentation."[317]

Effective catechesis should feature no opposition or artificial separation between content and method. Similar to the dynamic present in the pedagogy of God, catechetical methodology serves to transmit both the content of the entire Christian message and the source of that message, the Triune God. Catechetical methodology must be able to communicate that message, together with its sources and language, to particular ecclesial communities while always bearing in mind the particular circumstances of those to whom the message is addressed. Content and method interact and harmonize in the communication of the faith.

The communication of faith in catechesis is, first of all, "an event of grace" under the action of the Holy Spirit, "realized in the encounter of the word of God with the experience of the person. It is expressed in sensible signs and is ultimately open to mystery. It can happen in diverse ways, not always completely known to us."[318] An individual hears the word of God through catechesis and is moved by the Holy Spirit to listen, consider, assent to the truth, and respond through the obedience of faith.

Catechetical methods employ two fundamental processes that organize the human element in the communication of the faith: the *inductive*

---

314 *National Catechetical Directory*, no. 176.
315 CT, no. 51.
316 CT, no. 51.
317 GDC, no. 122.
318 GDC, no. 150.

method and the *deductive method*. "The inductive approach proceeds from the sensible, visible, tangible experiences of the person, and leads, with the help of the Holy Spirit, to more general conclusions and principles."[319] Since faith may be known through signs, the inductive method reflects the economy of Revelation insofar as we come to know God through his self-disclosure in the particular events of salvation history. The "inductive method consists of presenting facts (biblical events, liturgical acts, events in the Church's life as well as events from daily life) so as to discern the meaning these might have in divine Revelation."[320] The deductive method proceeds in the opposite manner, beginning with the general principles or truths of the faith and applying them to the concrete experiences of those to whom the catechesis is addressed. This method is used to interpret and explain the facts by proceeding from their causes. The deductive method, however, has full value only when the inductive process is completed.[321]

In the context of catechesis, the deductive method corresponds to the "*kerygmatic*" approach. This catechetical method begins with the proclamation of the faith as it is expressed in the principal documents of the faith, such as Sacred Scripture, the Creeds, or the Liturgy, and applies it to particular human experiences. This methodology begins with the principles and moves to the specifics in a descending direction. The inductive method, on the other hand, corresponds to a more "existential" approach, beginning with the specifics of human experience and examining them in the light of the word of God in an ascending direction. Both are legitimate approaches when properly applied and are distinct yet complementary methods for communicating the faith.

A. Learning Through Human Experience

Human experience is a constituent element in catechesis. It is the human element in the person's encounter with the word of God. Human experiences provide the sensible signs that lead the person, by the grace of the Holy Spirit, to a better understanding of the truths of the faith. They are the means through which human beings come to know themselves, one another, and God. They "give rise to concerns and questions, hopes and anxieties, reflections and judgments, which increase one's desire to penetrate more

---

319 *National Catechetical Directory*, no. 176.
320 GDC, no. 150.
321 Cf. *General Catechetical Directory*, no. 72.

deeply into life's meaning."[322] Human experience "serves in the examination and acceptance of the truths which are contained in the deposit of revelation."[323]

Jesus consistently used the ordinary human experiences of daily life to form his disciples, to point to the end of time, and to show the transcendent dimension of all of life and of God's eternal presence in it. Because the eternal Word assumed human nature, human experience is the *locus* for the manifestation and realization of salvation in him. By the grace of the Holy Spirit, persons come to know Christ, to know that he was sent from the Father, and to know that he died to save them in the midst of their human experience.

Human experience is affected by the fallen state of human nature; human beings are in need of redemption in Jesus Christ, and their experiences can lead to errors in judgment and action. However, human experience has been enlightened by Christ; for that reason, it can connect the person intimately with the Christian message and "is a necessary medium for exploring and assimilating the truths which constitute the objective content of Revelation."[324]

Catechesis links human experience to the revealed word of God, helping people ascribe Christian meaning to their own existence. It enables people to explore, interpret, and judge their basic experiences in light of the Gospel. Catechesis helps them relate the Christian message to the most profound questions in life: the existence of God, the destiny of the human person, the origin and end of history, the truth about good and evil, the meaning of suffering and death, and so forth. By recalling God's salvific action in human history, catechesis helps people to recognize their need for conversion and leads them to conversion in Christ.

B. Learning by Discipleship

An integral element in catechesis is learning by discipleship. The Christian faith is, above all, conversion to Jesus Christ, full adherence to his person and the decision to walk in his footsteps.[325] Discipleship is thus centered on the person of Jesus Christ and the kingdom he proclaims. "By following the

---

322 *National Catechetical Directory*, no. 176.
323 *General Catechetical Directory*, no. 74.
324 GDC, no. 152.
325 Cf. GDC, no. 152.

example of his self-giving love, we learn to be Christian disciples in our own time, place, and circumstances."[326] In learning to follow Christ, we become aware that there exist "facets of Christian life that come to full expression only by means of development and growth toward Christian maturity."[327] For disciples, saying "yes" to Jesus Christ means that they abandon themselves to God and give loving assent to all that he has revealed.

Mary is the first disciple, a unique instrument of Revelation and a model for all disciples. From all eternity the Father chose her, a young Jewish woman of Nazareth in Galilee, to conceive within her body, by the power of the Holy Spirit, the human body of his divine Son. God prepared her by his grace to cooperate freely with his will and to share her humanity with the divine Savior for whom she and all Israel confidently hoped. The Blessed Virgin Mary, by a singular grace from God, was preserved from sin from the first moment of her own conception until the end of her earthly life. "Most blessed among all women," Mary was "full of grace" and was a fitting vessel in which the word of God became flesh. Her faith, her sinlessness, her perpetual virginity, and her divine motherhood converged to cooperate with God's will to make her the perfect disciple.

Catechesis nourishes a living, explicit, and fruitful faith lived in discipleship to Jesus Christ. The disciple is brought to intimate communion with Jesus Christ and a deeper understanding that "by grace you have been saved through faith, and this is not from you; it is the gift of God."[328]

Here it is notable that, while children do not have the capacity to understand and articulate the content of the faith in the same way as do adults, they have a unique ability to absorb and celebrate the most profound truths of the faith. Children with cognitive disabilities often have an unusual intuitive understanding of the sacred. God's self-revelation unfolds in children in extraordinary ways, and his grace often develops within them a deep spirituality that continues to grow as they mature. Children are capable of being formed as disciples of the Lord from an early age. Their ongoing formation, which includes learning the basic truths of the Christian faith, increases their capacity to understand and articulate those truths more deeply later in life and disposes them to live Christ's message more faithfully.

---

326 USCCB, *Our Hearts Were Burning Within Us: A Pastoral Plan for Adult Faith Formation in the United States* (OHWB) (Washington, D.C.: USCCB, 1999), no. 46.

327 USCCB, *Called and Gifted for the Third Millennium* (Washington, D.C.: USCCB, 1995), 20.

328 Eph 2:8.

C. Learning Within the Christian Community

The witness of the Christian community—particularly the parish, family, parents, and catechists—is an important element in catechetical methodology.

The effectiveness of catechesis depends to a great extent on the vitality of the Christian community in which it is given. In either a parochial or non-parochial setting, the Christian community is the context in which individuals undertake their journey in faith toward conversion to Christ and discipleship in his name.

For most people, the parish, under the leadership of the pastor, is the door to participate in the ordinary Christian community. Therefore, "it is the responsibility of pastors and laity to ensure that those doors are always open."[329] It is the place where the Christian faith is first received, expressed, and nourished. It is where the Christian faith deepens and where the Christian community is formed. In the parish the members of the Christian community "become aware of being the people of God."[330] In the parish the faithful are nurtured by the word of God and nourished by the sacraments, especially the Eucharist. From the parish the faithful are sent on their apostolic mission in the world. "The parish is still a major point of reference for the Christian people, even for the non-practicing."[331] The parish serves as an effective catechetical agent precisely to the extent that it is a clear, living, and authentic sacrament of Christ. On the other hand, where a parish is lifeless and stagnant, it undermines both evangelization and catechesis. In such a situation, no catechetical "program" can be expected to overcome the catechetical message of the parish as a whole. Because of all this, it is the responsibility of the parish community and its leadership to ensure that the faith that it teaches, preaches, and celebrates is alive and that it is a true sign, for all who come in contact with it, that this truly is the living Body of Christ.

D. Learning Within the Christian Family

The Christian family is ordinarily the first experience of the Christian community and the primary environment for growth in faith. Because it

---

329   USCCB, *Welcome and Justice for Persons with Disabilities* (Washington, D.C.: USCCB, 1999), no. 6.
330   GDC, no. 257.
331   CT, no. 67.

is the "church of the home,"[332] the family provides a unique *locus* for catechesis. It is a place in which the word of God is received and from which it is extended. Within the Christian family, parents are the primary educators in the faith and "the first heralds of the faith with regard to their children."[333] But all the members make up the family, and each can make a unique contribution to creating the basic environment in which a sense of God's loving presence is awakened and faith in Jesus Christ is confessed, encouraged, and lived. Within the Christian family, the members first begin to learn the basic prayers of the tradition and to form their consciences in light of the teachings of Christ and the Church. Family members learn more of the Christian life by observing each other's strengths or weaknesses than by formal instruction. They learn intermittently rather than systematically, occasionally rather than in structured periods. Often extended family members take on a primary responsibility in transmitting the faith to the younger members. Their shared wisdom and experience often constitute a compelling Christian witness.

E. Learning Through the Witness of the Catechist

Next to home and family, the witness of the catechist may be pivotal in every phase of the catechetical process. Under the guidance of the Holy Spirit, catechists powerfully influence those being catechized by their faithful proclamation of the Gospel of Jesus Christ and the transparent example of their Christian lives. For catechesis to be effective, catechists must be fully committed to Jesus Christ. They must firmly believe in his Gospel and its power to transform lives.

Catechists must hand on the teachings of Christ to those being catechized; they must prepare them for the sacraments instituted by Christ; they must orient them toward life lived according to the moral teaching of Christ; and they must lead them to pray with Christ. Catechists must make the words of Christ their own: "My teaching is not my own but is from the one who sent me,"[334] and they confess with St. Paul, "I handed on to you . . . what I also received."[335]

---

332   FC, no. 38.
333   LG, no. 11.
334   Jn 7:16.
335   1 Cor 15:3.

F. Learning by Heart

Effective catechesis also incorporates learning "by heart." For centuries the living tradition of the faith was handed on principally through the oral tradition. From the earliest times catechesis has relied on the Creed, the sacraments, the Decalogue, and prayers, especially the Our Father, as primary instruments of transmitting the faith. In order to learn the principal truths of the faith, these instruments were easily committed to memory in lieu of textbooks or other printed materials and could be recalled often as the basis of catechetical instruction. "Use of memory, therefore, forms a constitutive aspect of the pedagogy of the faith since the beginning of Christianity."[336]

The principal formulations of the faith; basic prayers; key biblical themes, personalities, and expressions; and factual information regarding worship and Christian life should be learned by heart. These ensure an accurate exposition of the faith and foster a common language of the faith among all the faithful. The ability to express the one faith in a language that can be understood by all within the cultural diversity of the Church in the United States not only deepens the common understanding of the faith but also forms an indispensable condition for living that faith. Receiving the formulations of the faith, professing and internalizing them, and, in turn, sharing them with the community encourage the individual's participation in the received truth. "Faith is a personal act—the free response of the human person to the initiative of God who reveals himself. But faith is not an isolated act. No one can believe alone, just as no one can live alone. You have not given yourself faith as you have not given yourself life. The believer has received faith from others and should hand it on to others."[337]

While the content of the faith cannot be reduced to formulas that are repeated without being properly understood, learning by heart has had a special place in catechesis and should continue to have that place in catechesis today. "The blossoms, if we may call them that, of faith and piety do not grow in the desert places of a memory-less catechesis. What is essential is that the texts that are memorized must at the same time be taken in and gradually understood in depth, in order to become a source of Christian life on the personal level and the community level."[338] It

---

336   GDC, no. 154.
337   CCC, no. 166.
338   CT, no. 55.

should be introduced through a process that, begun early, continues gradually, flexibly, and never slavishly. In this way certain elements of the Catholic faith, tradition, and practice are learned for a lifetime, form a basis for communication, allow people to pray together in a common language, and contribute to the individual's continued growth in understanding and living the faith. Among those formulations that should be learned by heart are the following:

1. Prayers such as the Sign of the Cross; Lord's Prayer; Hail Mary; Apostles' Creed; Acts of Faith, Hope, and Charity; and the Act of Contrition
2. Factual information contributing to an appreciation of the place of the word of God in the Church and the life of the Christian through an awareness and understanding of the key themes of the history of salvation; the major personalities of the Old and New Testaments; and certain biblical texts expressive of God's love and care
3. Formulas providing factual information regarding the Church, worship, the church year, and major practices in the devotional life of Christians including the parts of the Mass, the list of the sacraments, the liturgical seasons, the holy days of obligation, the major feasts of our Lord and our Blessed Mother, the lives of the saints (especially those newly canonized or those special to particular regions), the corporal and spiritual works of mercy, the various Eucharistic devotions, the mysteries of the rosary of the Blessed Virgin Mary, and the Stations of the Cross
4. Formulas and practices dealing with the moral life of Christians including the Ten Commandments, the Beatitudes, the gifts of the Holy Spirit, the theological and moral virtues, the precepts of the Church, the principles of Catholic social teaching, and the examination of conscience[339]

In addition to the memorization of basic prayers and formulations of the faith, memorization of favorite psalms, songs, prayers, and poetry in praise of Christ our Savior is an effective form of catechesis that nourishes the human heart and helps to form the human spirit in Christ.

---

339   Cf. *National Catechetical Directory*, no. 176.

G. Making a Commitment to Live the Christian Life

In addition, learning by Christian living is an essential component of catechetical methodology. The active participation of all the catechized in their Christian formation fosters learning by doing. As a general condition of Christian life, the faithful actively respond to God's loving initiative through praying; celebrating the sacraments and the Liturgy; living the Christian life; fostering works of charity (meeting the immediate needs of those who are poor and vulnerable) and works of justice (working to address to address the injustices that exist in the systemic and institutional organizations of society); and promoting virtues from the natural law such as liberty, solidarity, justice, peace, and the protection of the created order. The participation of adults in their own catechetical formation is essential, since they have the fullest capacity to understand the truths of the faith and live the Christian life.

In the United States, Christian beliefs, practices, and values are often challenged by the dominant secular culture. The prevailing culture tends to trivialize, marginalize, or privatize the practice of religious faith. Both the private practice and the public witness of knowledgeable and committed Christians are indispensable factors in the sanctification of the world, a responsibility to which all the baptized are called. In such an environment, living an active Christian life becomes a crucial element in effective catechetical methodology.

H. Learning by Apprenticeship

Learning by apprenticeship is also an important human element in catechetical methodology. It links an experienced Christian believer, or mentor, with one who seeks a deeper relationship with Christ and the Church. The relationship that normally grows between a catechist and a catechumen provides a workable model of learning by apprenticeship.

All catechesis includes more than instruction. "It must be an integral Christian initiation."[340] Learning by apprenticeship ordinarily includes the profession of faith, education in the knowledge of the faith, celebration of

---

340 CT, no. 21.

the mysteries of the faith, practice of the Christian moral virtues, and dedication to the daily patterns of Christian prayer. It is a guided encounter with the entire Christian life, a journey toward conversion to Christ. It is a school for discipleship that promotes an authentic following of Christ based on the acceptance of one's baptismal responsibilities, the internalization of the word of God, and the transformation of the whole person to "life in Christ."

30. MEANS OF COMMUNICATION

The elements of human methodology in catechesis must be considered within the context of the revolution in communications technology. Much of what people today know and think about is conditioned by the various means of mass communications. In fact, for many people, experience itself is an experience of the media. The power of the mass media is so great that it largely determines not only what people perceive but also how people judge their perceptions. As the mass media become more dominant in people's lives, they influence how people understand the meaning of life itself. "Reality, for many, is what the media recognizes as real; what media do not acknowledge seems of little importance."[341]

The Church does not stand aside from these problems. Her mission requires her to be "in the very midst of human progress, sharing the experiences of the rest of humanity, seeking to understand and interpret them in the light of faith."[342] For the Church, "communication" is essentially the communication of the Good News of Jesus Christ. It is a proclamation of the Gospel of salvation and liberation to every human being. It articulates divine truth in an extremely secularized world in which truth is often an arbitrary and relative construct. Communication is a powerful witness for the transcendent nature and destiny of every person in the midst of a global culture that dehumanizes and diminishes the value of human life. It is a prophetic voice for the solidarity of all humanity against the radical individualism so typical of contemporary cultures. It holds out poverty of spirit as the desirable alternative to the lure of excessive materialism.

---

341   Pontifical Council for Social Communications, *On Social Communications on the Twentieth Anniversary of "Communio et Progressio"* (*Aetatis Novae*) (AN) (1992), no. 4, http://www.vatican.va/roman_curia/pontifical_councils/pccs (accessed on August 29, 2003).

342   John Paul II, Message for World Communications Day 1990.

Pope John Paul II has said that

> the first Areopagus of the modern age is the *world of communica-*
> *tions*, which is unifying humanity and turning it into what is
> known as a "global village." The means of social communication
> have become so important as to be for many the chief means of
> information and education, of guidance and inspiration in their
> behavior as individuals, families and within society at large.[343]

For this reason the effective use of mass media has become essential for
evangelization and catechesis.[344]

In addition to the numerous traditional means used in catechesis, all
the various instruments of the mass media should be employed to proclaim the Gospel message. Those to whom the Gospel message is
addressed today, both young and old, are, in a sense, children of the
media. They have been reared in the media age and have a high level of
comfort with using media:

> [For many,] the Internet, unknown to most until quite recently,
> is now an essential tool for business, education, and other kinds
> of communication. CD-ROM technology puts at our fingertips
> whole libraries and creates learning paths that enable users to
> grasp complex and unfamiliar subjects. Through satellite delivery
> and cable systems, consumers have access to many more TV
> channels, resulting in the availability of entertainment and infor-
> mation "on demand."[345]

Catechists must seriously commit themselves to learning how to use these
media to bring people to Christ. But that will not be enough.

Catechists also must learn the culture created by the mass media. "It
is not enough to use the media simply to spread the Christian message
and the Church's authentic teaching. It is also necessary to integrate that
message into the 'new culture' created by modern communications . . .
with new languages, new techniques and a new psychology."[346] Catechists

---

343   RM, no. 37. (The Areopagus was a public place in Athens where ideas were openly expressed and
      debated.)
344   Cf. AN, no. 11.
345   *Renewing the Mind of the Media*, 2.
346   RM, no. 37.

must also develop a critical sense with which to evaluate the media and be able to recognize the "shadow side" of the media, which at times promote "secularism, consumerism, materialism, dehumanization and lack of concern for the plight of the poor and neglected."[347]

31. CONCLUSION

The transmission of the Gospel message through the Church has always been and will always be the work of the Trinity. The Father's Word made flesh in Christ through the Holy Spirit bears witness to this truth and is the paradigm for all catechetical methodology. His word goes forth from his mouth and does not return to him without having realized the Father's objective. His divine command empowers and energizes humanity to put fear aside and to accomplish his intent, the announcement of the Good News to all peoples.

By God's grace, some people are called to proclaim the Gospel and to receive an apostolic mission as catechists. These catechists are the instruments of God's own methodology. Catechists do not merely transmit human knowledge; they transmit knowledge of the faith and, respecting "the absolute originality of faith,"[348] they do so according to "a pedagogy of faith"[349] that is patterned after God's own methodology. While catechists rightly employ a variety of methods and techniques in the transmission of the knowledge of faith, God's own methodology—the Father's self-revelation in Jesus Christ and through the Holy Spirit—always remains the model for all human methodologies.

Whatever method is used, all catechesis occurs within the life of a worshiping community. Drawn together by the Holy Spirit, this community gives praise and thanks to God. The next chapter will provide guidance on catechesis for worship, including sacramental catechesis.

---

347   AN, no. 13.
348   CT, no. 58.
349   CT, no. 58.

CHAPTER 5

Catechesis in a Worshiping Community

They devoted themselves to the teaching of the
apostles and to the communal life, to the breaking of
the bread and to the prayers. (Acts 2:42)

32. INTRODUCTION

The Jerusalem community of disciples concentrated on adherence to the
teachings of the Twelve, the Eucharistic Liturgy, living the way of Christ,
and prayer. These fundamental elements of ecclesial life have remained
constant for more than two thousand years. Faith and worship are as closely
related to one another as they were in the early Church: faith gathers the
community for worship, and worship renews the faith of the community.

The Holy Spirit draws together the community of the faithful as the
Church, the Body of Christ, and leads the Church in giving praise and
thanks to the Father. The Church, then, is a worshiping community of
believers in the Lordship of Jesus Christ—believers who, through the out-
pouring of the Holy Spirit, acknowledge their absolute dependence on
God, the Father. The Liturgy is the official worship of the Church. In her
Liturgy, the Church celebrates what she professes and lives, above all the
Paschal Mystery, by which Christ accomplished the work of our salvation.

The rites of the Church are now—more than before the Second Vatican Council—clearly identified with the Paschal Mystery of Christ, adequately integrated with the Eucharist as the principal celebration of that
mystery, and directly related to the experiences of individual Christians
and communities of faith. The retrieval of Sacred Scripture in the Lec-
tionary and the restoration of the liturgy of the word are an integral component in all sacramental celebrations and other liturgical rites. This

restoration is a significant achievement in the renewal of the Liturgy. Liturgical renewal has also brought the Christian ecclesial communities closer to one another in their faith and forms of worship and has emphasized the common riches that they share on the road to full communion.

This chapter describes the relationship between catechesis and Liturgy. It also treats liturgical and personal prayer, catechesis for the sacramental life, sacred time and space, and sacramentals, popular piety, and popular devotions.

33. THE RELATIONSHIP BETWEEN CATECHESIS AND LITURGY

In the Church's mission of evangelization, catechesis and Liturgy are intimately connected. "Catechesis is intrinsically linked with the whole of liturgical and sacramental activity."[350] Catechesis and Liturgy originate in the faith of the Church; they proclaim the Gospel; they call its hearers to conversion to Christ; they initiate believers into the life of Christ and his Church; and they look for the coming of the kingdom in its fullness when "God may be all in all."[351] "The liturgy is the summit toward which the activity of the Church is directed; it is also the fount from which all her power flows."[352] The history of salvation, from the creation of the world to its redemption and eschatological fulfillment in Jesus Christ, is celebrated in the sacraments, especially in the Eucharist. That is why the Liturgy is "the privileged place for catechizing the People of God."[353]

Catechesis both precedes the Liturgy and springs from it. It prepares people for a full, conscious, and active participation in the Liturgy by helping them understand its nature, rites, and symbols. It stems from the Liturgy insofar as it helps people to worship God and to reflect on their experience of the words, signs, rituals, and symbols expressed in the Liturgy; to discern the implications of their participation in the Liturgy; and to respond to its missionary summons to bear witness and offer service. And Liturgy itself is inherently catechetical. As the Scriptures are proclaimed and reflected upon and as the Creed is articulated, the truths

---

350   CT, no. 23.
351   1 Cor 15:28.
352   SC, no. 10; cf. CCC, no. 1069.
353   CCC, no. 1074.

of the faith shape more and more profoundly the faith of the People of God. Through the Eucharist, the People of God come to know the Paschal Mystery ever more intimately and experientially. They come not simply to the knowledge of God—they come to know the living God.

"Liturgical catechesis aims to initiate people into the mystery of Christ . . . by proceeding from the visible to the invisible, from the sign to the thing signified, from the 'sacraments' to the 'mysteries.'"[354] It promotes a more informed knowledge and a more vital experience of the Liturgy. Liturgical catechesis fosters a deeper sense of the meaning of the Liturgy and the sacraments. "In other words, sacramental life is impoverished and very soon turns into hollow ritualism if it is not based on serious knowledge of the meaning of the sacraments, and catechesis becomes intellectualized if it fails to come alive in sacramental practice."[355]

34. LITURGICAL AND PERSONAL PRAYER

God draws every human being toward himself, and every human being desires communion with God. Prayer is the basis and expression of the vital and personal relationship of a human person with the living and true God: "God tirelessly calls each person to that mysterious encounter known as prayer."[356] His initiative comes first; the human response to his initiative is itself prompted by the grace of the Holy Spirit. That human response is the free self-surrender to the incomprehensible mystery of God. In prayer, the Holy Spirit not only reveals the identity of the Triune God to human persons, but also reveals the identity of human persons to themselves. It has been expressed throughout the history of salvation in the words and actions of prayer.

Liturgical prayer is the participation of the People of God in Christ's work. "Every liturgical celebration, because it is an action of Christ the Priest and of his Body, which is the Church, is a sacred action surpassing all others. No other action of the Church can equal its efficacy by the same title and to the same degree."[357] The sacraments, especially the Eucharist, are the Church's preeminent experiences of liturgical prayer.

354 CCC, no. 1075.
355 CT, no. 23.
356 CCC, no. 2567.
357 SC, no. 7.

"In the liturgy, all Christian prayer finds its source and goal."[358] The rhythms of prayer within the life of the Church are both liturgical and personal. Liturgical prayer is the public prayer of the Church. It is the work of Christ, and as such it is the work of the Church. Personal prayer is an essential aspect of the human person's relationship with God, which can find expression in and be nourished by various devotional prayers, such as the Holy Rosary, Stations of the Cross, and novenas.

Since the time of the apostles, the Church has abided by the exhortation "to pray constantly" (1 Th 5:17) The Liturgy of the Hours, or the Divine Office, is the daily public prayer of the Church; in it "the whole course of the day and night is made holy by the praise of God."[359] Catechists especially would benefit greatly from participating in the Liturgy of the Hours. "Pastors of souls should see to it that the principal hours, especially Vespers, are celebrated in common in church on Sundays and on the more solemn feasts. The laity, too, are encouraged to recite the divine office, either with the priests, or among themselves, or even individually."[360]

The living Tradition of the Church, however, contains more than the great treasury of liturgical prayer. Personal prayer is God's gift to the "humble and contrite heart."[361] It expresses the covenant relationship that binds God to the person and the person to God. The connection is Christ, the Son of God made flesh. He is the new and eternal covenant whose blood "will be shed on behalf of many for the forgiveness of sins"[362] so that humanity may be redeemed and restored to communion with God. Personal prayer expresses communion with the life of the Blessed Trinity. The Holy Spirit inspires hearts to pray, removes obstacles to living life in Christ, and leads humanity into communion with the Father and the Son. Personal prayer permeates the daily life of the Christian and disposes him or her toward liturgical, communal, or public prayer.

Because catechesis seeks to lead persons and communities to deeper faith, it is oriented to prayer and worship. Catechesis for prayer emphasizes

---

358   CCC, no. 1073.
359   SC, no. 84.
360   SC, no. 100.
361   Ps 51:19.
362   Mt 26:28.

the major purposes for prayer—adoration, thanksgiving, petition, and con-trition—and includes various prayer forms: communal prayer, private prayer, traditional prayer, spontaneous prayer, gesture, song, meditation, and contemplation. Catechesis for prayer accompanies a person's continual growth in faith. It is most effective when the catechist is a prayerful person who is comfortable leading others to prayer and to participation in liturgi-cal worship. "When catechesis is permeated by a climate of prayer, the assimilation of the entire Christian life reaches it summit."[363]

Catechesis for prayer begins when children see and hear others pray-ing and when they pray with others, especially in the family. Young chil-dren seem to have a special sense of wonder, a recognition of God's pres-ence in their lives, and a capacity for prayer. They should be encouraged by parents and catechists to call upon the Father, the Son, and the Holy Spirit as well as the Mother of God, the angels, and the saints. From infancy they should be inculturated into the daily prayer life of the fam-ily, thereby learning the prayers and prayer forms of the Catholic tradition and becoming accustomed to praying daily: e.g., morning and evening prayer, prayer before and after meals, and prayer at special moments in the life of the family.

35. CATECHESIS FOR THE SACRAMENTS IN GENERAL

A. Sacraments as Mysteries

The liturgical life of the Church revolves around the sacraments, with the Eucharist at the center. "The sacraments are efficacious signs of grace, instituted by Christ and entrusted to the Church," by which divine life is given to us and celebrated.[364] The Church celebrates seven sacraments: Baptism, Confirmation or Chrismation, Eucharist, Penance, Anointing of the Sick, Holy Orders, and Matrimony.[365]

---

363   GDC, no. 85.
364   CCC, no. 1131.
365   Many Eastern Traditions call this sacrament of Matrimony the mystery of "Holy Crowning." Cf. below in this *Directory*, no. 36 ("Catechesis for the Particular Sacraments"), section C ("The Sacraments at the Service of Communion"), subsection 2 ("Catechesis for the Sacrament of Matrimony").

B. General Principles for Sacramental Catechesis

Some fundamental principles apply to catechesis for each of the sacraments. Dioceses and parishes should present sacramental catechesis that

- Is a comprehensive and systematic formation in the faith, one that integrates knowledge of the faith with living the faith
- Is fundamentally Trinitarian and centers on initiation into the life of the Triune God
- Presents Christian life as a lifelong journey to the Father in the Son and through the Holy Spirit
- Is appropriate to the age level, maturity, and circumstances of those being catechized
- Is intended for all members of the Christian community, takes place within the community, and involves the whole community of faith
- Involves parents in the preparation of their children for the sacraments
- Is integrated into a comprehensive catechetical program
- Focuses primarily on the symbols, rituals, and prayers contained in the rite for each sacrament
- Enables the believer to reflect on the meaning of the sacrament received by implementing a thorough experience of *mystagogia* following the celebration

C. Catechetical Guidelines for Celebration of the Sacraments

The Church provides official catechetical norms and guidelines for the celebration of the sacraments. These are essential tools for sacramental catechesis. The *General Instruction of the Roman Missal*[366] provides the general guidelines for the celebration of the Eucharist. The introductions to each rite contain catechetical norms and guidelines appropriate to each sacrament. The *Rite of Christian Initiation of Adults* sets forth the directives to be followed throughout the process of the initiation of adults

---

366   Cf. *General Instruction of the Roman Missal* (GIRM) (2001) (Washington, D.C.: USCCB, 2003).

and children of catechetical age into the life of the Church. Our 1995 statement entitled *Guidelines for the Celebration of the Sacraments with Persons with Disabilities*[367] stresses the need to include persons with disabilities in the celebration of all the sacraments and provides general catechetical guidelines for celebrating the sacraments with persons with a variety of disabilities. The *Directory for Masses with Children*[368] contains the norms for Eucharistic liturgies with children. The *Directory for the Application of Principles and Norms on Ecumenism* outlines Catholic principles and practice in sacramental sharing with other Christians.[369] The *Directory on Popular Piety and the Liturgy*[370] addresses the need for multicultural parishes to make special efforts to celebrate culture and traditions and employ the language, music, and art of each culture represented. In addition to the documents listed above, the prayers that are the form of the sacraments are also essential tools for sacramental catechesis.

D. Baptismal Catechumenate: Inspiration for All Catechesis

The baptismal catechumenate is the source of inspiration for all catechesis. This process of formation includes four stages, as well as rituals that mark those stages. The first stage, the pre-catechumenate, coincides with the first evangelization, in which the primary proclamation of the Gospel and the initial call to conversion to Christ takes place. The handing on of the Gospels accompanies the second stage, the catechumenate, and begins the period in which a more integral and systematic catechesis is presented to the catechumens and candidates. The third stage, purification and enlightenment, is characterized by the celebration of the scrutinies, by more intense prayer, and by the study and conferral of the Creed and the Lord's Prayer. This time is characterized by a more intense preparation for the sacraments of initiation. Fourth, the mystagogy, or post-baptismal catechesis, marks the time in which the neophyte experiences the sacraments

---

367 Cf. USCCB, *Guidelines for the Celebration of the Sacraments with Persons with Disabilities* (Washington, D.C.: USCCB, 1995).

368 Cf. Sacred Congregation for Divine Worship, *Directory for Masses with Children* (1973).

369 Cf. Pontifical Council for Promoting Christian Unity, *Directory for the Application of Principles and Norms on Ecumenism* (Washington, D.C.: USCCB, 1993), Chapter 4.

370 Cf. Congregation for Divine Worship and the Discipline of the Sacraments, *Directory on Popular Piety and the Liturgy: Principles and Guidelines* (2002), http://www.vatican.va/roman_curia/congregations/ccdds /documents/rc_con_ccdds_doc_20020513_vers-direttorio_en.html (accessed on August 29, 2003).

and enters fully into the life of the community.[371] "These stages, which reflect the wisdom of the great catechumenal tradition, also inspire the gradual nature of catechesis."[372]

While a distinction is made between catechumens and those already baptized who are being catechized,[373] some elements of the baptismal catechumenate are instructive for post-baptismal catechesis. In that sense, the baptismal catechumenate inspires a continuing catechesis. It reminds the Church that her catechesis accompanies a continual conversion to Christ and an ongoing initiation into the celebration of the sacraments and the life of the Church. Just as the baptismal catechumenate is the responsibility of the entire Christian community, so too does the whole Church bear the obligation to provide an ongoing catechesis for the faithful. The baptismal catechumenate accompanies the catechumen's passage with Christ from the initial proclamation of his name, through "burial together with him in the death of baptism,"[374] and then to the newness of life. All catechesis should provide those being catechized with the opportunity to journey with Christ through the stages of his Paschal Mystery. The baptismal catechumenate is where the Gospel message deliberately engages the culture of the catechumens. All catechesis must "take flesh" in the various cultures and environments in which the Gospel message is proclaimed.

The baptismal catechumenate is both "a process of formation and a true school of the faith."[375] It is a fruitful blend of instruction and formation in the faith; it progresses through gradual stages; it unfolds the Church's rites, symbols, and biblical and liturgical signs; and it incorporates the catechumens into the Christian community of faith and worship. While mystagogical, or post-baptismal, catechesis should not slavishly imitate the structure of the baptismal catechumenate, it should recognize that the baptismal catechumenate provides an admirable model for the whole of the Church's catechetical efforts and especially emphasizes the necessity for lifelong catechesis.[376]

---

371 Cf. RCIA, nos. 9-40.
372 GDC, no. 89.
373 Cf. *Directory for the Application of Principles and Norms on Ecumenism*, nos. 92-100.
374 Congregation for Divine Worship, *Rite of Baptism* (1969), no. 91.
375 GDC, no. 91.
376 Cf. Synod of Bishops, *Message to the People of God* (October 28, 1977), no. 8.

More specifically, the time that follows the celebration of the sacraments of initiation—i.e., the period of post-baptismal catechesis, or mystagogy—"is a time for the community and the neophytes together to grow in deepening their grasp of the paschal mystery and in making it part of their lives through meditation on the Gospel, sharing in the Eucharist, and doing the works of charity."[377] It is the phase of liturgical catechesis that aims to incorporate the neophytes more deeply into the mystery of Christ through reflection on the Gospel message and the experience of the sacraments they have received. It gives them the opportunity to relive the great events of salvation history and helps them to open themselves to the spiritual understanding of the economy of salvation. Mystagogical, or post-baptismal, catechesis also helps the newly baptized to internalize the sacraments of initiation to deepen and nourish their life of faith and to enter more deeply into the community.

Through the period of post-baptismal catechesis, the neophytes "should experience a full and joyful welcome into the community and enter into closer ties with the other faithful. The faithful, in turn, should derive from it a renewal of inspiration and of outlook."[378] Sunday Masses during the Easter season following the neophytes' reception of the sacraments of initiation provide particularly favorable opportunities for them to gather with the community of faith, to hear readings from the Word of God specifically chosen for the period of post-baptismal catechesis, and to partake fully in the Eucharist. "Out of this experience, which belongs to Christians and increases as it is lived, [the neophytes] derive a new perception of the faith, of the Church, and of the world."[379]

In the broader sense, mystagogy represents the Christian's lifelong education and formation in the faith. By analogy it signifies the continuous character of catechesis in the life of the Christian. Conversion to Christ is a lifelong process that should be accompanied at every stage by a vital catechesis that leads Christians on their journey towards holiness. Lifelong catechesis should take many forms and use a variety of means: participation in the Sunday Eucharist and study of the Liturgy, the study and exploration of Sacred Scripture and the social teachings of the Church, reflection on the important events of life in the light of Christian

---

377 RCIA, no. 244.
378 RCIA, no. 246.
379 RCIA, no. 245.

faith, opportunities for prayer, spiritual exercises, acts of charity that involve self-sacrifice, especially toward those in need, and more formal theological and catechetical instruction. Among these forms of continuing catechesis, the homily occupies a privileged position since it "takes up again the journey of faith put forward by catechesis, and brings it to its natural fulfillment."[380]

36. CATECHESIS FOR THE PARTICULAR SACRAMENTS

A. Sacraments of Initiation

Christian initiation is celebrated in Baptism, Confirmation or Chrismation, and Eucharist. These sacraments are efficacious signs of God's love and stages of a person's journey toward communion with the Trinity. Through these sacraments, a person is incorporated into the Church, is strengthened for participation in the Church's mission, and is welcomed to partake of the Body and Blood of Jesus Christ. As indicated above, the Rite of Christian Initiation of Adults provides the norm for catechetical as well as liturgical practice for the sacraments of initiation. In the Eastern Churches, Baptism, Chrismation, and Eucharist are celebrated together in infancy, and their intimate relationship is apparent. While the Latin Church has separated the celebration of Baptism from Confirmation and Eucharist, she also recognizes their essential interconnection.

Dioceses and parishes should present catechesis for Christian initiation that

- Summons the catechumen to profess faith in the person of Jesus Christ from the heart, to follow him faithfully, and to become his disciple
- Recognizes that Christian initiation is an apprenticeship of the entire Christian life and so should include more than instruction[381]

---

380 CT, no. 48.
381 GDC, no. 67.

- Presents a comprehensive and systematic formation in the faith so that the catechumen or candidate can enter deeply into the mystery of Christ
- Incorporates the catechumen into the life of the Christian community, which confesses, celebrates, and bears courageous witness to the faith of Jesus Christ
- Includes instruction on the rites of Christian initiation, their basic symbols and forms, and the offices and ministries at work in them

For the purpose of Christian initiation, children who have reached the age of reason, generally understood as seven years of age, are considered adults in a limited sense.[382] As much as possible, their formation in the faith should follow the general pattern of the ordinary catechumenate, making use of the appropriate adaptations permitted in the rite. "They should receive the sacraments of baptism, confirmation, and eucharist at the Easter Vigil, together with the older catechumens."[383]

The initiation of children who have not been baptized as infants, but who have attained the use of reason and have reached catechetical age, is ordinarily sought by their parents or guardians or, with parental permission, by the children themselves. These children are capable of receiving and nurturing a personal faith. They are also capable of a conversion appropriate to their age. They can receive a catechesis that is suited to their circumstances. The process of their initiation must be adapted to their ability to grow in faith and their capacity to understand the faith. Their initiation should proceed through the same steps that the initiation of adults does. While the process may take several years before they receive the sacraments, "their condition and status as catechumens . . . should not be compromised or confused, nor should they receive the sacraments of initiation in any sequence other than that determined in the ritual of Christian initiation."[384]

Children's catechetical formation should lead up to and follow the steps of the initiation process. Ordinarily the children to be initiated are part of a group of children of similar age and circumstances, some of whom have already been baptized and are preparing for Confirmation and

---

382   Cf. Canon Law Society of America (CLSA), *Code of Canon Law, Latin-English Edition, New English Translation* (CIC) (Washington, D.C.: CLSA, 1999), c. 852 §1.
383   RCIA, Appendix III, no. 18.
384   RCIA, Appendix III, no. 19.

Eucharist. In general, catechesis for such children should incorporate the appropriate elements of the same thorough and systematic catechetical instruction of baptized children before their reception of the Sacraments of Confirmation and the Eucharist.

The family is the child's first experience of a faith community and, as such, deserves careful attention in all catechetical endeavors. Throughout the period of initiation of children of catechetical age, the parents of the children should be encouraged to be involved. If the children are determined to be ready to receive the sacraments, the final period of preparation should proceed, if possible, during the season of Lent; the final step, the celebration of the sacraments of initiation, should normally take place at the Easter Vigil.[385] "Celebration at this time must also be consistent with the program of catechetical instruction they are receiving, since the candidates should, if possible, come to the sacraments of initiation at the time that their baptized companions are to receive confirmation or eucharist."[386]

1. Catechesis for Baptism

Catechesis for Baptism is directed primarily to adults: that is, catechumens—including children who have reached the age of reason—as well as the parents and godparents of infants who are to be baptized. Catechumens and candidates should be led through the stages of Christian initiation set forth in the *Rite of Christian Initiation of Adults*. This process provides helpful guidelines for the catechesis of parents and godparents who are preparing for the Baptism of an infant or child. All those preparing for Baptism, including parents and godparents, need the prayerful support and apostolic witness of the people of the local community of faith—the parish. This preparation is an especially important opportunity for the Church to encourage the parents and godparents of infants to reexamine the meaning of the Christian message in their own lives. It is also the proper time to remind the parents and godparents that "an infant should be baptized within the first weeks after birth. If the child is in danger of death, it is to be baptized without delay."[387] For pastoral reasons, Baptism

---

385   Cf. RCIA, Part II, no. 256.
386   RCIA, Part II, no. 256.
387   Congregation for Divine Worship, *Rite of Baptism of Children*, no. 8, in *The Rites of the Catholic Church* (New York: Pueblo Publishing, 1983).

may be deferred if there is no assurance that the child's faith will be nurtured. The parish should give attention to the families of these children through pastoral outreach and evangelization.

Dioceses and parishes should present baptismal catechesis that

- Teaches that Baptism (1) is the foundation of the Christian life because it is the journey into Christ's death and Resurrection, which is the foundation of our hope; (2) gives sanctifying grace, that is, God's life; (3) gives them a new birth in which they become children of God, members of Christ, and temples of the Holy Spirit; (4) cleanses people from original sin and from all personal sins; (5) incorporates them into the life, practices, and mission of the Church; and (6) imprints on their souls an indelible character that consecrates them for Christian worship and is necessary for salvation in the case of all those who have heard the Gospel and have been able to ask for this sacrament[388]
- Teaches that through Baptism we receive a share in the mission of Christ as king, priest, and prophet
- Teaches that Baptism "symbolizes the catechumen's burial into Christ's death, from which he rises up by resurrection with him, as 'a new creature'"[389]
- Teaches that Baptism is "the basis of the whole Christian life, the gateway to life in the Spirit . . . and the door which gives access to the other sacraments"[390]
- Teaches that through Baptism the faithful "share in the priesthood of Christ, in his prophetic and royal mission"[391]
- Teaches that "the Most Holy Trinity gives the baptized sanctifying grace, the grace of *justification*" (thus "the whole organism of the Christian's supernatural life has its root in baptism")
  - "enabling them to believe in God, to hope in him, and to love him through the theological virtues"
  - "giving them the power to live and act under the prompting of the Holy Spirit through the gifts of the Holy Spirit"

---

388   Cf. CCC, no. 1257.
389   CCC, no. 1214.
390   CCC, no. 1213.
391   CCC, no. 1268.

— "allowing them to grow in goodness through the moral virtues"[392]

- Teaches that "having become a member of the Church, the person baptized belongs no longer to himself, but to him who died and rose for us. From now on he is called to be subject to others, to serve them in the communion of the Church, and to 'obey and to submit' to the Church's leaders, holding them in respect and affection"[393]

- Includes a thorough explanation of the Rite of Baptism together with the fundamental signs and symbols that it employs: immersion in or the pouring of water, the words of the Trinitarian formula, and the anointing with oil

- Teaches that the ordinary minister for the Sacrament of Baptism is a priest or deacon (in the Eastern Catholic Churches the priest is the only ordinary minister of Baptism, since Chrismation follows immediately) but that, in the case of necessity, any person who intends to do what the Church does can baptize by pouring water on the candidate's head and saying the Trinitarian formula

2. Catechesis for Confirmation/Chrismation

The revised *Rite of Confirmation*[394] indicates that episcopal conferences may designate the appropriate age for Confirmation. In the United States the age of Confirmation in the Latin Church for children and young people varies widely from diocese to diocese; it can be designated between the age of discretion through around sixteen years. Since the sacramental practice for Confirmation in the United States is so diverse, a single catechesis cannot be prescribed for Confirmation. However, some general guidelines can be articulated.

Catechesis for adults preparing for Confirmation follows the pattern recommended in the *Rite of Christian Initiation of Adults*. Dioceses and parishes should present catechesis for the Sacrament of Confirmation that

---

392   CCC, no. 1266.
393   CCC, no. 1269.
394   Cf. Sacred Congregation for Divine Worship, *Rite of Confirmation* (1971).

- Teaches that Confirmation increases and deepens the grace of Baptism, imprinting an indelible character on the soul
- Teaches that Confirmation strengthens the baptismal conferral of the Holy Spirit on those confirmed in order to incorporate them more firmly in Christ, strengthen their bond with the Church, associate them more closely with the Church's mission, increase in them the gifts of the Holy Spirit,[395] and help them bear witness to the Christian faith in words and deeds
- Teaches about the role of the Holy Spirit, his gifts, and his fruits
- Is developmentally appropriate and includes retreat experiences
- Includes instruction on the Rite of Confirmation and its basic symbols: the imposition of hands, the anointing with Sacred Chrism, and the words of the sacramental formula
- Ensures that parents and sponsors are involved in the catechetical preparation of the children for Confirmation
- Teaches that the bishop is the ordinary minister of the Sacrament of Confirmation (in the Eastern Catholic Churches, however, the priest is the ordinary minister of Chrismation)

3. Catechesis for Eucharist[396]

The Sacrament of the Eucharist is one of the sacraments of Christian initiation. "Those who have been raised to the dignity of the royal priesthood by Baptism and configured more deeply to Christ by Confirmation participate with the whole community in the Lord's own sacrifice by means of the Eucharist."[397]

The Eucharist is the ritual, sacramental action of giving thanks and praise to the Father. It is the sacrificial memorial of Christ and his body, the Church, and is the continuing presence of Christ in his Word and in his Spirit.

---

395 Cf. CCC, no. 1303.
396 Cf. Congregation for Rites, *Instruction on Eucharistic Worship* (1967). In this document is a seven-part article (article 3) that deals specifically with "The Principal Points of Doctrine" and eleven articles (articles 5-15) that deal specifically with "Some General Principles of Particular Importance in the Catechesis of the People on the Mystery of the Eucharist." Cf. also John Paul II, *On the Eucharist* (*Ecclesia de Eucharistia*) (EE) (Washington, D.C.: USCCB, 2003).
397 CCC, no. 1322.

In the Mass, or "the Divine Liturgy" as it is termed in the Eastern Catholic Churches, the Eucharist constitutes the principal liturgical celebration of the Paschal Mystery of Christ and the ritual memorial of our communion in that mystery. Acting through the ministry of the priests, the bread and wine become—through Transubstantiation—Christ himself. Christ offers the Eucharistic sacrifice and is really present under the species of bread and wine.

Since the Eucharist is the "source and summit of the Christian life,"[398] catechesis for the Eucharist recognizes it as the heart of Christian life for the whole Church, for the dioceses and parishes, and for each individual Christian. Dioceses and parishes should present lifelong catechesis for the Eucharist that

- Helps people understand that the Eucharist is the mystery in which Christ's sacrifice on the cross is perpetuated; that it is a memorial of Christ's passion, death, and Resurrection; and that it is a sacred banquet in which the People of God share the benefits of the Paschal Mystery, renew the covenant that God has made through the blood of Christ, and anticipate the heavenly banquet
- Helps people understand that the work of salvation accomplished by these events is made present by the liturgical action that Christ himself offers in every celebration of the Eucharist
- Teaches that through the priest—the other Christ—the bread and wine are transformed, through the Eucharistic Prayer, into the Body and Blood of Christ
- Includes instruction that the Eucharist is the Body and Blood of Christ, his real presence under the appearances of bread and wine, and that the Eucharist nourishes the Body of Christ, the Church, and each individual communicant
- Teaches that Christ is present whole and entire, God and man, substantially and permanently, and in a unique way under the species of bread and wine[399]
- Teaches that Christ is also present in his word, in the body of the faithful gathered in his name, and in the person of the priest who acts in the person of Christ, the Head of his Body, the Church

---

398 LG, no. 11.
399 Cf. USCCB, *The Real Presence of Jesus Christ in the Sacrament of the Eucharist: Basic Questions and Answers* (Washington, D.C.: USCCB, 2001), 1-2.

- Includes the effects of the sacrament: unity in the Body of Christ and provision of spiritual food for the Christian's journey through life
- Teaches that the reception of the Body and Blood of Christ signifies and effects communion with the most Holy Trinity, forgives venial sins, and, through the grace of the Holy Spirit, helps the communicant to avoid mortal sin
- Helps the People of God to understand that, through the power of the Holy Spirit, the Eucharist forms the Church
- Helps the faithful to understand that, in the Eucharist, "Christ associates his Church and all her members with his sacrifice of praise and thanksgiving offered once for all on the cross to his Father"[400]
- Gives instruction about the meaning of the ritual, symbols, and parts of the Mass
- Presents the Jewish roots of the Last Supper as the renewal of God's covenant with his people in the blood of his beloved Son
- Teaches that essential signs of the Eucharistic sacrament are bread and wine, on which the power of the Holy Spirit is invoked and over which the priest pronounces the words of consecration spoken first by Jesus during the Last Supper
- Teaches that the "bread and wine are changed, a change traditionally and appropriately expressed by the word 'Transubstantiation,' so that, while the appearances of bread and wine remain, the reality is the Body and Blood of Christ"[401]
- Teaches that the Eucharist commits those who receive it to serve the poor[402]
- Reminds the faithful that the Sacrament of the Eucharist is the preeminent sign of the unity of the Church
- Teaches that the Eucharist is an effective sign of the unity of all Christians and that one day—that is, the Parousia—by the grace of the Holy Spirit, the divisions that separate Christians will be healed
- Presents the guidelines for Eucharistic sharing that have been set forth by the United States Catholic bishops[403]

---

400   CCC, no. 1407.
401   *National Catechetical Directory*, no. 121.
402   Cf. CCC, no. 1397.
403   Cf. USCCB, *Guidelines for the Reception of Communion* (November 14, 1996).

- Considers the mystery of the Eucharist in all its fullness and consequently teaches that the celebration of the Eucharist in the sacrifice of the Mass is the origin and consummation of the worship shown the Blessed Sacrament outside of Mass[404]
- Encourages visits to the Blessed Sacrament and other Eucharistic devotions, and teaches appropriate devotional gestures, postures, and proper conduct in church
- Includes instruction on the implications of the Eucharist for the Church's mission in the world and for social justice
- Clarifies the roles and ministries within the sacred action so that all may experience full, active, and conscious participation in the celebration of the Mass
- Includes an explanation of the theology and practice of celebrating the Eucharist in the Eastern Churches
- Makes people aware of their obligation to be free of mortal sin before receiving Holy Communion
- Teaches that Catholics must receive Holy Communion at least once a year during the Easter season
- Recommends that the faithful receive Holy Communion when they participate in the celebration of the Eucharist
- Instructs the faithful concerning the Eucharistic fast and the conditions under which Holy Communion may be received a second time on the same day
- Instructs the faithful that we are called to realize that we become what we receive—which has great implications for how we live and act

3a. Catechesis for Children's First Reception of the Eucharist

Children's preparation for first reception of the Eucharist begins in the home. The family has the most important role in communicating the Christian and human values that form the foundation for a child's understanding of the Eucharist. Children who participate with their family in the Mass experience the Eucharistic mystery in an initial way and gradually learn to join with the liturgical assembly in prayer.

---

404   Cf. Sacred Congregation for Divine Worship, *Holy Communion and Worship of the Eucharist Outside of Mass* (1973).

Parents and the parish catechetical leader or catechist, together with the pastor, are responsible for determining when children have attained the age of reason and are ready to receive First Communion.[405] Because reception of the Eucharist, especially for the first time, is integral to the child's full incorporation into the ecclesial community, the pastor has a responsibility in determining every child's readiness to receive First Communion. Parents also have the right and the duty to be involved in preparing their children for First Communion. The catechesis offered should help parents grow in their own understanding and appreciation of the Eucharist and enable them to catechize their children more effectively.

The *Directory for Masses with Children* "sets the framework for catechizing children for eucharistic celebration."[406] Catechesis on the Mass provided in systematic parish catechetical programs is an indispensable part of the preparation of children for their first reception of the Eucharist. Suited to the children's age and abilities, catechesis should help children participate actively and consciously in the Mass. During planning, it is essential to remember that children around the age of reason ordinarily think concretely. Dioceses and parishes should present catechesis in preparation for the first reception of the Eucharist that

- Teaches that the Eucharist is the living memorial of Christ's sacrifice for the salvation of all and the commemoration of his last meal with his disciples
- Teaches not only "the truths of faith regarding the Eucharist but also how from First Communion on . . . they can as full members of Christ's Body take part actively with the People of God in the Eucharist, sharing in the Lord's table and the community of their brothers and sisters"[407]
- Ensures that the baptized have been prepared, according to their capacity, for the Sacrament of Penance prior to their First Communion
- Develops in children an understanding of the Father's love, of their participation in the sacrifice of Christ, and of the gift of the Holy Spirit

---

405 Cf. CIC, cc. 914, 777 2°; cf. *Code of Canons of the Eastern Churches* (CCEO), c. 619.

406 *National Directory for Catechesis*, no. 135.

407 *Directory for Masses with Children*, no. 12.

- Teaches that "the Holy Eucharist is the real body and blood of Christ" and that "what appear to be bread and wine are actually His living body"[408]
- Teaches the difference between the Eucharist and ordinary bread
- Teaches the meaning of reception of the Holy Eucharist under both species of bread and wine
- Helps them to participate actively and consciously in the Mass
- Helps children to receive Christ's Body and Blood in an informed and reverent manner

Traditional practice in some Eastern Churches in the United States calls for the newly baptized and chrismated infant or adult to receive the Holy Eucharist. The infant's first reception of the Eucharist, therefore, occurs in conjunction with the sacraments or mysteries of Baptism and Chrismation, because the culmination of initiation into the community of faith is sharing in the communal meal. In these situations, Eucharistic catechesis ordinarily follows reception of the sacrament and supports the young Christian's growth into the mystery of the Eucharist and the life of the Church.

3b. The Eucharistic Liturgy for Special Groups

The parish Sunday Mass, or Divine Liturgy, is the normative celebration of the Eucharistic Liturgy. It is the whole parish community's central act of worship, through which Christ unites the faithful to himself and to one another in his perfect sacrifice of praise. While every parish is made up of different groups, associations, and smaller religious communities, through the Sunday Eucharist Christ provides the opportunity for everyone to move beyond their particular circles to celebrate in common the sacrament of unity. "This is why on Sunday, the day of gathering, small group Masses are not to be encouraged: it is not only a question of ensuring that parish assemblies are not without the necessary ministry of priests, but also of ensuring that the life and unity of the Church community are fully safeguarded and promoted."[409] Occasionally, however, Mass may be celebrated

---

408   *National Catechetical Directory*, no. 122.
409   John Paul II, *On Keeping the Lord's Day Holy* (*Dies Domini*) (DD) (Vatican City, 1998), no. 36, http://www.vatican.va/holy_father/john_paul_ii/apost_letters/documents/hf_jp-ii_apl_05071998_dies-domini_en.html (accessed on August 29, 2003).

with groups whose members share special ties or a particular need. Such celebrations should help the members to grow in their faith and unite them more deeply to one another, to the parish community, and to the whole Church.

The *General Instruction of the Roman Missal* is the normative point of reference for the celebration of the Mass. Only the Holy See can change the liturgical books of the Roman Rite. Only the United States Conference of Catholic Bishops can propose adaptations of those rites to the Holy See, for the regulation of the Liturgy is strictly assigned to bishops alone. "'No other person, not even if he is a priest, may on his own initiative add, remove, or change anything in the liturgy.' Inculturation is not left to the personal initiative of celebrants or to the collective initiative of an assembly."[410] Only in those instances clearly indicated in the *Roman Missal* may the celebrant choose from the options provided or add his own words to those prescribed. Catechists are often called upon to assist in planning these Masses and in preparing the groups to participate in them. The catechists should themselves have adequate liturgical preparation and should always work closely with these special groups, their pastors, and others trained in Liturgy.

3b-1. Children

Young children sometimes are not able to participate fully in Masses that are prepared primarily for adults since they may have difficulty understanding the words, symbols, and actions of the Eucharist. The *Directory for Masses with Children* is the normative reference for the preparation and celebration of Masses with children. It is "concerned with children who have not yet entered the period of pre-adolescence."[411] Such Eucharistic celebrations "must lead children toward the celebration of Mass with adults, especially the Masses at which the Christian community must come together on Sundays."[412] The authorization for the adaptation of the Liturgy given by the *Directory for Masses with Children* does not apply to Masses with adolescents or other special groups. While particular sensitivity to the cultural and age-specific needs of every group is a pre-condition

---

410 Congregation for Divine Worship and Discipline of the Sacraments, *Inculturation and the Roman Liturgy* (*Varietates Legitimae*), no. 37 (quoting SC, no. 22), Appendix B in *Liturgiam Authenticam: Fifth Instruction on Vernacular Translation of the Roman Liturgy* (Washington, D.C.: USCCB, 2001).

411 *Directory for Masses with Children*, no. 6.

412 *Directory for Masses with Children*, no. 21.

for every celebration of the Eucharist, the requirements of the *Roman Missal* must always determine the parameters of such adaptation.

3b-2. Racial, Cultural, and Ethnic Groups

The celebration of the Liturgy should reflect the particular gifts and cultures of the different peoples; however, only those cultural adaptations approved by the Holy See for use in the United States or in the country of origin of a particular group are suited for use in the Liturgy. People express their worship of God most fruitfully through their particular culture as it has been assumed and transformed by Christ. In these celebrations, "homogenous cultural, racial, or ethnic communities have the right to use their own language and cultural expressions of faith in ritual, music, and art."[413]

Such liturgical diversity can be a source of enrichment to the whole Church, but it must not diminish the unity of the Church. Any adaptation must avoid all distortion of the celebration of the Liturgy as it is prescribed in the universal liturgical laws of the Church. No matter which particular group is celebrating the liturgy, it must express the one faith of the Church, always respecting "the *substantial unity of the Roman Rite* as expressed in the liturgical books."[414] "The liturgical assembly derives its unity from the 'communion of the Holy Spirit' who gathers the children of God into the one Body of Christ. This assembly transcends racial, cultural, social—indeed, all human affinities."[415]

3b-3. Persons with Disabilities[416]

Catholics with disabilities have the right to participate in the sacraments as full functioning members of the local ecclesial community. All forms of the liturgy should be completely accessible to persons with disabilities, since these forms are the essence of the spiritual tie that binds the Christian community together. As much as possible they should also be invited

---

413 *National Catechetical Directory*, no. 137.

414 John Paul II, *On the Twenty-Fifth Anniversary of the Constitution on the Sacred Liturgy* (*Vicesimus Quintus Annus*) (VQA) (Vatican City, 1988), no. 16, http://www.vatican.va/holy_father/john_paul_ii/ apost_ letters/documents/hf_jp-ii_apl_04121988_vicesimus-quintus-annus_en.html (accessed on August 29, 2003).

415 CCC, no. 1097.

416 For a fuller presentation of the participation of persons with disabilities in the Church's sacramental life see *Guidelines for the Celebration of the Sacraments with Persons with Disabilities* (1995) and *Pastoral Statement of U.S. Catholic Bishops on Persons with Disabilities* (Washington, D.C.: USCCB, 1978).

to play a more active role in the liturgy and should be provided with proper training and aids to do so. In some situations, special liturgies for persons with disabilities may be appropriate.

It is the responsibility of the pastor and lay leaders to make sure that the door to participation in the life of the Church is always open for persons with disabilities. To that end, the physical design of parish buildings must include easy accessibility for persons with disabilities.

Guidelines for the Celebration of the Sacraments with Persons with Disabilities provides general catechetical guidelines for the celebration of the sacraments, including the Eucharist, with persons with a variety of disabilities. Special liturgies for persons with disabilities, however, should never replace their inclusion in the larger worshiping community. Rather, these liturgies should always orient the participants back to the parish celebration of the Eucharist where the fundamental encounter between Christ and his people unfolds. Parishes should provide the means for inclusion of persons with disabilities, for example, sign language interpreters, hearing devices, Braille texts, etc. The Church "must recognize and appreciate the contributions that persons with disabilities can make to the Church's spiritual life and encourage them to do the Lord's work in the world according to their God-given talents and capacity."[417]

B. Sacraments of Healing

Through the sacraments of initiation, believers are drawn into the communion of the Holy Trinity. They become partakers in God's own life, are incorporated into the Body of Christ, and are strengthened for discipleship by the Holy Spirit. Ever present in the sacraments of initiation, however, is the sacrifice of Christ, which has reconciled the believers to the Father through the action of the Holy Spirit. This constant awareness of the redemptive sacrifice of Christ in the sacraments of initiation reminds the faithful of their need for conversion, penance, and forgiveness, because they "hold this treasure in earthen vessels."[418] This treasure of new life in Christ can be gradually squandered or lost entirely by sin.

But the Father's design for his creation intends that all people be saved by Christ's self-sacrificial love. Toward that end, Christ founded his

---

417   *Welcome and Justice for Persons with Disabilities*, no. 7.
418   2 Cor 4:7.

Church to continue his work of healing and salvation through the power of the Holy Spirit. Immediately after he called his first disciples, Christ cured many who were sick with various diseases,[419] exorcized demons, cleansed lepers, and forgave the sins of a paralytic, restoring him to physical and spiritual health. Christ's healing and reconciling ministry is carried on in the Church principally through the two sacraments of healing: the Sacrament of Penance and Reconciliation and the Sacrament of the Anointing of the Sick.

1. Catechesis for the Sacrament of Penance and Reconciliation[420]

On the evening of his Resurrection, Jesus sent his apostles out to reconcile sinners to his Father and commissioned them to forgive sins in his name: "'Peace be with you. As the Father has sent me, so I send you.' And when he had said this, he breathed on them and said to them, 'Receive the holy Spirit. Whose sins you forgive are forgiven them, and whose sins you retain are retained.'"[421]

Catechesis for the Sacrament of Penance and Reconciliation first depends on the person's acknowledgment of God's faithful love, of the existence of sin, of the capacity to commit sin, and of God's power to forgive sin and reconcile the sinner with himself and with the Church. "If we say, 'We are without sin,' we deceive ourselves, and the truth is not in us."[422] The normative point of reference for catechesis for the Sacrament of Penance and Reconciliation is the *Rite of Penance*.[423]

Dioceses and parishes should present catechesis for the Sacrament of Penance and Reconciliation that

- Emphasizes God's plan for the salvation of all, his desire for every person to be reconciled with him and live in communion with him, and his gift of the grace of conversion

---

419 Cf. Mk 1:21-2:12.

420 In addition to using the term "sacrament of Penance and Reconciliation" for this sacrament, the *Catechism of the Catholic Church* also uses "sacrament of Conversion," "sacrament of Confession," and "sacrament of Forgiveness." Cf. nos. 1423-1424.

421 Jn 20:21-23.

422 1 Jn 1:8.

423 Cf. Sacred Congregation for Divine Worship, *Rite of Penance* (1973).

- Reveals a merciful and loving father who runs to greet the repentant sinner, throws his arms around him, and welcomes him home with a banquet[424]
- Reveals the love of Christ, the Redeemer who, through the action of the Holy Spirit, pours himself out with a "love more powerful than death, more powerful than sin"[425]
- Teaches that Christ is at work giving actual graces in the sacrament, thereby effecting what the sacrament signifies, namely "reconciliation with God by which the penitent recovers grace; reconciliation with the Church; remission of the eternal punishment incurred by mortal sins; remission, at least in part, of temporal punishments resulting from sin; peace and serenity of conscience, and spiritual consolation; and an increase of spiritual strength for the Christian battle"[426]
- Teaches that "individual, integral confession and absolution remain the only ordinary way for the faithful to reconcile themselves with God and the Church, unless physical or moral impossibility excuses from this kind of confession";[427] the faithful are "obliged to confess in kind and in number all serious sins committed after baptism and not yet directly remitted through the keys of the Church nor acknowledged in individual confession, of which [they are] conscious after diligent examination of conscience"[428]
- Teaches that the Sacrament of Penance and Reconciliation consists of repentance, confession, reparation on the part of the penitent, and the priest's absolution
- Teaches that "mortal sin is sin whose object is grave matter and which is also committed with full knowledge and deliberate consent"[429]
- Teaches that one who desires to obtain sacramental Reconciliation with God and the Church must confess to a priest all unconfessed mortal sins; calls attention to the obligation to celebrate

---

424   Cf. Lk 15:11-32.
425   John Paul II, *Rich in Mercy* (*Dives in Misericordia*) (Vatican City, 1980), no. 8, http://www.vatican. va/edocs/eng0215/_index.htm (accessed on August 29, 2003).
426   CCC, no. 1496.
427   Introduction, *Rite of Penance*, no. 31.
428   CIC, c. 988 § 1.
429   John Paul II, *Reconciliation and Penance* (*Reconciliatio et Paenitentia*) (RP) (Washington, D.C.: USCCB, 1984), no. 17.

the sacrament whenever one has committed mortal sin, at least once a year[430]

- Teaches that "only priests who have received the faculty of absolving from the authority of the Church can forgive sins in the name of Christ"[431]
- Informs the faithful that priests are bound by the seal of confession, under the most severe penalties,[432] to keep absolute secrecy regarding the sins that penitents have confessed to them
- Instructs those being catechized about the forms and options for celebrating the sacrament, the words and gestures of the rite, how to examine one's conscience, and how to make a good confession
- Reminds the faithful that the Penitential Rite in the Eucharistic Liturgy is a means of repentance for venial sin and that the confession of venial sins—"sin that merits merely temporal punishment"[433]—is strongly recommended by the Church
- Prepares the community to celebrate in ritual the realities of repentance, conversion, and reconciliation
- Challenges the individual and the community to recognize the presence of evil in the social order, to evaluate that evil in light of the Gospel values as articulated in the Church, to accept appropriate individual and corporate responsibility, and to seek forgiveness for participation in social evil, or the evil of society
- Reminds even those who have "put on Christ"[434] in the sacraments of initiation that they are all sinners and that, in the Sacrament of Penance and Reconciliation, they have an opportunity to acknowledge their sinfulness, their estrangement from God and his Church, and their need for conversion and forgiveness
- Encourages Christians to grow in their awareness of their solidarity with other human beings, to seek forgiveness from them, and to offer forgiveness to them when necessary

---

430 Cf. CIC, c. 989.
431 CCC, no. 1495.
432 Cf. CIC, c. 1388 §1; cf. CCEO, c. 728 1°.
433 CIC, c. 988 §2.
434 Cf. Gal 3:27.

2. Catechesis for Children's First Reception of the Sacrament of Penance and Reconciliation

Like preparation for Confirmation and First Communion, parents and the parish catechetical leader, together with the pastor, are responsible for determining when children are ready to receive First Penance and Reconciliation. Readiness for reception of this sacrament includes knowledge of the person of Jesus and the Gospel message of forgiveness, knowledge of sin and its effect, and understanding and experience of sorrow, forgiveness, and conversion.

In the Latin Church, children must receive the Sacrament of Penance and Reconciliation for the first time prior to their first reception of the Eucharist.[435] Since the celebration of First Confession precedes First Communion,

> catechesis for the Sacrament of Reconciliation is to precede First Communion and must be kept distinct by a clear and unhurried separation. This is to be done so that the specific identity of each sacrament is apparent and so that, before receiving First Communion, the child will be familiar with the revised Rite of Reconciliation and will be at ease with the reception of the sacrament.[436]

Catechesis for children prior to their first reception of the Sacrament of Penance and Reconciliation must always respect their natural disposition, ability, age, and circumstances. Since the family is intimately involved with the formation of a child's moral conscience and ordinarily integrates the child into the wider ecclesial communities, parents should be involved in the preparation of their children for this sacrament so that they can affirm and reinforce frequent participation in the sacraments. They orient the child toward God and encourage continual growth in the understanding of God's mercy and love.

Dioceses and parishes should present catechesis for the first reception of the Sacrament of Penance and Reconciliation that helps children to

- Acknowledge God's unconditional love for us
- Turn to Christ and the Church for sacramental forgiveness and reconciliation

---

435 Cf. *General Catechetical Directory*, Addendum, no. 5.
436 *National Catechetical Directory*, no. 126.

- Recognize the presence of good and evil in the world and their personal capacity for both
- Recognize their need for forgiveness, not only from parents and others close to them, but from God
- Explore the meaning of the symbols, gestures, prayers, and scriptures of the Rite of Reconciliation
- Understand how to celebrate the Rite of Reconciliation
- Understand that "sacramental Confession is a means offered children of the Church to obtain pardon for sin, and furthermore that it is even necessary *per se* if one has fallen into serious sin"[437]

Since conversion is a lifelong process, catechesis for the Sacrament of Penance and Reconciliation is ongoing. Children have a right to a fuller catechesis each year.[438]

3. Catechesis for the Sacrament of the Anointing of the Sick

The Gospels are filled with signs of Jesus' compassion for the sick, both in spirit and in body. Jesus charged his disciples and with them the whole Church to "cure the sick."[439] His love for the sick continues in the Church today. His healing power is a definitive sign that the Kingdom of God is close at hand and is a clear announcement of his victory over sin, suffering, and death. His Spirit draws all Christians to care for those who suffer in body and soul. Jesus, the divine physician of our souls and bodies, is at work in the Sacrament of the Anointing of the Sick: touching our wounds in order to heal us and restoring us to communion with his Father in the Holy Spirit. Christ's personal solicitude for the sick is expressed in the words of James: "Is anyone among you sick? He should summon the presbyters of the church, and they should pray over him and anoint [him] with oil in the name of the Lord, and the prayer of faith will save the sick person, and the Lord will raise him up. If he has committed any sins, he will be forgiven."[440] In the Latin Church, the normative reference point

---

437   *General Catechetical Directory*, Addendum, no. 3.
438   Cf. *National Catechetical Directory*, no. 126.
439   Mt 10:8.
440   Jas 5:14-15.

for catechesis for the Anointing of the Sick is the *Pastoral Care of the Sick: Rites of Anointing and Viaticum.*[441]

Dioceses and parishes should present a catechesis for the Sacrament of the Anointing of the Sick that

- Examines the meaning of human suffering, sickness, aging, healing, and death in the light of the Christian faith
- Emphasizes the solidarity with the suffering Christ that Christians experience through their own illness—Christ was no stranger to the world of human suffering, for he took human suffering upon himself, voluntarily and innocently
- Includes instruction on the basic symbols of the sacrament: the laying-on of hands, the anointing of the head and hands with blessed oil, and the words of the sacramental formula[442]
- Teaches that "like all the sacraments the Anointing of the Sick is a liturgical and communal celebration, whether it takes place in the family home, a hospital or church, for a single sick person or a whole group of sick persons"[443]
- Clarifies that the Sacrament of the Anointing of the Sick "is not a sacrament intended only for those who are at the point of death,"[444] but that any baptized person who is seriously or chronically ill or in danger of death from advancing age may receive this sacrament
- Makes clear, equally, that the Anointing of the Sick is also a preparation for death, to be received by those at the point of death; integral to the last rites with which the Church fortifies her faithful in their last hours and which Catholics value so highly, Anointing of the Sick, with the Sacrament of Penance and the Eucharist as Viaticum, form the sacraments of departure[445]
- Explains the effects of the sacrament: "the uniting of the sick person to the passion of Christ, for his own good and that of the whole Church; the strengthening, peace, and courage to endure

---

441 Cf. USCCB, *Pastoral Care of the Sick: Rites of Anointing and Viaticum* (1982).
442 Cf. CCC, no. 1519.
443 CCC, no. 1517.
444 SC, no. 73.
445 Cf. CCC, nos. 1523, 1525.

in a Christian manner the sufferings of illness or old age; the forgiveness of sins, if the sick person was not able to attain it through the Sacrament of Penance and Reconciliation; the restoration of health, if it is conducive to the salvation of his soul; and the preparation for passing over to eternal life"[446]

- Teaches that a person who has previously received the Sacrament of the Anointing of the Sick may receive it again if the condition worsens still or if the condition initially improves and then worsens again
- Explains that those preparing for serious surgery, the elderly whose infirmity declines further, and seriously ill children should ask for sacramental anointing
- Encourages the members of the parish to visit and care for the sick and express concern and love for them
- Teaches that only bishops and priests are ministers of the Sacrament of the Anointing of the Sick

In some of the Eastern Churches, the Sacrament of the Anointing of the Sick is available to all the baptized on the Wednesday or Thursday before Easter and on certain other occasions, such as in the context of a pilgrimage. In these Churches, different parts of the body are anointed, according to the particular Eastern tradition.

Faithful to Christ's command to "heal the sick," the Church offers to those who are about to leave earthly life the Eucharist as *viaticum*, the Body and Blood of Christ, that goes "on the way with" or accompanies the dying person as he or she passes from this life to the next. In these circumstances, the Eucharist is the seed of eternal life that completes the pilgrim's earthly journey from birth through death to life. Catechesis on *viaticum* should include careful instruction so that the faithful can arrange for *viaticum* to be brought while the dying person is able to receive it.

C. The Sacraments at the Service of Communion

Jesus Christ, the only Son of God, leads all people to the Father through the Holy Spirit into communion with the Holy Trinity. This is the end toward

---

446   CCC, no. 1532.

which the Father's eternal plan for the salvation of humanity advances. To achieve this end, Christ pours out the Holy Spirit in the Church through the sacraments at the service of communion so that the baptized may bear witness to him and join themselves to his sacrificial offering of praise to the Father. Holy Orders and Matrimony are the sacraments at the service of communion because they "confer a particular mission in the Church and serve to build up the People of God."[447] The Eastern Catholic Churches call these the "Mysteries of Vocation."

1. Catechesis for the Sacrament of Holy Orders

Catechesis for the Sacrament of Holy Orders should be given to all members of the Christian community. Catechesis should teach that the whole Church is a priestly people and that through Baptism all the faithful share in the priesthood of Christ, the common priesthood of the faithful. Those who have been consecrated by the Sacraments of Baptism, Confirmation or Chrismation, and Eucharist share the vocation to holiness and to the mission of proclaiming the Gospel to all nations.[448] That call, issued by Jesus Christ, establishes the common priesthood of the faithful.

Within this common priesthood of the faithful, some are consecrated through the Sacrament of Holy Orders as members of the ministerial priesthood "to nourish the Church with the word and grace of God."[449] Catechesis should, therefore, teach that "based on this common priesthood and ordered to its service, there exists another participation in the mission of Christ: the ministry conferred by the Sacrament of Holy Orders, where the task is to serve in the name and in the person of Christ the Head in the midst of the community."[450] Catechesis should teach that "the ministerial priesthood differs in essence from the common priesthood of the faithful because it confers a sacred power for the service of the faithful."[451] It should teach that there are three degrees of the ordained ministry: that of bishops, that of priests, and that of deacons.

The ministerial priesthood and the common priesthood of the faithful participate "each in its own proper way, in the one priesthood of

447   CCC, no.1534.
448   Cf. CIC, c. 1008.
449   LG, no. 11.
450   CCC, no. 1591.
451   CCC, no. 1592.

Christ."[452] Though they are ordered to each other, they differ essentially.[453] The ministerial priesthood is at the service of the common priesthood of the faithful. It is essential that all the faithful understand that the Sacrament of Holy Orders "is the sacrament through which the mission entrusted by Christ to his apostles continues to be exercised in the Church until the end of time."[454]

Catechesis concerning the Sacrament of Holy Orders should be provided for all the faithful so that they may have a clear understanding that bishops, priests, and deacons are called by Christ and, through sacramental ordination, are empowered to minister in his name and in the name of the Church. Such catechesis clarifies the specific roles and tasks of those in Holy Orders. It emphasizes the intimate connection between the ministerial priesthood and the common priesthood of the faithful. It encourages support for bishops, priests, and deacons so that they may remain faithful to their call and be effective in their ministry. It includes prayer for those in Holy Orders and for new vocations to the ordained ministry. Finally, such catechesis provides opportunities for young men to consider the call to the ministerial priesthood.

Dioceses and parishes should present catechesis for the Sacrament of Holy Orders that

- Explains that the whole Church is a priestly people and that, through Baptism, all the faithful share in the priesthood of Christ, the common priesthood of the faithful
- Teaches that "the ministerial priesthood differs in essence from the common priesthood of the faithful because it confers a sacred power for the service of the faithful"[455]
- Sets forth the effects of the sacrament: that it configures a man to Christ either in the priesthood or diaconal service by a special grace of the Holy Spirit and imprints an indelible sacramental character that marks him permanently
- Teaches that "Church authority alone has the responsibility and right to call someone to receive the Sacrament of Holy Orders"[456]

---

452 CCC, no.1547.
453 Cf. LG, no 10.
454 CCC, no. 1536.
455 CCC, no. 1592.
456 CCC, no. 1598.

- Teaches that the Church, in the person of the bishops, confers the Sacrament of Holy Orders only on baptized men: "priestly ordination, which hands on the office entrusted by Christ to his Apostles of teaching, sanctifying, and governing the faithful, has in the Catholic Church from the beginning always been reserved to men alone"[457]
- Teaches the symbols, gestures, prayers, and scriptures of the Rite of Ordination,[458] including the laying-on of hands and the bishop's prayer of consecration
- Describes the three degrees of the ordained ministry: that of bishops, that of priests, and that of deacons
- Explains that the grace of the Holy Spirit empowers bishops, priests, and deacons—each in ways particular to their order—to share in the saving action of Jesus Christ's ministry of teaching, sanctifying, and building up the Church
- Makes clear that the Latin Church calls ordained ministers, with the exception of permanent deacons, to consecrate themselves with undivided heart to the Lord by committing themselves to celibacy as a sign of the new life of service to which they are consecrated; ordinarily, the Sacrament of Holy Orders is conferred only on men who freely promise to embrace celibacy for the length of their lives[459]
- Teaches that, in the Eastern Churches, priests and deacons are ordinarily permitted to marry before their ordination
- Teaches that permanent deacons may be men who are already married but that, after ordination to the deaconate, they cannot enter into another marriage

Catechesis on the value and importance of religious life should also be provided for the faithful. It should teach that religious life "derives from the mystery of the Church"[460] and is "distinguished from other forms of consecrated life by its liturgical character, public profession of the evangelical counsels" of poverty, chastity, and obedience; of "fraternal life led

---

457   John Paul II, *Reserving Priestly Ordination to Men Alone (Ordinatio Sacerdotalis)* (OS) (Washington, D.C.: USCCB, 1994), no. 1.

458   Cf. CCC, no. 1573.

459   Cf. CCC, no. 1579.

460   CCC, no. 926.

in common"; and of "witness given to the union of Christ with the Church."[461] It should also include instruction on secular institutes, societies of apostolic life, and other forms of consecrated life recognized by the Church.[462]

2. Catechesis for the Sacrament of Matrimony

Christian marriage is the union of a baptized man and woman who freely enter into a loving covenant with each other in Christ. "The matrimonial covenant, by which a man and a woman establish between themselves a partnership of the whole of life and which is ordered by its nature to the good of the spouses and the procreation and education of offspring, has been raised by Christ the Lord to the dignity of a sacrament between the baptized."[463]

This self-giving love of husband and wife represents the mutual love of Christ for his bride, the Church, and the love of the Church for her bridegroom, Christ. "Thus, the *marriage bond* has been established by God himself in such a way that a marriage concluded and consummated between baptized persons can never be dissolved."[464] It gives permanent witness to the fidelity of love. "This bond, which results from the free human act of the spouses and their consummation of the marriage, is a reality, henceforth irrevocable, and gives rise to a covenant guaranteed by God's fidelity. The Church does not have the power to contravene this disposition of divine wisdom."[465]

Catechesis for the Sacrament of Matrimony is addressed to the whole parish community. It is addressed directly to couples intending to marry in the parish and often takes the form of a diocesan or parish preparation program. Catechesis specifically for adults should be offered through all the stages of married life and should be the model for all other forms of catechesis on Christian marriage. Catechesis on Christian marriage and distinctively Christian family values should be given to adolescents and teenagers during their high school years. Children begin learning the meaning of married love at a very early age from their parents, both through the example

---

461 CCC, no. 925.
462 Cf. CCC, nos. 914-933.
463 CIC, c. 1055 §1; cf. CCEO, c. 776 §§1-2.
464 CCC, no. 1640.
465 CCC, no. 1640.

of their lives and through their more formal instruction. The family is the most effective school for catechesis on Christian marriage and family life.

Dioceses and parishes should present catechesis on the Sacrament of Matrimony that

- Encourages the care and concern of the whole Christian community for married couples by public recognition of couples planning marriage, modeling by couples in successful marriages, and support of couples in challenged marriages
- Stresses marriage as a distinct and dignified vocation in the Church
- Explains the effects of the Sacrament of Matrimony: the establishment of a perpetual and exclusive bond between the spouses that is sealed by God himself,[466] the perfection of the mutually exclusive and permanent love of the couple, the strengthening of their indissoluble unity, and the experience of a foretaste of the Kingdom of God
- Encourages marriages within the Catholic faith and explains why this is desirable (the Church requires marriage within the Catholic faith; permission or a dispensation from the bishop is necessary for a Catholic to marry a non-Catholic or an unbaptized person, respectively)
- Teaches that marriage is a covenant of love in which God participates as an active member
- Acknowledges that it is in the love and struggles of marriage that a couple attains the holiness of their vocation
- Teaches that in Christian marriage the unity of the couple is a unity founded in an equal personal dignity and expressed in an unreserved mutuality of self-giving
- Teaches that the family is the first and essential center of faithful living, the domestic Church
- Teaches that the home is the first school of Christian life and human enrichment
- Teaches that a couple's marriage in Christ is a sacred relationship that is supported for the length of their lives by the grace to love each other with the love Christ has for the Church

---

466   Cf. Mk 10:9.

- Teaches that fidelity, indissolubility, and openness to children are essential to Christian marriage
- Teaches that Christian marriage is for the mutual support of the spouses, their growth in love, and the procreation and education of their children
- Includes a clear presentation of the Church's teaching on the morally acceptable methods of regulating birth and the immorality of artificial birth control, of sterilization for that purpose, and of abortion
- Emphasizes their personal responsibility to protect the human life that they co-create with God from the moment of conception to natural death
- Includes a clear presentation of the Church's teaching on mixed and interreligious marriages
- Includes instruction on the rite of the sacrament
- Teaches that the couple themselves are the ministers of the sacrament and that their consent should be publicly exchanged in their vows before a priest or deacon (or a witness authorized by the Church) and two other witnesses, ideally in the presence of an assembly of the faithful[467]
- Assists the couple in deepening their understanding of the nature of Christian marriage as a covenant between a man and a woman whereby the spouses establish between themselves a partnership of their whole life that is ordered to the well-being of the spouses and to the procreation and upbringing of children

Catechesis for those preparing for ecumenical or interreligious marriages should encourage them to discuss openly and honestly the challenges and opportunities that the respective faith traditions present for their relationship, the education and formation of their children, and the harmony of the family. It should also recognize the sacramental nature of a marriage between a baptized Catholic and a spouse baptized in another Christian tradition. Catechesis is also needed for non-sacramental marriages between a baptized Catholic and an unbaptized person. It should clarify that for marriages between a Catholic and another Christian, the Catholic spouse must request a canonical dispensation from the diocesan bishop; likewise, the

---

467 In Byzantine Catholic Churches, the priest is the minister of the sacrament. In addition, the vows are optional because the statement of the intention is made in a different manner.

Catholic spouse must request a canonical dispensation in order to marry a member of a non-Christian religion or of no religion.

Dioceses and parishes should also present catechesis to the whole Catholic community that

- Encourages the care and concern of the whole Christian community for those who have suffered the trauma of divorce
- Encourages the Christian community to welcome divorced persons and their children into the parish as truly integral members
- Makes clear that, while the fact of divorce itself does not prevent reception of the sacraments, Catholics who are divorced and remarried without having obtained a declaration of nullity cannot participate in the sacramental life of the Church
- Explains that a Church annulment or "declaration of nullity" is an official decision by the Church that a marriage was invalid from the beginning, but that it does not affect the legitimacy of children resulting from the union
- Encourages those Catholics who are divorced and remarried outside the Church to seek to regularize their marriage if possible, "to listen to the word of God, to attend the sacrifice of the Mass, to persevere in prayer, to contribute to works of charity and to community efforts in favor of justice, to bring up their children in the Christian faith, to cultivate the spirit and practice of penance and thus implore, day by day, God's grace"[468]

37. THE SACRED: TIME (LITURGICAL YEAR) AND SPACE (ART)

A. Sacred Time: The Liturgical Year

"*In Christianity time has a fundamental importance.*"[469] Christ inaugurates "the last days"[470] and the time of the Church that extends to the definitive coming of the Kingdom of God in Jesus Christ. "*In Jesus Christ, the*

---

468 FC, no. 84.
469 TMA, no. 10.
470 TMA, no. 10, citing Heb 1:2.

Word made flesh, time becomes a dimension of God, who is himself eternal."[471] Because of God's presence in time in the person of Jesus Christ, time is sacred. Christians mark time itself in relation to Christ.

The Latin Church lives and celebrates the mystery of Christ in the span of a calendar year that re-presents the mystery of the incarnation and redemption beginning with the First Sunday of Advent and concluding on the Solemnity of Christ the King. The Eastern Catholic Churches begin and end the liturgical year in accord with their particular traditions and follow the pattern of the Church year by means of their own particular lectionaries.

The economy or history of salvation unfolds throughout the liturgical year. Each day of the liturgical year is sanctified primarily by Christ's presence in it, but also by the prayer and the liturgical celebrations of the People of God, especially by the Mass and the Divine Office. The liturgical year exerts "a special sacramental power and influence which strengthens Christian life."[472]

From the time of the apostles, beginning with the actual day of Christ's Resurrection, the Church has celebrated the Paschal Mystery every first day, Sunday, the Lord's Day. "The intimate bond between Sunday and the Resurrection of the Lord is strongly emphasized by all the Churches of the East and West."[473] Sunday is the weekly Easter. The day of Christ's Resurrection is both the first day of the week in the new creation and the "eighth day" of the week, the image of eternity, which anticipates the glorious return of Christ and the fulfillment of God's reign. In the Byzantine Liturgy, Sunday is called "the day that knows no evening."

"The weekdays extend and develop the Sunday celebration."[474] As the Church celebrates the mystery of Christ throughout the liturgical year, she honors especially Mary, the Mother of God, and Mother of the Church, who is "inseparably linked with her son's saving work. In her the Church admires and exalts the most excellent fruit of redemption, and joyfully contemplates, as in a faultless image, that which she herself desires and hopes wholly to be."[475] The Church also commemorates the lives of the apostles,

---

471 TMA, no. 10.
472 Sacred Congregation of Rites, *Maxima Redemptionis Nostrae Mysteriis* (1955).
473 DD, no. 19.
474 *National Catechetical Directory*, no. 144.
475 SC, no. 103.

martyrs, and other saints, for they have been glorified with Christ. They are heroic examples of Christian life and intercede for the faithful on earth.

The liturgical year is divided into seasons that correspond to the major events in the history of salvation in Christ. The Christmas season celebrates the birth of the Savior in the mystery of the incarnation. In the Eastern Churches, after the close of the Christmas cycle, the Baptism of the Lord, called the "Theophany," is celebrated with great solemnity. Christ's baptism is seen as the paradigm or model for our own baptism.

For all the baptized, Lent is likewise the time to deepen and renew our own baptismal commitment. It is the primary penitential season in the Church's liturgical year, during which the faithful embrace the traditional practices of fasting, prayer, and almsgiving in preparation to renew their baptismal promises on Easter. These expressions of penance and self-denial manifest the Christian's continual need for conversion. Lent reflects the forty days that Jesus spent in the desert in fasting and prayer. It is also the time when the Church journeys with her catechumens and draws them toward the celebration of the Paschal Mystery in the final stages of their Christian initiation.

The Easter Triduum celebrates the Lord's passion, death, and Resurrection and is the culmination of the entire liturgical year. The Easter Vigil marks the sacramental initiation of the catechumens into God's own life and the life of the Church. The Easter season extends for fifty days to the celebration of Pentecost, which commemorates the mission of the Holy Spirit from the Father and the Son to the Church.

In the Latin Church, Ordinary Time, which spans the periods from Christmas to Lent and from Pentecost to the Feast of Christ the King, celebrates different aspects of the fullness of the mystery of Christ from week to week. The Eastern Catholic Churches do not designate a season of Ordinary Time, but some dedicate a season to the power of the cross, beginning with the Feast of the Holy Cross, in which the cross is celebrated with great solemnity as the standard for Christian living as the believers await the second coming of Christ.

Catechesis for recognizing God's presence in time, for keeping time holy, and for the interiorization of the liturgical year is directed to every Christian. The *Commentary on the Revised Liturgical Year* and the *General Norms for the Liturgical Year and the Calendar*[476] provide many examples for

---

476   Cf. USCCB, *Roman Calendar, Text and Commentary* (1976).

the development of catechesis for the liturgical year. The religious customs and traditions of the diverse cultural and ethnic heritages of the many peoples who make up the Catholic Church in the United States also offer countless opportunities to mark the more significant moments throughout the liturgical year. The celebration of these religious customs and traditions provide genuine opportunities to evangelize the culture and cultures of the United States.

B. Sacred Art, Architecture, and Music

1. Sacred Art

In sacred art human hands express the infinite beauty of God and prompt praise and thanks. "*Sacred art* is true and beautiful when its form corresponds to its particular vocation: evoking and glorifying, in faith and adoration, the transcendent mystery of God—the surpassing invisible beauty of truth and love visible in Christ."[477] While the particular expressions of sacred art vary from culture to culture, authentic sacred art turns human minds, hearts, and souls toward God. "Art is meant to bring the divine to the human world, to the level of the senses, then, from the spiritual insight gained from the senses and the stirring of the emotions, to raise the human world to God, to his inexpressible kingdom of mystery, beauty and life."[478] Sacred art "should be worthy, becoming, and beautiful, signs and symbols of things supernatural."[479]

Sacred art also has both a liturgical and catechetical purpose. Sacred art expresses the reverence and honor that are due the sacred. It conveys faith and fosters the expression of faith in the Liturgy. Sacramental celebrations depend on signs, symbols, and gestures to effect the grace they signify. Sacred art forms an essential part of the sacred Liturgy; it is "integral to the Church at prayer because these objects and actions are [sacred] 'signs and symbols of the supernatural world' and expressions of the divine presence."[480] Whether traditional or contemporary, sacred art

---

477 CCC, no. 2502.
478 Paul VI, Address to the Pontifical Commission for Sacred Art in Italy (December 17, 1969).
479 SC, no. 122.
480 USCCB, *Built of Living Stones: Art, Architecture, and Worship* (Washington, D.C.: USCCB, 2000), no. 146.

is suitable for religious worship as long as it expresses the divine in the midst of the human and leads to prayer.

Especially in the Eastern Churches, the liturgical icon portrays the sacred images of Christ, the Mother of God, the saints, or the angels. These icons represent various aspects of the mystery of the incarnation of the Son of God. "Christian iconography expresses in images the same Gospel message that Scripture communicates by words. Image and word illuminate each other."[481] In Eastern spirituality, iconography depicts redeemed creation as a manifestation of the Divine Creator. Sacred images of the Mother of God, the angels, and the saints signify Christ, who is glorified in them. These sacred images lead the faithful to contemplate the mystery they depict, to meditate on the Word of God, and to enter more deeply into communion with God.

Dioceses and parishes should present catechesis on sacred art that

- Includes an introduction to the religious art of the past and the present in both the Eastern and Latin Churches
- Revives the tradition of using great works of art, such as music, stained glass windows, paintings, mosaics, and sculpture to instruct the faithful on the fundamental truths of the faith
- Employs contemporary examples of sacred art of different cultures to imprint the mystery of Christ on the memories and experiences of those being catechized
- Encourages the placement of religious art in the home, such as the crucifix, statuary, sculpture, painting, mosaics, and other sacred images of Christ, the Virgin Mary, and the saints

2. Sacred Architecture

In sacred architecture, the Church "demonstrates God's reign over all space by dedicating buildings to house the Church and its worship."[482] Christians build churches to worship God, but churches are not simply gathering spaces for the Christian assembly. Rather, "the church building is a sign and reminder of the immanence and transcendence of God—who chose to dwell among us and whose presence cannot be contained or limited to any

---

481   CCC, no. 1160.
482   *Built of Living Stones*, no. 20.

single place."[483] A church is the house of God, his dwelling with those who have been reconciled to him by Christ and united to him by the Holy Spirit. A church building signifies the Church, the Body of Christ, alive in a particular place and among a particular people. It is the building in which the Christian community gathers to hear the word of God, to celebrate the Eucharist, to receive the sacraments, and to pray. It must have a place of great honor for God to dwell and for the faithful to pray. It should be a place appropriate for the reservation of the Eucharist and befitting the adoration of the Blessed Sacrament. It should be a form of worship itself, lifting the hearts and minds of the people to give praise and thanks to God. A church also signifies the Father's house, toward which his people journey and for which his people long. It should be easily accessible to all. The church building, in short, is a "sign of the pilgrim Church on earth and reflects the Church dwelling in heaven."[484]

3. Sacred Music

Because sacred music gives glory and praise to God, it has been an integral part of the life of the Church from the very beginning. Jesus sang hymns with his apostles at the Last Supper,[485] and the first Christian writers attested to the customary inclusion of sacred music even in the earliest forms of Eucharistic Liturgy. Sacred music can be sung or performed on instruments. It can take a variety of forms, such as chant or polyphony, and can be ancient, medieval, modern, or contemporary. "Among the many signs and symbols used by the Church to celebrate its faith, music is of preeminent importance."[486]

Thus, sacred music forms an integral part of the Church's Liturgy. More than just hymns, sacred music especially includes the Mass parts, so as to enrich the people's active participation in the Liturgy. It exhibits a "certain holy sincerity of form"[487] and performs a ministerial role in the celebration of divine worship. It serves—but does not dominate. "Liturgical worship is

---

483   *Built of Living Stones*, no. 50.
484   Congregation for the Sacraments and Divine Worship, *Rite of Dedication of a Church and an Altar* (1978), ch. 1, no. 2.
485   Cf. Mk 14:26.
486   USCCB Bishops' Committee on the Liturgy, *Music in Catholic Worship*, rev. ed. (Washington, D.C.: USCCB, 1983), no. 23.
487   Sacred Congregation of Rites, *Instruction on Music in the Liturgy* (*Musicam Sacram*) (MusSacr), no. 4, in Flannery.

given a more noble form when divine offices are celebrated solemnly in song with the assistance of sacred ministers and the active participation of the people."[488]

In the Roman Liturgy, "Gregorian chant holds pride of place."[489] Along with it, polyphony in particular is allowed, and other forms of sacred music as well, "provided that they correspond to the spirit of liturgical action and that they foster the participation of all the faithful."[490] It is also desirable that everywhere the faithful "know how to sing together at least some parts of the Ordinary of the Mass in Latin, especially the Creed and the Lord's Prayer, set to the simpler melodies."[491]

Consequently, sacred music also has a distinct catechetical purpose. Sacred music invites the faithful to give glory to God; it enhances their prayer, fosters the unity of their minds and hearts, and aims to draw them closer to Christ. Sacred music "should assist the assembled believers to express and share the gift of faith that is written within them and to nourish and strengthen their interior commitment of faith."[492] Within the scope of sacred music, special attention should be given "to the *songs used by the assembly*, since singing is a particularly apt way to express a joyful heart, accentuating the solemnity of the celebration and fostering the sense of a common faith and a shared love."[493] Parishes should provide opportunities for their people to learn sacred hymns in order that they may fully participate in the liturgical life of the Church.

38. SACRAMENTALS AND POPULAR DEVOTIONS[494]

A. Sacramentals

Sacramentals "are sacred signs which bear a resemblance to the sacraments. They signify effects, particularly of a spiritual nature, which are

---

488 SC, no. 113.
489 GIRM, no. 41.
490 GIRM, no. 41.
491 GIRM, no. 41.
492 *Music in Catholic Worship*, no. 23.
493 DD, no. 50.
494 Cf. *Directory on Popular Piety and the Liturgy: Principles and Guidelines*.

obtained through the Church's intercession."[495] They prepare the faithful to receive and cooperate with grace and so are catechetical by nature. They are liturgical actions in which the faithful are invited to participate. In general, sacramentals sanctify the lives of the faithful by linking them to Christ's Paschal sacrifice.

Sacramentals are instituted by the Church in order to sanctify certain ministries, certain states of life, and certain objects Christians use in their daily lives. Sacramentals are often concrete examples of the inculturation of the faith since they express the faith in the particular language, customs, and traditions of a specific culture. "They always include a prayer, often accompanied by a specific sign, such as the laying on of hands, the sign of the cross, or the sprinkling of holy water (which recalls Baptism)."[496]

Blessings of persons, meals, occasions, objects, and places are the most important kinds of sacramentals.[497] Certain blessings consecrate persons to God, such as the abbot or abbess of a monastery, virgins or widows, and the members of vowed communities. Other blessings designate persons for ministry in the Church, such as catechists, lectors, acolytes, and so forth. Still other blessings consecrate objects for liturgical use. Thus, the church building, the altar, the baptistry, oils to be used in celebrating the sacraments, sacred vessels, vestments, holy water, crosses and crucifixes, rosaries, palms, ashes, candles, medals, and various types of religious art and artifacts are all sacramentals. Some cultures have emphasized some sacramentals; the faith has been inculturated through them.

Catechesis on sacramentals should describe their relationship to faith in Jesus Christ and their function in the Church and in the lives of individual Christians. It should especially seek out examples of sacramentals that are common to all cultures in order to reveal their relationships to the Christian message.

B. Popular Piety and Popular Devotion

Especially in light of the cultural, ethnic, and religious diversity of the United States, popular piety is a vital element in Catholic life that is expressed in a wide variety of popular devotions, such as various forms of

---

495 SC, no. 60.
496 CCC, no. 1668.
497 Cf. *Book of Blessings* (New York: Catholic Book Publishing Co., 1989).

prayers for the souls in purgatory, the use of sacramentals, and pilgrimages to shrines of Christ, the Blessed Virgin Mary, and the saints.[498] In the United States, popular piety is a mode of the inculturation of the faith that is deeply rooted in the many cultures represented in its population. All racial, ethnic, and cultural groups have devotional practices that spring from their particular expressions of the one faith. Popular piety and the popular devotion it inspires provide many opportunities to encounter Christ in the particular circumstances of ethnic, cultural, and religious customs. If popular piety "is well oriented, above all by a pedagogy of evangelization, it is rich in values. It manifests a thirst for God which only the simple and poor can know. It makes people capable of generosity and sacrifice even to the point of heroism, when it is a question of manifesting belief."[499]

The large and growing number of immigrants in the United States requires careful attention to the role of popular piety in many people's lives.[500] This is true, for example, in the lives of Catholics whose roots are in Africa. The Church "recognizes that it must approach these Americans from within their own culture, taking seriously the spiritual and human riches of that culture which appear in the way they worship, their sense of joy and solidarity, their language and their traditions."[501] As another example, Hispanics/Latinos "tend to view all of life as sacred and have generally developed a profound sense of the divine in daily living. This is evident in their popular religiosity. . . . In small communities, [they] find support to retrieve this sense of popular piety and to reaffirm the values contained in these celebrations."[502]

Asian and Pacific Catholic Americans and immigrants sustain their faith through devotional prayers and practices. They "migrated with the experience and sensibilities of the great religions and spiritual traditions of the world . . . together with Christianity. Their experience of the great religions and spiritual traditions teaches them to live with profound presence of the sacred, a holistic approach to life and salvation, and spirituality

---

498   Cf. EA, no. 16.
499   EN, no. 48.
500   Cf. USCCB, *Together a New People: Pastoral Statement on Migrants and Refugees* (Washington, D.C.: USCCB, 1986), no. 31.
501   EA, no. 16.
502   USCCB Committee on Hispanic Affairs, *Communion and Mission: A Guide for Bishops and Pastoral Leaders on Small Church Communities* (Washington, D.C.: USCCB, 1995), no. 5.

adapted to their needs and a life-giving vitality."[503] They "bring popular devotions from their homelands and share them with fellow parishioners."[504]

In the Latin Church in the United States, the Blessed Sacrament, the Sacred Heart, the Blessed Virgin Mary, and many saints are very important in popular devotion. "Hispanic/Latino spirituality," for example, "places strong emphasis on the humanity of Jesus, especially when he appears weak and suffering, as in the crib and in his passion and death. . . . The Blessed Virgin Mary, especially under the titles of Our Lady of Guadalupe (Mexico), Our Lady of Providence (Puerto Rico), and Our Lady of Charity (Cuba), occupies a privileged place in Hispanic/Latino popular piety."[505]

African Americans likewise weave the message of evangelization into the cultural environment of their distinctive spirituality. The roots of African American spirituality are found in the family and issue from their history and lived experience. Their art, music, language, dance, and drama—as well as those of other Black cultures—should be incorporated into liturgical celebrations that are always "authentically black . . . truly Catholic . . . well-prepared and well-executed."[506] The Kingship of Jesus Christ, the pouring of libations, and an emphasis on Mary as the "Great Mother" are a few examples of popular devotion that express the profound biblical themes of freedom and hope that are so integral to African American culture and spirituality.

In Eastern Catholic communities, *Akathistos, Paraklesis, Molebens*,[507] devotion to the Blessed Virgin Mary, reverence for icons, and offices to the saints are important forms of popular devotion.

C. Marian Devotion

Devotion to the Blessed Virgin Mary deserves special attention because it is such an important part of worship in the United States. The United States of America is under the patronage of the Immaculate Conception.

---

503   USCCB, *Asian and Pacific Presence: Harmony in Faith* (Washington, D.C.: USCCB, 2001), 15.

504   *Asian and Pacific Presence*, 16.

505   USCCB, *The Hispanic Presence: Challenge and Commitment* (1983), no. 12, in *Hispanic Ministry: Three Major Documents* (Washington, D.C.: USCCB, 1995).

506   *What We Have Seen and Heard*, 31.

507   *Akathistos, Paraklesis,* and *Molebens* are various types of prayer services. *Akathistos*, literally "standing prayer," is the oldest version and involves prayers of devotion to Mary, to Jesus, or to the Sacred Hearts of Jesus or Mary. *Paraklesis* is a prayer service of intercession to a saint. *Molebens* is a somewhat shorter version of a *Paraklesis*.

The various forms of devotion to the Blessed Virgin Mary reflect the many different cultures, religious convictions, and popular sensibilities that make up the Church in the United States. Catholic people of all cultures have a deep love for the Mother of God. They employ many different expressions of that love to show the one faith that characterizes their particular prayer life and spirituality.

In this country, as well as throughout the world, the Rosary holds a place of honor as the most popular prayer devotion to the Blessed Virgin Mary. In October 2002, Pope John Paul II called for a renewed focus on the Rosary in his apostolic letter *On the Most Holy Rosary* (*Rosarium Virginis Mariae*).[508] In that letter, the Holy Father also suggested five new Mysteries, which he called the "Luminous Mysteries." These Mysteries focus on events in the public life of Jesus.

Dioceses and parishes should present catechesis on piety that

- Promotes the exercise of sound pastoral judgment in order to ensure that popular devotions and the religious sensibility that underlies them lead the faithful to a deeper knowledge of the mystery of Jesus Christ and a true encounter with him
- Promotes Marian devotion that clearly expresses "intrinsic Trinitarian, Christological and ecclesiological aspects of mariology"[509]
- Discovers the authentic spiritual values present in popular piety and enriches it with genuine Catholic doctrine so that it might lead to a sincere conversion and a practical exercise of charity[510]
- Recognizes the cultural and religious diversity of the United States and promotes awareness of how important popular piety and popular devotion are in the lives of many of the Christian faithful
- Provides opportunities for a more complete inculturation of the Gospel so that the seeds of the Word found in the culture may come to their fulfillment in Christ
- Ensures that the various forms of popular devotion radiate from the Church's sacramental life but do not replace it
- Leads the faithful to a deeper sense of their membership in the Church, which increases the fervor of their love for the

---

508   Cf. John Paul II, *On the Most Holy Rosary* (*Rosarium Virginis Mariae*) (Washington, D.C.: USCCB, 2002).
509   GDC, no. 196.
510   Cf. EA, no. 16.

Church and offers an effective response to the challenges of today's secularization[511]
- Distinguishes between appropriate popular devotion and the requirements of the Christian faith
- Relies on valid elements of popular piety to be effective instruments in the new evangelization

39. CONCLUSION

Gathered to worship the Father in Christ and through the Holy Spirit, the whole Church is one and is profoundly aware of her mission to the world. In the Liturgy, the Church at once expresses her faith and by God's grace deepens that faith. In the Eucharist, Christ leads the community of the baptized to continual conversion in him, to deeper communion with the Father, and to life in the Holy Spirit. The Liturgy both enables and inspires the faithful to live the Christian faith: dedication to the teaching of the apostles, the communal life, the breaking of the bread, and prayer. The participation in the liturgical life of the Church presupposes support of and engagement in all forms of catechetical life in the parish and in the home. The liturgical life of the Church is integrated with her moral life. The next chapter describes how catechesis prepares and strengthens the believer for life in Christ: a life of faith, hope, charity, justice, and peace.

---

511 Cf. EA, no. 16.

CHAPTER 6

Catechesis for Life in Christ

I live, no longer I, but Christ lives in me; insofar as I now live in the flesh, I live by faith in the Son of God who has loved me and given himself up for me. (Gal 2:20)

---

40. INTRODUCTION

What the Christian faith confesses, the Christian sacraments celebrate and the Christian life animates. Christ calls his disciples in every age to live lives "worthy of the gospel."[512] We are enabled to do so by the Father's love, the grace of Christ, and the gifts of the Holy Spirit that are diffused through the Church. The Christian moral life is living the call to holiness through transformation in Christ.

Through Baptism we have become "children of God"[513] and "share[rs] in the divine nature"[514] and are incorporated into Christ; and so we participate in the life of the Risen Lord.[515] United with Christ, conformed to him, we follow his example in word and deed. The actions of our lives reflect "the fruit of the Spirit . . . love, joy, peace, patience, kindness, generosity, faithfulness, gentleness, self control."[516] We have been "justified in the name of the Lord Jesus Christ and in the Spirit of our God."[517] We "have been sanctified in Christ Jesus, called to be holy."[518] Christ has

---

512 Phil 1:27.
513 Jn 1:12.
514 2 Pt 1:4.
515 Cf. Col 2:12.
516 Gal 5:22-23.
517 1 Cor 6:11.
518 1 Cor 1:2.

invited us to "be perfect, just as your heavenly Father is perfect."[519] And he has given us the Holy Spirit to enlighten and strengthen us to achieve "every kind of goodness and righteousness and truth."[520] The life of holiness in Christ proceeds from him, is guided by him, and leads to him.

The discipleship to which he has called all believers costs personally and dearly; the Gospel demands love and self-surrender. The way of Christ is the way of his cross: "If anyone wishes to come after me, he must deny himself and take up his cross daily and follow me."[521] From the cross of Christ flows the water of life. The way of Christ leads to life.

Catechesis for life in Christ reveals both the joy and the demands of the way of Christ. Catechesis for the newness of life in Christ should be a catechesis of the Holy Spirit, the interior guide who inspires, corrects, and strengthens us on the journey to the Father in Christ. It is a catechesis of grace, the love of God, which prompts our good works and by which we are saved. It is a catechesis of the Beatitudes, the blessings that anticipate the eternal beatitude of life in communion with God. It is a catechesis about sin and forgiveness that helps us confront our sinfulness and accept God's mercy. It is a catechesis of the human virtues, themselves gifts of grace, which incline us towards goodness. It is a catechesis of the Christian virtues of faith, hope, and charity that allow us to enter into union with the Holy Trinity. It is a catechesis of the twofold commandment of charity: to love God above all things, and to love our neighbor as ourselves. And it is a catechesis of the Church in which the Christian life is received, nourished, and perfected in Christ.[522] This catechesis always begins and ends in Christ, who is "the way and the truth and the life."[523]

This chapter describes the catechetical principles and guidelines needed for both personal and social moral formation. It also addresses the witness to the new life in Christ that is to be given by both the individual person and the community of faith.

---

519 Mt 5:48.
520 Eph 5:9.
521 Lk 9:23.
522 Cf. CCC, no. 1697.
523 Jn 14:6.

41. THE DIGNITY OF THE HUMAN PERSON

A. Creation in the Image and Likeness of God

The dignity of human persons is initially rooted in our creation by God in his image and likeness. The divine image is present in every person. The Father has created human beings in Christ, and in Christ we come to know ourselves and our exalted vocation. Our redemption in Christ intensifies our inherent dignity.

Endowed with a spiritual and immortal soul, humans beings are "the only creatures on earth that God has wanted for [their] own sake."[524] By reason, we are capable of understanding the created order; by free will we are capable of directing our lives toward the good and away from evil. Yet we know how deeply these gifts have been wounded by original sin. Human beings also find perfection in seeking and loving "what is true and good."[525] From our conception, we are destined for eternal happiness. We have a desire for happiness that God has placed in our hearts in order to draw us to himself. "The beatitude of eternal life is a gratuitous gift of God. It is supernatural, as is the grace that leads us there."[526] Life in the Holy Spirit makes the fulfillment of this desire possible.

In Christ, God reveals how we human beings are to live our lives. God created human beings with the freedom to initiate and direct their own actions and to shape their own lives. "Freedom is the power, rooted in reason and will, to act or not to act, to do this or that, and so to perform deliberate actions on one's own responsibility."[527] Freedom makes human beings responsible for their actions to the extent that they are voluntary. Every human person is a free and responsible agent with an inalienable right to exercise freedom, especially in moral and religious matters. In fact, action is human action insofar as it is free.

This human freedom does not, however, entitle the person to say or do just anything. Human beings are not fully self-sufficient. We are capable of sin. Yet Christ redeemed us from the sin that held us in bondage and set us free. As St. Paul said, "For freedom Christ set us free."[528]

---

524 GS, no. 24.
525 GS, no. 15.
526 CCC, no. 1727.
527 CCC, no. 1731.
528 Gal 5:1.

Human freedom, therefore, is the capacity to choose good or evil. The more one chooses to do what is good, the more free one becomes. The choice to do evil, on the other hand, is an abuse of freedom and leads to the "slavery of sin."[529] In Christ, human beings freely direct themselves to life in the Holy Spirit. "Where the Spirit of the Lord is, there is freedom."[530] Freely choosing to do the good, to obey the universal and unchanging moral norms, in no way diminishes the freedom and dignity of the human person. "*The Crucified Christ reveals the authentic meaning of freedom; he lives it fully in the total gift of himself* and calls his disciples to share in his freedom."[531]

B. Some Challenges to the Dignity of the Human Person

The moral situation in the United States today poses some serious challenges to the Church's catechetical mission. Although religious faith is a strong force in the lives of many, the country's dominant secular culture often contradicts the values on which this nation was established. There is a tendency to privatize religious faith, to push its considerations to the margins of society and to banish its concerns from the public conversation in which social policy is formed.

At the center of the moral vision contained in this nation's founding documents are two basic principles: (1) the recognition of the dignity and rights of the human person as endowed by the Creator and (2) liberty and justice for all. While the people of the United States can rightly be proud of what we have achieved in pursuing those noble principles, unfortunately they are sometimes contradicted in practice and even in law.

In a society that publicly proclaims that life is an inalienable right and affirms the value of life, the inherent dignity and incomparable value of every human person is being threatened: "The very right to life is being denied or trampled upon, especially at the more significant moments of existence: the moment of birth and the moment of death."[532] Abortion and euthanasia directly attack innocent life itself, the most fundamental human right and the basis of all other rights. They attack the weakest and

---

529   Rom 6:17.
530   2 Cor 3:17.
531   John Paul II, *The Splendor of Truth* (*Veritatis Splendor*) (VS) (Washington, D.C.: USCCB, 1993), no. 85.
532   John Paul II, *The Gospel of Life* (*Evangelium Vitae*) (EV) (Washington, D.C.: USCCB, 1995), no. 18.

most defenseless members of society, the unborn and the sick. "Such direct attacks on human life, once crimes, are today legitimized by governments sworn to protect the weak and marginalized."[533] Without the benefit of carefully considered ethical analysis, some current biological and technological developments undermine the dignity of the human person and even attempt to create human life itself by artificial means.

In addition, the treatment of immigrants, of illegal aliens, of those in prison, and of criminals and their victims must be shaped by this recognition of the inherent dignity of every human person.

> The new evangelization calls for followers of Christ who are unconditionally pro-life: who will proclaim, celebrate and serve the Gospel of life in every situation. A sign of hope is the increasing recognition that the dignity of human life must never be taken away, even in the case of someone who has done great evil. Modern society has the means of protecting itself, without definitively denying criminals the chance to reform. I renew the appeal I made most recently at Christmas for a consensus to end the death penalty, which is both cruel and unnecessary.[534]

In a society that publicly proclaims that liberty is an inalienable right, freedom has come to mean an unlimited individual autonomy in which many people find their ultimate sense of fulfillment in the exercise of unrestricted personal choice. Individual freedom becomes the absolute and the source of other values. Such an excessively individualistic notion of freedom distorts the true meaning of freedom, pits the individual person against society, and empties social life, even family life, of its significance. "Yet between life itself and freedom there is an inseparable bond, a link. And that link is love or fidelity."[535]

In a society that values power, utility, productivity, and profit, the helpless, the weak, and the poor are seen as liabilities. The unprecedented economic and military power of the United States has sometimes led to grave injustices both at home and abroad.

At home, it has fueled self-absorption, indifference and consumerist excess:

---

533 *Living the Gospel of Life*, no. 5.
534 John Paul II, Mass at St. Louis, Mo. (January 27, 1999).
535 USCCB, *Faithful for Life: A Moral Reflection* (Washington, D.C.: USCCB, 1995), 9.

Overconfidence in our power, made even more pronounced by advances in science and technology, has created the illusion of a life without natural boundaries and actions without consequences. The standards of the marketplace, instead of being guided by sound morality, threaten to displace it. We are now witnessing the gradual restructuring of American culture according to the ideals of utility, productivity and cost-effectiveness. It is a culture where moral questions are submerged by a river of goods and services and where the misuse of marketing and public relations subverts public life.[536]

The gradual erosion of the principles on which this country was founded contributes to a growing secularism, materialism, and an *"ethical relativism, which would remove any sure moral reference point from political and social life."*[537] In a secularist society there is a grave danger that people will live as if God did not exist. When the sense of God is lost, the sense of humanity is lost as well. In a materialist society there is a grave danger that people will begin to believe that they are what they have. "In a widely dechristianized culture, the criteria employed by believers themselves in making judgments and decisions often appear extraneous or even contrary to those of the Gospel."[538] People wonder if they should hold any truths as sacred. Their ability to make moral decisions based on objective criteria is severely diminished or eliminated altogether. "In turn, the systematic violation of the moral law, especially in the serious matter of respect for human life and its dignity, produces a kind of progressive darkening of the capacity to discern God's living and saving presence."[539]

In general, dioceses and parishes should offer catechesis on Christian morality that

- Upholds the right to life from conception to natural death
- Presents the distinctively Christian understanding of human freedom
- Teaches that freedom reaches its authentic goal in love of the weak and defenseless and in defense of their rights

---

536   *Living the Gospel of Life*, no. 3.
537   VS, no. 101.
538   VS, no. 88.
539   EV, no. 21.

- Promotes the public expression of the Christian faith in the formation of social policy
- Encourages concern for the lives of the poor, the weak, the disabled, and the sick, as well as action on their behalf
- Helps the faithful to make practical moral decisions in the light of the Gospel
- Encourages the faithful to understand that power, wealth, utility, and productivity must be subordinated to and guided by higher moral values

42. MORAL FORMATION IN CHRIST

Christ is the norm of morality. "Christian morality consists, in the simplicity of the Gospel, in *following Jesus Christ*, in abandoning oneself to him, in letting oneself be transformed by his grace and renewed by his mercy, gifts which come to us in the living communion of his Church."[540]

Christian moral formation involves a journey of interior transformation in light of Christ's Paschal Mystery, which brings about a deep personal conversion to Christ. Conversion to Christ involves confession of faith in him, adherence to his person and his teaching, following in his footsteps, taking on his attitudes, and surrendering the old self in order to take up the new self in Christ. "The Sermon on the Mount, in which Jesus takes up the Decalogue, and impresses upon it the spirit of the beatitudes, is an indispensable point of reference for the moral formation which is most necessary today."[541] Moral catechesis involves more than the proclamation and presentation of the principles and practice of Christian morality. It presents the integration of Christian moral principles in the lived experience of the individual and the community. This moral testimony must always demonstrate the social consequences of the Gospel.[542]

A. Grace

Grace conforms the Christian to Christ. It is God's free initiative, which only he can give. It enables us to give ourselves freely in response. Even

---

540 VS, no. 119.
541 GDC, no. 85.
542 Cf. CT, no. 29.

our preparation for grace is itself a work of grace. It is the free and undeserved help that God gives us to, in turn, respond to his call to become his adopted children, partakers of the divine nature and of eternal life.[543] Sanctifying grace is a participation in God's own life that introduces us into the life of the Holy Trinity. Through the grace of Baptism, we are brought into union with the Father; we become members of Christ's Body; and we are joined to the Spirit of the Father and the Son in the Church. "Whoever is in Christ is a new creation: the old things have passed away; behold, new things have come. And all this is from God, who has reconciled us to himself through Christ."[544] The Eastern Churches understand grace as divinization, or being perfected in order to live in communion with God and act by his love.

B. Virtue

Human beings are wounded by sin and need help to live morally good lives. Divine grace transforms human nature. It elevates and purifies virtue so that a person may lead a morally good life. Virtue is the habit of tending toward the good and choosing the good in the concrete actions of a person's life. This gift of grace can also take the form of the cardinal virtues: prudence, justice, fortitude, and temperance, which dispose the person to live in harmony with God, with others, and with the whole created order. The virtuous person freely practices the good. By the grace of the Holy Spirit, the virtuous person consistently seeks communion with God and becomes like God.

This gift of grace takes the form of the theological virtues of faith, hope, and charity. These virtues have God as their origin and object. They are the foundation of Christian moral living—life in Christ. They transform the human capacity to do good into a participation in the divine nature. By the virtue of faith, we believe in God—all he has revealed to us and all the Church proposes for belief. By the virtue of hope, we trust in God's promise of eternal life and his grace to deserve it. And by the virtue of charity, "the bond of perfection,"[545] we love God above all else and our neighbor as ourselves for love of God.

---

543 Cf. CCC, no. 1996; cf. *Joint Declaration on the Doctrine of Justification*, nos. 37-39.
544 2 Cor 5:17-19.
545 Col 3:14.

C. The Formation of Moral Conscience

Moral conscience is a person's "most secret core and . . . sanctuary."[546] It "is a judgment of reason whereby the human person recognizes the moral quality of a concrete act."[547] It bears witness to the truth and judges particular choices, decisions, and actions to be either good or evil. By the judgment of conscience, a person recognizes the prescriptions of the moral law. One's conscience obliges one to follow faithfully what one knows to be good.

The dignity of the human person implies and requires uprightness of moral conscience. While moral conscience reflects God's law written in the human heart, it needs to be formed and informed. The judgments it renders must be enlightened. The formation of a conscience is a lifelong task. In the formation of a conscience, the Word of God illumines the way.

The formation of conscience is influenced by many human factors, such as the person's age, intellectual capacity, psychological capacity, emotional maturity, family experience, and cultural and social conditions. But the example of Christ's life and his teachings are the norm in the formation of conscience. The person's relationship with Christ, expressed by frequent participation in the sacramental and prayer life of the Church, is the basis for the formation of the Christian moral conscience.

Christ's gift of the Spirit of Truth to the Church also ensures that the Church's teachings are true and consequently are necessary in the formation of one's conscience. The Church is the indispensable guide to the complete richness of the teachings of Christ. Thus, "Catholics should always measure their moral judgments by the Magisterium, given by Christ and the Holy Spirit to express Christ's teaching on moral questions and matters of belief and so enlighten personal conscience."[548]

One's conscience can make an erroneous judgment when one faces a moral decision. While a human being must always obey the certain judgment of conscience, conscience can be poorly informed or simply ignorant. Persons are responsible for ensuring that their consciences are well formed and that their actions are determined accordingly. If the poorly formed or ignorant conscience is the result of personal neglect in its formation, the individual is culpable for the choices that are made. If the

---

546   GS, no. 16.
547   CCC, no. 1778.
548   *National Catechetical Directory*, no. 190.

moral decisions made are the result of poor conscience formation or igno-rance for which the person is not responsible, the person is not culpable for the evil committed as a result. The transformed experience through grace is more than the human life development. It is growth "into Christ." Christians deepen their relationship with the Risen Lord, which draws them into the very heart of Christ. Therefore, the transformation of self to the authenticity of being made in the image of God becomes a graced happening and a lifelong commitment to live in freedom, self-assurance, joy, and love. Those involved in catechesis have the moral responsibility to nourish the development of properly informed consciences in those entrusted to their care.

D. Sin

Sin wounds the loving relationship that God has initiated with his crea-tures. It is an offense against God that turns the human heart away from his love. It wounds human nature and injures human solidarity. Our sinfulness is the object of God's great mercy, for which the Church continually prays.

Original sin is the first obstacle to life in Christ. It is the loss of the holiness and grace that Adam and Eve received from God. It is transmit-ted to every person, weakening human nature and leaving it subject to suffering and death. In this state one cannot consistently or persistently avoid personal sin.

Personal sin, whether mortal or venial, is committed by an individual. It is an offense against God, an act contrary to reason. Personal sin wounds human nature, harms the Christian community, and damages human sol-idarity. Because sin wounds, one needs to be both forgiven and healed of sin, a healing that needs to begin within the heart and soul of the sinner.

Mortal sin is a person's deliberate choice to do something seriously con-trary to divine law. "Mortal sin is sin whose object is grave matter and which is committed with full knowledge and deliberate consent."[549] It attacks the principle of life within the human person, namely God's love; it kills or breaks one's relationship with God and his Church, places the person in danger of eternal separation from God, and leads to everlasting death.

Venial sin is a less serious offense against God. It is the failure to observe the less serious matters of the moral law, or the failure to observe

---

549   *Rite of Penance*, no. 12.

the moral law in grave matter, but without full knowledge or complete consent. It diminishes or wounds the divine life in the soul and impairs the sinner's relationship with God. The repetition of individual acts of sin can lead one into a state of sinfulness. In addition, repetitive, deliberate, and unrepentant venial sin can lead to mortal sin.

E. Challenges to Communicate These Fundamental Realities

In order to communicate these fundamental moral teachings in ways that are persuasive and fruitful, dioceses and parishes should present catechesis that

- Restores a sense of the sacred and transcendent in life
- Reassures the faithful that God is present to all and offers his grace to each one
- Prompts the faithful to cooperate with God's grace and live in communion with the Holy Trinity
- Convinces believers that, through Baptism, God shares his own life with them, adopts them as his own children, forgives their sins, and sustains them in his unfailing love
- Encourages and models dependence on God
- Disposes the faithful to live in harmony with God and the created order
- Encourages the faithful to understand that true happiness is communion with God, not material, social, or political success
- Assists the faithful in developing their capacity to discern God's will, becoming ever more ready and able to choose the greater good
- Encourages the faithful to commit themselves to a deep personal relationship with Christ
- Encourages believers to encounter Christ frequently in the celebration of the sacraments
- Helps the faithful to recognize and obey the law that is based on universal truths revealed by God and inscribed by him in their hearts
- Teaches the norms and principles of Christian morality in devoted adherence to the Church's leadership
- Helps believers to understand that true freedom involves doing what ought to be done

- Helps believers form their consciences through careful consideration of the life and teachings of Christ and the Church, the advice of competent people, and the help of the Holy Spirit
- Helps the faithful to identify sins of commission and sins of omission
- Helps believers to identify the effects of original, personal and social sin
- Helps believers to recognize that sin can deter or prevent them from achieving their lifetime goal: union with God
- Helps the faithful to make concrete moral judgments by applying the principles of Christian morality to the ordinary situations of everyday life
- Helps believers to persevere in the pursuit of virtues
- Reaches out in love to those who seem not to respond

43. THE HUMAN COMMUNITY

The model for the human community is the Holy Trinity: the unity of Father, Son, and Holy Spirit. The very nature of the Trinity is communal and social. "God reveals himself to us as one who is not alone, but rather as one who is relational, one who is Trinity. Therefore, we who are made in God's image share this communal, social nature. We are called to reach out and to build relationships of love and justice."[550] The relationships that men and women are to establish among themselves resemble the relationships between and among the divine persons within the Triune God. Those human relationships transcend the boundaries of language, race, ethnicity, gender, culture, and nation to bind people together in one human family. Every single member of that one human family is of inestimable worth, since each is made in the image of God and was created to be happy with God for all eternity.

A. The Communal Character of Life in Christ

People are social by nature. We need other people, and we need to live in society. The family, the community, and the state are the essential social contexts for the development of individual human beings. Ideally these

---

550   USCCB, *Sharing Catholic Social Teaching: Challenges and Directions* (Washington, D.C.: USCCB, 1998), 1.

social units bind people together by a principle of unity that goes beyond each individual. They are necessary structures within which human beings develop their individual potential and collaborate on the achievement of objectives that could not be accomplished by any single person. But these social structures can also present dangers. They can threaten personal freedom and exploit individual ability. The human person "is and . . . ought to be the beginning, the subject and the object of every social organization."[551]

The fact that human beings are social by nature forms a fundamental tenet of Catholic social teaching. Since societies are essential to human development, and all human beings are called to communion with God, the way societies contribute to or impede the achievement of that end involves profound moral questions. Societies are organized around certain social, political, economic, and legal principles—whether clearly articulated or not—and societies function within the institutions and structures that those principles initiate. "Catholic social teaching provides principles by which the Church as an institution, and Christians as individuals, can evaluate political, economic, social, and legal structures."[552]

Society ought to promote the exercise of virtue, not obstruct it. Catholic social teaching recognizes a hierarchy of values within human society that "subordinates . . . material and instinctive dimensions to . . . interior and spiritual ones."[553] Since it is composed of human beings made in God's image and called to communion with him, human society ought to be primarily ordered to the spiritual dimension of the human persons who constitute it. Respect for the inherent dignity of every human person is the foundation of a just society, and its ultimate end is the development of those persons to their fullest potential. Persons cannot be viewed merely as the means to a productive and profitable society. Rather, they should be seen as the architects and beneficiaries of the society that they have conceived and built. Men and women ought to be able to exercise their rights and fulfill their obligations without undue interference from social institutions. The society to which they belong should inspire them to develop themselves as followers of Christ and to develop their families, their communities, and their cultures. The economic, social, political,

---

551 GS, no. 25.
552 *National Catechetical Directory*, no. 158.
553 CA, no. 36.

and legal institutions set up by a society ought to enhance the development of the human person, not restrict it. "Human society must primarily
be considered something pertaining to the spiritual."[554]

B. Moral Conversion and Society

Christian morality has a distinctly social dimension that derives from both
the nature of the human person and the Church's social mission. The
Christian person simply cannot live in society without recognizing the
duties and responsibilities that naturally arise within that relationship.
Our faith in the sovereignty of God and the destiny of the human person
compels us to work for justice, to serve those in need, to seek peace, and
to defend the life, dignity, and rights of every person. "Catholics are called
by God to protect human life, to promote human dignity, to defend those
who are poor, and to seek the common good. This social mission of the
Church belongs to all of us. It is an essential part of what it is to be a
believer."[555] We are called to be leaven in society, applying Christian values to every aspect of our lives. Our society needs the witness of Christians who take the social demands of the Gospel seriously and who
actively practice the virtue of social justice. Christians, by virtue of their
Baptism, must be the "servant" leaders that Jesus Christ challenged the
disciples to be. They must remember that it is "the right and duty of
Catholics and all citizens to seek the truth with sincerity and to promote
and defend, by legitimate means, moral truths concerning society, justice,
freedom, respect for human life and the other rights of the person. . . ."[556]

C. Principles of
Catholic Social Teaching

The call to work for social justice is imbedded in the Gospel message of
Jesus Christ, who came "to bring good tidings to the poor / . . . liberty to
captives / and recovery of sight to the blind."[557] That call has been further

---

554   John XXIII, *Peace on Earth* (*Pacem in Terris*) (PT) (Washington, D.C.: USCCB, 1963), no. 36.
555   USCCB, *Everyday Christianity: To Hunger and Thirst for Justice* (Washington, D.C.: USCCB, 1998), 1.
556   Congregation for the Doctrine of the Faith, *Doctrinal Note on Some Questions Concerning the Participation
         of Catholics in Political Life* (Washington, D.C.: USCCB, 2004), no. 6.
557   Lk 4:18.

specified by the official teachings of the Church. The Church's social teaching comprises a body of doctrine, but it is not merely a series of documents. Rather, it is a living tradition of thought and action. This teaching is a

> call to conscience, compassion, and creative action in a world confronting the terrible tragedy of widespread abortion, the haunting reality of hunger and homelessness, and the evil of continuing prejudice and poverty. [It] lifts up the moral and human dimensions of major public issues, examining the "signs of the times" through the values of the Scriptures, the teaching of the Church, and the experience of the People of God.[558]

The Church's social doctrine is part of a systematic moral framework that includes the totality of Christ's moral teachings and those proposed by the Church in his name. The Church's social teachings are deeply integrated in her comprehensive vision of Christian morality. They cannot be treated as if they were peripheral or optional. They are constituent elements of her Magisterium, and the values on which they are based are indispensable components of life in Christ.

The Church's social teaching seeks to apply the Gospel command of love to and within social systems, structures, and institutions. It "proposes principles for reflection; it provides criteria for judgment; it gives guidelines for action."[559] We bishops have articulated seven key themes that form the heart of Catholic social teaching: (1) life and dignity of the human person; (2) call to family, community, and participation; (3) rights and responsibilities; (4) the option for the poor and vulnerable; (5) the dignity of work and the rights of workers; (6) solidarity; and (7) care for God's creation.[560]

D. Social Sin

The Church's emphasis on the social dimension of morality has led to the development of the concept of social sin. The effect of sin over time in society that causes society to create structures of sin is, by analogy, called "social sin." Personal sin expressed in the structures of society—personal

---

558 USCCB, *A Century of Social Teaching: A Common Heritage, a Continuing Challenge* (Washington, D.C.: USCCB, 1991), 3.

559 CCC, no. 2423.

560 Cf. *Sharing Catholic Social Teaching*, 4-6.

sin that has social implications—is social sin. Social sin resembles original sin because it can exist in structures, because we can participate in an evil not of our own creation, and because it is sometimes the inheritance of our families and communities. Sinful structures set up social relationships that in turn cause systematic denial or abuse of the rights of certain groups or individuals. Organized social injustice, institutionalized racism, systemic economic exploitation, and the destruction of the environment are examples of the social consequences of sin.

Social sin can affect large numbers of people, yet it is very difficult to hold individuals accountable for it. Social injustice can be so deeply rooted and ingrained into the life of a society that it almost defies eradication. But individual persons are moral agents—structures or systems are not moral agents. Individuals devise structures and systems; individual people are responsible for the evil consequences of systematic social injustice and should work with others to change those structures and systems that cause evil.

44. MORAL FORMATION IN THE GOSPEL MESSAGE

The Church has the responsibility to form the members of Christ's Body in light of the Gospel message and to teach them how to apply Christian moral principles to contemporary problems in specific and practical ways. The Ten Commandments (or Decalogue) and the Beatitudes are the primary reference points for the application of Christian moral principles. The Decalogue, the expression of God's covenant with his people, is also a privileged expression of the natural law that sums up love of God and neighbor. In the Sermon on the Mount, Jesus took up the Ten Commandments and challenged his disciples to live them in the spirit of the Beatitudes. The Beatitudes proclaim the salvation brought about through the Kingdom of God. In them, Jesus teaches the attributes and virtues that should be cultivated in those who follow him. They sum up the way of Christ, the only way that leads to eternal beatitude, communion with God. Those being catechized not only should know the Ten Commandments and the Beatitudes by heart but should also understand how the spirit of the Beatitudes permeates the Decalogue.

Other sources for the application of Christian moral principles are the spiritual and corporal works of mercy, the theological and moral virtues, the seven capital sins, and traditional moral formulations that express the wisdom of the Church. Catechesis in Christian moral living should also include instruction in the laws of the Church, chief among which are the precepts of the Church. Sacred Scripture and the lives of the saints provide concrete positive examples of Christian moral living.

45. CATECHESIS ON THE DECALOGUE

Catechesis on the Ten Commandments, or Decalogue, is an important part of the catechetical process. In general, catechesis should present the teaching of the *Catechism of the Catholic Church* on the Decalogue in the light of Christ's teaching in the Sermon on the Mount. Specific guidelines for catechesis on the Ten Commandments follow.

A. The First Commandment: I, the Lord, am your God. You shall not have other gods besides me.

Catechesis on the first commandment awakens belief in God, inspires hope in him, and encourages believers to love him above all else. Such catechesis

- Presents compelling evidence from reason and faith for belief in the existence of a transcendent and loving God
- Helps believers to perceive themselves in a loving relationship with God and to express that relationship in adoration, prayer, and worship
- Teaches that no one or no thing occupies God's place in one's life and demonstrates the futility of divinizing what is not God, such as power, pleasure, money, success, and so forth

B. The Second Commandment: You shall not take the name of the Lord, your God, in vain.

Catechesis on the second commandment encourages recognition of a sense of the sacred in life. Such catechesis

- Encourages reverence for the sacred and teaches that respect for God's name characterizes the creature's relationship with the Creator
- Teaches that the holiness of God's name requires that it not be used for trivial purposes
- Teaches that promises, vows, and oaths made in God's name are serious matters[561]
- Enables believers to bear witness to the Lord's name in their confession of the faith
- Promotes respect for the names of God, Jesus Christ, the Holy Spirit, the Blessed Virgin Mary, and all the saints
- Explains that God calls each one by name[562] and that proper address shows reverence for the person

C. The Third Commandment: Remember to keep holy the sabbath day.

Catechesis on the third commandment begins with the conviction that creatures and their Creator are bound together in a loving relationship and that creatures owe their Creator worship and praise. On Sunday, the faithful are also asked "to abstain from those works and affairs which hinder the worship to be rendered to God, the joy proper to the Lord's Day, or the suitable relaxation of mind and body."[563] Catechesis on the third commandment

- Helps believers to recognize the transcendent dimension of life and the presence of God in time
- Teaches that Sunday, the Lord's Day, is the first day of the week and the day on which the Church commemorates the Resurrection of the Lord
- Teaches that Sunday "must be observed in the universal Church as the primordial holy day of obligation"[564] and that "on Sundays and other holy days of obligation, the faithful are obliged to participate in the Mass"[565]

---

561 Cf. CCC, nos. 2147, 2149.
562 Cf. Is 43:1.
563 CIC, c. 1247.
564 CIC, c. 1246 §1; CCEO, c. 880 §3.
565 CIC, c. 1247; CCEO, c. 881 §1.

- Encourages the faithful to set Sunday aside as a day of rest, reflection, and the cultivation of their familial, cultural, social, and religious lives

D. The Fourth Commandment: Honor your father and your mother.

Catechesis on the fourth commandment begins with the understanding that the family is a communion of persons and a sign and image of the communion of the Father and the Son in the Holy Spirit. Such catechesis

- Proceeds with the knowledge that the family is "the sanctuary of life,"[566] "the vital cell of society,"[567] and the church of the home[568]
- Recognizes and promotes in parents an awareness that the witness of Christian life given by parents in the family is particularly formative
- Teaches the responsibilities of parents toward their children and of children toward parents
- Nourishes an attitude of gratitude and respect in parents and their children
- Promotes an awareness of the rights and responsibilities of civil authorities and citizens
- Teaches the right relationship between the Church and the political community

E. The Fifth Commandment: You shall not kill.

Catechesis on the fifth commandment fosters respect for human life and an understanding of the sacredness of human life, recognizes the complexities involved in the moral analysis of life issues, yet provides specific guidelines for that analysis. Such catechesis

---

566 EV, no. 6.
567 AA, no. 11.
568 Cf. LG, no. 11.

- Teaches that the human person has the right to life from the moment of conception and that, according to church teaching, any form of direct abortion is a crime against life[569] and is gravely contrary to the moral law; so serious is this sin that involvement in a deliberate act of abortion can result in automatic excommunication

- Explains that the human embryo is a person at every stage and "must be defended in its integrity, cared for, and healed like every other human being"[570]

- Teaches that the production and cloning of human embryos as disposable biological material, even in the name of scientific advancement, for the purpose of exploitation, experimentation, or research is gravely immoral

- Explains that euthanasia and assisted suicide—no matter what forms they take or for what reasons they are undertaken—are morally wrong because they are gravely contrary to divine law and the dignity of the human person; that suicide is a grave moral evil; and that those who are disabled or sick "deserve special respect" and "should be helped to lead lives as normal as possible"[571]

- Includes instruction on legitimate personal and civil defense, proportionate punishment for crimes, and the fact that non-lethal means for defending society from criminals are to be preferred as being "more in conformity to the dignity of the human person"[572]

- Explains "the evils and injustices that accompany all war,"[573] "the strict conditions for *legitimate defense by military force*,"[574] the immorality of indiscriminate use of weapons, the danger of the excessive accumulation of armaments, and the risk of unregulated production and sale of arms

- Includes instruction on the integrity of the person, the moral evil of creating scandal, the responsibility for one's own health and the health of others, the contributions and dangers of scientific research, and the proper treatment of the dead

---

569   Cf. GS, no. 27.
570   CCC, no. 2323.
571   CCC, no. 2276.
572   EV, no. 56, citing CCC, no. 2276.
573   CCC, no. 2307.
574   CCC, no. 2309.

F. The Sixth Commandment:
You shall not commit adultery.
The Ninth Commandment:
You shall not covet your neighbor's wife.

Catechesis on the sixth and ninth commandments includes instruction on the gift of human sexuality, its inherent goodness, and the proper place of that gift within the context of a faithful, fruitful, and lifelong marriage. Such catechesis

- Explains the difference, complementarity, and essential equality of the sexes
- Explains the virtue of chastity, its meaning, and its various forms
- Teaches the follower of Christ to reject the values and practices of a sexually permissive society
- Teaches the practice of chastity through modest behavior, dress, and speech, resisting lustful desires and temptations, pornography, and indecent entertainment
- Promotes marital fidelity and teaches that sexual intercourse is a moral and human good reserved for married spouses
- Explains that for Christians, premarital sex, extramarital sex, adultery, masturbation, homosexual acts, and other acts of impurity are forbidden
- Invites consideration of a vocation to the priesthood or religious life, in which Christian chastity is lived and witnessed out of love for Christ and for the sake of the kingdom
- Explains that the procreation and education of children is the supreme gift of Christian marriage and that the methods of birth regulation based on self-observation and the use of infertile periods are in conformity with the objective criteria of morality[575]
- Explains that direct sterilization, contraception, and any form of artificial fertilization or human cloning are morally unacceptable
- Includes instruction on the immorality of adultery, polygamy, incest, common-law marriage, premarital cohabitation, rape, and all forms of sexual abuse

---

575   Cf. Paul VI, *On the Regulation of Birth (Humanae Vitae)* (HV) (Washington, D.C.: USCCB, 1968), no. 16.

- Teaches that living a chaste life requires the practice of prayer and purity of intention and self-control
- Includes instruction on the virtue of temperance, modesty, and proper discretion
- Explains that immodest thoughts, words, and actions are morally wrong and can lead to morally permissive behavior
- Recognizes that the family is the most suitable environment for gradual education in human sexuality and the harmonious integration of Christian moral principles
- Recognizes that parents have the basic right, duty, and primary responsibility to provide education in human sexuality for their children and to decide what kind of formal education in human sexuality is best for children, and that they may ask the Church to assist them in providing this education[576]
- Recognizes that the most effective education in human sexuality for children comes from the wholesome example of their parents and other adults
- Recognizes the duty of the pastors and parish catechetical leaders to support and encourage parents as they carry out their role as educators of their children in human sexuality as well as to provide additional instructions regarding Catholic teaching and values that complement and complete the formation provided by parents
- Supports parents in their role as educators in human sexuality and involves them in planning, presenting, and evaluating programs of education in human sexuality
- Helps parents to teach their children that the positive values inherent in human sexuality derive from the dignity of each human person created in God's image and called to communion with him
- Helps parents to ensure that their children's education in human sexuality occurs within the context of the moral principles and values of the Church
- Helps parents to ensure that proactive education formation in chastity and timely information regarding sexuality is provided in the broadest context of education for love

---

576 FC, no. 37.

G. The Seventh Commandment: You shall not steal. The Tenth Commandment: You shall not covet anything that belongs to your neighbor.

Catechesis on the seventh and tenth commandments focuses on social and economic justice, for "social justice is an integral part of evangelization, a constitutive dimension of preaching the gospel, and an essential part of the Church's mission."[577] Such catechesis

- Explains that the fundamental belief on which the social teachings of the Church are based is the inherent dignity of the human person, created in the image and likeness of God, and the call to communion with God
- Teaches that "theft" is taking goods, property, or time against the will of their legitimate owner
- Is derived from the sources of the Church's social doctrine: the Old and New Testaments, the life and ministry of Jesus, and the papal, conciliar, and episcopal teaching developed throughout the history of the Church
- Includes thorough instruction on the social doctrine of the Church, justice and solidarity among nations, the Church's preferential option for the poor and vulnerable, and the dignity of human labor
- Explains the relationship of personal morality to social morality by illustrating in concrete ways how stealing, vandalism, and fraud are violations of the rights of people to their property
- Sets forth the moral principles that Christians have a duty to apply carefully to particular situations
- Explains that the "goods of creation are destined for the entire human race"[578] and encourages respect for the integrity of creation and the obligation of all human persons to protect and preserve the environment for future generations

---

577 USCCB, *Communities of Salt and Light: Reflections on the Social Mission of the Parish* (Washington, D.C.: USCCB, 1994), 3.
578 CCC, no. 2452.

- Fosters the desire for authentic happiness that can be found only in God, when one is poor in spirit and detached from riches
- Helps Christians to overcome the seduction of pleasure, power, and wealth by teaching the virtue of humility and abandonment to the providence of God
- Provides instruction on the meaning of immoderate desires and the particular meanings of greed, envy, and avarice
- Explains that the Church's mission of evangelization proceeds from the Gospel imperative of loving one's neighbor, especially the neighbor who suffers or is in need
- Presents the Church's social teachings completely, faithfully, and enthusiastically, enabling Christians to renew their own experience of Christ and also to evangelize others
- Integrates the Church's social doctrine into her catechetical mission and weaves the substance of the Church's social teaching throughout a person's education and formation in the faith
- Recognizes that the action of human beings brings about the social consequences of sin: social injustice, greed, selfishness, and violence
- Includes instruction on commutative justice, reparation, and restitution of stolen goods
- Calls for a renewal of heart based on the recognition of sin in its individual and social manifestations,[579] helping people to recognize their individual and collective responsibility to work for justice in the world and their dependence on God to achieve that end
- Develops the human capacity to reflect on society and its values and to evaluate the social structures and economic systems that shape human lives
- Promotes action on behalf of justice, emphasizing the corporal works of mercy
- Promotes collaboration among Christians as an important dimension of action on behalf of justice
- Helps Catholics to fulfill their duties as citizens and encourages them to consider positions in public service

---

579   Cf. Synod of Bishops, *Justice in the World* (1971), III, in *Justice in the Marketplace: Collected Statements of the Vatican and the U.S. Catholic Bishops on Economic Policy, 1891-1984* (Washington, D.C.: USCCB, 1985).

- Integrates the principles of Catholic social teaching in a systematic and comprehensive catechetical program, as well as in more occasional and informal settings
- Explains that "the commitment to human life and dignity, to human rights and solidarity, is a calling all Catholic educators must share with their students"[580]
- Passes on the history of the Church's involvement in social justice, offering the example of the lives of the saints and other outstanding Catholics who have embodied the Church's commitment to social justice
- Encourages the practice of works of charity and stewardship on the part of all Catholics, according to their understanding and ability
- Includes activities that bring Catholics into direct contact with the reality of injustice, enabling them to effect change for the common good and to foster respect for human and Christian values in society
- Recognizes that social justice ministry is a valid and necessary service in the Church and encourages Catholics to consider vocations and careers in social justice work

H. The Eighth Commandment: You shall not bear false witness against your neighbor.

Catechesis for the eighth commandment teaches that God is the source of all truth and that the fullness of truth is revealed in the person of Jesus Christ. Such catechesis

- Explains that Christians are to testify to the truth by bearing witness to the Gospel and living in conformity to its obligations
- Recognizes the difficulty in bearing witness to the truth in a society that considers truth to be relative and influenced by the bias of the mass media

---

580 *Sharing Catholic Social Teaching*, 7.

- Teaches respect for the truth, respect for the good name and honor of others, and the immorality of rash judgment, calumny, detraction, and any other action that causes unjust injury to the reputation of another
- Explains that "lying" is saying what is false in order to deceive another and that the "gravity of a lie is measured against the nature of the truth which it deforms, the circumstances, the intentions of the one who lies, and the harm suffered by its victims"[581]
- Teaches that one must repair the damage one has caused by lies
- Teaches that the right to the truth has certain limits and also that society has a right to expect the truth from the public means of mass communication

I. The Decalogue in the Spirit of the Beatitudes

The Ten Commandments and the Beatitudes describe the paths that lead to the Kingdom of God. Just as the Ten Commandments were at the heart of the Mosaic Law, the Beatitudes are at the heart of Jesus' preaching. They fulfill the promises God made to the chosen people and teach the people of the new covenant the final end to which God calls us, the Kingdom of Heaven. They reflect the desire for happiness that is written upon the human heart and reveal the goal of human existence, eternal happiness in communion with God.

> The Beatitudes depict the countenance of Jesus Christ and portray his charity. They express the vocation of the faithful associated with the glory of his Passion and Resurrection; they shed light on the actions and attitudes characteristic of the Christian life; they are the paradoxical promises that sustain hope in the midst of tribulations; they proclaim the blessings and rewards already secured, however dimly, for Christ's disciples; they have begun in the lives of the Virgin Mary and all the saints.[582]

---

581   CCC, no. 2484.
582   CCC, no. 1717.

The Beatitudes are as follows:

Blessed are the poor in spirit,
for theirs is the kingdom of heaven.
Blessed are those who mourn,
for they shall be comforted.
Blessed are the meek,
for they will inherit the land.
Blessed are they who hunger and thirst for righteousness,
for they will be satisfied.
Blessed are the merciful,
for they will be shown mercy.
Blessed are the clean of heart,
for they will see God.
Blessed are the peacemakers,
for they will be called children of God.
Blessed are they who are persecuted for the sake of righteousness,
for theirs is the kingdom of heaven.[583]

Catechesis on the Beatitudes

- Explains that "all people seek happiness: life, peace, joy, wholeness . . . of being"[584]
- Teaches that the happiness which all people seek and for which they were created is given in Jesus
- Gives hope in time of difficulty
- Describes the vocation of all the faithful, shedding light on the actions and attitudes characteristic of the Christian life
- Challenges the Christian with decisive moral choices
- Encourages the Christian to strive for perfection and work for the coming of the Kingdom

46. CONCLUSION

Life in Christ is a way of being, a way of loving. It is not a plan of action, even action on behalf of justice. Life in Christ shapes human beings anew

---

583 Mt 5:3-10.
584 *National Catechetical Directory*, no. 100.

and provides a new vital principle for all their activity. It is the radical integration of the person with Christ, the indwelling of Christ in the heart and soul of the Christian, a fusion of the Christian with the Son of God. "Christ lives in me" is the singular confession of the Christian who has been led by God's grace and who trusts, at the deepest level of being, that true life comes only through the redemptive sacrifice of Jesus Christ.

Catechesis for life in Christ stirs the heart, enlightens the mind, and inspires the soul. It aims to enable Christians to love God with their hearts, all their souls, all their minds, and all their strength. It seeks to help people form correct consciences, choose what is morally good, avoid sin and its occasions, and live in this world according to the prompting of the Holy Spirit. It teaches people their obligations in love toward God, others, and themselves. It summons them to recognize their inherent dignity and to act in accord with the divine life in which they share. Catechesis for life in Christ offers them the way of Christ, the way that leads away from death and toward life.

Now that the content that makes up the catechetical message has been presented, we turn our attention to those who are waiting to hear this good news. The next chapter will provide guidance for how to catechize the People of God.

CHAPTER 7

Catechizing the People of God in Diverse Settings

On another occasion he began to teach by the sea.
A very large crowd gathered around him so that he
got into a boat on the sea and sat down. And the
whole crowd was beside the sea on land. And he
taught them at length in parables. (Mk 4:1-2)

47. INTRODUCTION

Teaching was central to the ministry of Jesus. He was sent by the Father to proclaim the coming of the Kingdom of God and to draw humanity into communion with the life of the Holy Trinity. The Father identified himself with Jesus, favored him, and commended his teaching to those to whom he was sent. "This is my beloved Son, with whom I am well pleased; listen to him."[585] Jesus was anointed by the Spirit "to bring glad tidings to the poor . . . / to proclaim liberty to captives / and recovery of sight to the blind, / to let the oppressed go free, / and to proclaim a year acceptable to the Lord."[586] He taught with authority; and people from every walk of life and from every age and circumstance followed him into synagogues, up hillsides, through towns and villages, and to the seashore. He taught them in places familiar

585   Mt 17:5.
586   Lk 4:18-19.

to them, and he taught them according to their capacity to understand his message. He taught them that the Kingdom he came to announce was intended for all, especially the poor and vulnerable. And he commissioned his disciples to continue his teaching ministry "for all time."[587]

For two thousand years the Church has taken up Christ's command to go, make disciples, and teach.[588] The Church must proclaim the Gospel message or she would not be faithful to Christ's command. Conversely the people of God need his Word made flesh and the words of his teaching if they are to be saved by the sacrifice of Christ, sanctified by the Holy Spirit, and brought into communion with the Father. All the faithful have a right to receive Christ's authentic teaching. Hearing Christ's proclamation of the Good News that the Kingdom of God is at hand is essential to their salvation. Because the word of God is a saving word, the faithful, who are called to salvation in Christ, must have access to it and to him. "All the baptized, because they are called by God to maturity of faith, need and have therefore a right to adequate catechesis."[589]

The Church, the Body of Christ, is both the principal agent of catechesis and the primary recipient of catechesis. In fact, the life of the Church is a kind of catechesis itself. Every individual has the responsibilities to grow in faith and to contribute to the growth in faith of the other members of the Church.

Just as Christ instructed his followers according to their capacity to understand his message, the Church also must take serious account of the circumstances and cultures in which the faithful live in order to present the meaning of the Gospel to them in understandable ways. There is one saving word—Jesus Christ—but that word can be spoken in many different ways. The "adaptation and preaching of the revealed Word must ever be the law of all evangelization."[590]

This chapter describes those conditions involved in the catechetical process and gives principles, guidelines, and criteria for presenting the Gospel to different groups in their diverse settings.

---

587   Cf. Acts 1:8.
588   Mt 28:19.
589   GDC, no. 167.
590   GS, no. 44.

48. CATECHESIS ACCORDING TO READINESS AND AGE LEVELS

Growth in faith is related to human development and passes through stages. Individuals develop as human beings and faithful followers of Christ in different ways and according to their own pace. No matter what style or rate of growth in faith, such growth always means gradually becoming more like Christ. It means growing into communion with the Father and the Son in the Holy Spirit through active participation in the sacraments, the prayer life of the Church, and generous service to others. The Church's catechesis—and even more so, the catechist—must take into consideration all the human factors of a particular age level in order to present the Gospel message in a vital and compelling way. From infancy through maturity, "catechesis is thus a permanent school of the faith and follows the major stages of life."[591]

A. Adult Catechesis

Most adults are capable of a free and informed response of faith to God's initiative of love. They "have a right and a duty to bring to maturity the seed of faith sown in them by God."[592] They have experienced the joys and challenges of life and have the capacity to question the truth and meaning of life. "The catechesis of adults . . . is the principal form of catechesis, because it is addressed to persons who have the greatest responsibilities and the capacity to live the Christian message in its fully developed form."[593] The catechetical formation of adults is essential for the Church to carry out the commission given the apostles by Christ. "Because of its importance and because all other forms of catechesis are oriented in some way to it, the catechesis of adults must have high priority at all levels of the Church."[594]

This formation needs to be addressed to adults at different stages in the development of their faith. Many Catholic adults practice their faith and desire to deepen it. They "require to be constantly nourished by the word of God so that they may grow in their Christian life."[595] Others who

---

591 CT, no. 39.
592 GDC, no. 173.
593 CT, no. 43.
594 *National Catechetical Directory*, no. 188.
595 GDC, no. 50.

have been baptized but who have not received a comprehensive catechesis or who no longer practice their faith need to be renewed through an enthusiastic preaching of the word and a vibrant re-evangelization. Still others, who are not baptized, may desire to be incorporated into the catechumenate, wherein they can gradually proceed through the stages of Christian initiation and be incorporated into the life of the Church.

Adult catechesis should be the "*organizing principle*, which gives coherence to the various catechetical programs offered by a particular Church. . . . This is the axis around which revolves the catechesis of childhood and adolescence as well as that of old age."[596]

Adult catechesis promotes mature adult faith: the faith of the disciple who has been saved by Christ's redemptive love and who is being continually converted to him. Adult catechesis fosters this discipleship by providing "a comprehensive and systematic presentation and exploration of the core elements of Catholic faith and practice—a complete initiation into a Catholic way of life."[597]

1. The Goals of Adult Catechesis

Adult catechesis has three major goals.[598]

1. It invites and enables adults "to acquire an attitude of *conversion to the Lord*."[599] This attitude views the Christian life as a gradual transformation in Christ, in which the Christian takes on the mind of Christ, trusts in the Father's love, accepts the Spirit's guidance in searching out and obeying God's will, and seeks holiness of life within the Church. It fosters a baptismal spirituality in which the Christian's faith in Jesus is continuously deepened through participation in the sacraments, the works of charity and justice, and the prayer life of the Church.

2. Catechesis for adults helps them to make "a conscious and firm decision to live the gift and choice of faith through *membership in the Christian community*."[600] It fosters active participation in the

---

596   GDC, no. 275.

597   OHWB, no. 65.

598   Cf. OHWB, nos. 67-73.

599   International Council for Catechesis, *Adult Catechesis in the Christian Community: Some Principles and Guidelines* (Washington, D.C.: USCCB, 1992), no. 36.

600   *Adult Catechesis in the Christian Community*, no. 37.

Church as she is realized in families, small faith-based communities, parishes, dioceses, and the communion of saints. It helps adults to develop a deeper sense of their cooperation with the Holy Spirit for the mission of the Church in the world and for her internal life as well.

3. Catechesis for adults helps them to become "more willing and able to be a *Christian disciple in the world*."[601] It enables adult disciples to accept their rightful place in the Church's mission to evangelize, to hear the cry for justice, to promote unity among Christians, and to bear witness to the salvation won by Jesus Christ for all.

2. The Tasks of Adult Catechesis

The general task of adult catechesis is to "propose the Christian faith in its entirety and in its authenticity, in accordance with the Church's understanding. It must give priority to the proclamation of salvation, drawing attention to the many challenges to living a Christian life posed by American society and culture. It must introduce adults to a faith-filled reading of Sacred Scripture and the practice of prayer."[602] In particular, the major tasks of adult catechesis are as follows:

- To promote formation and development of life in the Risen Christ through the sacraments, prayer life of the Church, works of charity and justice, retreats, and spiritual direction
- To promote evangelization as the means of bringing the Good News to all states of humanity[603]
- To educate toward the development of an informed moral conscience
- To clarify religious and moral questions
- To clarify the relationship between the Church and the world, especially in light of the Church's social doctrine
- To develop the rational foundations of the faith and demonstrate the compatibility of faith and reason

---

601   *Adult Catechesis in the Christian Community*, no. 38.
602   GDC, no. 175.
603   Cf. EN, no. 18.

- *"To encourage adults to assume [their baptismal] responsibility for the Church's mission and to be able to give Christian witness in society"*[604]
- To develop creative ways to interest and encourage adults to take advantage of the various programs of enrichment and spiritual development being offered

3. The Content of Catechesis

Since adults are called to be disciples of Christ, the content of adult catechesis should be a catechesis directed toward discipleship. The content of such catechesis is *"cognitive, experiential, [and] behavioral."*[605] The richness of the content is developed by "word, memorial and witness—doctrine, celebration and commitment in living."[606] The content of adult catechesis should be as comprehensive and diverse as the Church's mission. It should help adults to better understand the faith of the Church as well as its practical application in Christian living.

Sacred Scripture and Tradition form the basic content for adult catechesis because they constitute "the supreme rule of . . . faith."[607] "And such is the force and power of the Word of God that it can serve the Church as her support and vigor,"[608] imparting robustness to the faith of its daughters and sons. The *Catechism of the Catholic Church* is the normative reference text for the catechesis of adults. It presents the Catholic faith as a symphony in which several distinct strains blend into a rich harmony.

Adult catechesis aims to foster the development of all the distinct yet complementary aspects of the Catholic faith, for each one is a dimension of Christian discipleship. "The maturation of the Christian life requires that it be cultivated in all its dimensions: knowledge of the faith, liturgical life, moral formation, prayer, belonging to community, missionary spirit. When catechesis omits one of these elements, the Christian faith does not attain full development."[609]

A fuller treatment of the content of adult catechesis is contained in our 1999 statement *Our Hearts Were Burning Within Us*. In brief, adult catechesis should include

---

604   GDC, no. 175.
605   GDC, no. 35.
606   CT, no. 47.
607   DV, no. 21.
608   DV, no. 21.
609   GDC, no. 87.

- Study of Sacred Scripture and Tradition, the Creeds and doctrines of the faith, the hierarchy of truths, and the history of the Church
- Study of the Mass, the sacraments, and the daily prayer life of the Church
- A focus on the universal call to holiness, including a study of the Ten Commandments, the Beatitudes, and Jesus' commandment to love one another as he has loved us
- The Church's teaching on the dignity of the human person, sin, grace, the virtues, and conscience formation
- The Church's social teachings and the implications for social sin
- Prayer and the various traditions of spirituality within Catholicism
- The Church, her structure and authority, and the rights and responsibilities of the baptized
- Marriage and family life; single life
- The ecumenical movement and interreligious dialogue
- The Church's mission in the world and for the world, and the nature of the lay apostolate

4. Catechetical Methodology for Adults

Whatever method is chosen for adult catechesis, it is always a basic organic formation in the faith that includes a serious study of Christian doctrine integrated with formation in Christian living. Effective adult catechesis relates the content of the faith to life experience. It enables the Christian to read the signs of the times in light of the Gospel.

Several principles should guide the selection of effective methods for adult catechesis:

- Since adults "have a right and a duty to bring to maturity the seed of faith sown in them by God,"[610] they should identify their catechetical needs and, with the help of those responsible for religious education, plan ways to meet those needs.
- Those responsible for adult catechesis should identify the principal characteristics of adult Catholics, develop catechetical objectives based on those characteristics, and design a catechetical plan to meet those objectives.

610 GDC, no. 173.

- Those responsible for adult catechesis should determine the most effective methods and choose formats and models that represent a "variety of forms: systematic and occasional, individual and community, organized and spontaneous."[611]
- Those responsible for catechesis should identify the members of the community who can serve as catechists for adults and should provide for their training, formation, and spiritual enrichment.
- Adult catechesis should respect the experiences of adults and make use of their personal experiences, skills, and talents.
- Adult catechesis should be based on the circumstances of those to whom it is addressed: their situations as adults; their racial, cultural, religious, social, and economic conditions; their experiences and problems; and their educational and spiritual maturity.
- Adult catechesis should recognize the specific conditions of lay Catholics and consistently call them to holiness and to "seek[ing] the Kingdom of God by engaging in temporal affairs and ordering them according to the plan of God."[612]
- Adult catechesis should involve the whole community so that it may be a welcoming and supportive environment.
- Adult catechesis requires a comprehensive, multifaceted, and coordinated approach and a variety of learning activities, such as participation in liturgical experiences, Scripture reading and study, retreats and experiences of prayer, family or home-centered activities, ecumenical dialogue, small-group experiences, large-group experiences, and individual activities.[613]
- As much as possible, adult catechesis should involve adults themselves in the catechetical process so that they can teach and learn from one another.

Many forms of special catechesis complement the "ongoing, systematic, catechetical courses which every ecclesial community must provide for all adults."[614] Among these special forms are the following:

---

611   *General Catechetical Directory*, no. 19.
612   CL, no. 9.
613   Cf. OHWB, nos. 100-112.
614   GDC, no. 176.

- Catechesis for Christian initiation as set forth in the *Rite of Christian Initiation of Adults*
- Catechesis for parents
- Catechesis adapted to the liturgical year
- Catechesis that is more missionary by intention
- Catechetical formation of catechists and those involved in the lay apostolate in the world
- Catechetical formation of Catholic school teachers
- Catechesis for special moments and experiences (e.g., reception of the sacraments, critical times in life, sickness, beginning a new job, military service, emigration, death and bereavement)
- Catechesis for the use of leisure time, holidays, travel, and pilgrimage
- Catechesis for special events in the life of the Church and society[615]

B. Catechesis of the Elderly

By 2030, about seventy million Americans, or 20 percent of the population, will be more than seventy-five years of age. The growing number of elderly people in the United States represents a new pastoral challenge to the Church. They are "a gift of God to the Church and to society."[616] The practical experience, wisdom, attitude, and example of many older people make them especially valued gifts to the life of the Church. Since Christ calls everyone to proclaim the Gospel, he calls the elderly as well, which enhances the richness of intergenerational catechesis. "The Church still needs you," Pope John Paul II has said; "the service of the Gospel has nothing to do with age!"[617] Nevertheless, the Church owes the elderly "adequate catechetical care. In catechesis, they have the same rights and duties as all Christians."[618]

The catechesis of older people takes into account the diversity of their personal, family, and social conditions. It notes the significant contributions that they make to the entire community through their wisdom and witness. It pays particular attention to the maturity of their faith.

---

615   Cf. OHWB, no. 176.
616   GDC, no. 186.
617   John Paul II, *Letter to the Elderly* (Washington, D.C.: USCCB, 1999), nos. 13, 7.
618   GDC, no. 186.

Many of the elderly come to old age with a strong and vibrant faith. Catechesis for them should help develop an attitude of thanksgiving and hopeful expectation. Others have not practiced their faith as well as they might have; therefore, catechesis for them becomes a new opportunity to see the light of the Gospel and rediscover the experience of God in their lives. Still others come to old age severely "wounded in body and soul."[619] Catechesis for them fosters an attitude of "prayer, forgiveness and inner peace."[620] In all situations, catechesis for the elderly should encourage the theological virtue of Christian hope by which all Christians confidently await eternal life and the grace to merit it. The catechesis of the elderly is a catechesis of hope.

The most effective catechesis for older persons occurs within the context of a comprehensive program of pastoral care specifically developed for and with them. Such programs should be built on several fundamental principles:

- Older people are providers, not simply recipients, of pastoral care.
- Older people themselves should help to identify their pastoral needs and decide how they are met.
- Older people are as diverse as other generational groups, if not more so.
- Older people need a mix of activities that connect them with each other as well as the larger faith community.
- Spiritual health affects and is affected by the individual's physical, emotional, mental, and social health. While the faith community is especially concerned about meeting spiritual needs, it cannot ignore these other realities.[621]

The elderly should participate fully in the catechetical life of the Christian community. "Older persons have a responsibility, commensurate with health, abilities, and other obligations, to undertake some form of service to others."[622] Elderly people themselves can provide some of the

---

619   GDC, no. 187.
620   GDC, no. 187.
621   USCCB, *Blessings of Age: A Pastoral Message on Growing Older Within the Faith Community* (Washington, D.C.: USCCB, 1999), 22-24.
622   *Blessings of Age*, 13.

most effective catechesis for the aged. They should be offered equivalent opportunities for formation that are provided all catechists. Such programs give them the chance to discover the storehouse of wisdom within themselves and, like the head of the household in Matthew's Gospel, to bring forth from that storehouse "both the new and the old."[623] In light of the courageous and faithful witness they have born to the Gospel over many years, the elderly are natural catechists, especially for their own grandchildren. Their unique catechesis has the invaluable element of intergenerational dialogue that adds a significant dimension to the proclamation of the Gospel within the family and within the community of faith.

C. Catechesis of Young Adults

Some special consideration should be given to the catechesis of young adults. Young adults are persons in their late teens, twenties, and thirties who represent diverse cultural, racial, ethnic, educational, vocational, social, political, and spiritual backgrounds. They are college and university students, workers, and professionals; they are persons in military service; they are single, married, divorced, or widowed; they are with or without children; they are newcomers in search of a better life. Young adults have many gifts to offer the Church: their faith, their hope, their desire to serve, their spiritual hunger, their vitality, their optimism and idealism, their talents and skills. The world also looks with hope to young adults to bring about a better future. Many young adults have vast reservoirs of goodness, generosity, and enthusiasm. They earnestly search for meaning in their lives; they value solidarity with the rest of humanity and seek to commit themselves to the cause of social justice. On the other hand, many young adults have been captivated by the consumerism and materialism of the society in which they grew up and have become apathetic and cynical. Young adulthood is sometimes a world of boredom, disillusionment, and indifference to the Church. Young adults are often "the first victims of the spiritual and cultural crisis gripping the world."[624] Nevertheless, Pope John Paul II confidently exhorted the young people of the world, "Do not be afraid to go out on the street and into public places like the first apostles, who preached Christ and the good news of salvation in the squares of the

---

623   Mt 13:52.
624   GDC, no. 181.

cities, towns and villages. This is no time to be ashamed of the Gospel. It is the time to preach it from the rooftops."[625]

The inspiration for catechesis for young adults is Christ's proposal to the young man: "Come, follow me."[626] Many young adults welcome Christ's invitation. They are looking for opportunities to grow in the knowledge of their faith and in their ability to make good moral decisions. They need a non-threatening place where they can freely express their questions, doubts, and even disagreements with the Church and where the teachings of the Church can be clearly articulated and related to their experience. A series of evening or weekend sessions, special one-time presentations, days of recollection, retreats, discussion groups, Scripture study groups, mentoring relationships, hands-on social justice programs, and mission education projects can all be attractive means for involving busy young adults. But dioceses and parishes are challenged to develop new and creative ways to provide significant points of contact for young adults with the Church.

Ordinarily, in the period of early adulthood, young adults make some of the most important decisions in their lives about their Christian vocation, their career, and their choice of spouse. These choices condition and often even determine their futures. Effective catechesis will assist young adults in examining their lives and engaging in dialogue about the great questions they face. Catechesis with young adults helps them to make these crucial decisions in accord with God's will and their Catholic faith.

Catechesis with young adults should form them in Christ, helping them to make moral decisions in light of the teachings of Christ and the Church. "Good and evil, grace and sin, life and death will more and more confront one another within them, not just as moral categories but chiefly as fundamental options which they must accept or reject lucidly, conscious of their own responsibility."[627]

Catechesis with young adults draws them into the liturgical life and mission of the Church. It invites them to commit themselves to Christ, live fully Christian lives, and carefully consider their vocational call, whether it be to the priesthood, diaconate, religious life, married life, or chaste single life. This can also be an opportunity to consider a future of lay ecclesial ministry in the Church. Young adults should also be given the opportunity

---

625   Pope John Paul II, Homily at World Youth Day Vigil, August 14, 1993.

626   Mt 19:21.

627   CT, no. 39.

to receive formation and training to serve as liturgical ministers. The Rite of Christian Initiation of Adults is an especially fruitful experience for young adults. It provides the opportunity for some young people to enter into the Catholic faith and for others to be sponsors or catechists. It is especially important that parishes and campus ministry programs offer sacramental preparation to young adults who have been baptized but have not made their First Penance, received their First Communion, or received the Sacrament of Confirmation. Outside of Sunday Mass, marriage preparation often is the most significant point of contact for young adults and the Church. It is a crucial moment for their evangelization and can be a "journey of faith, which is similar to the catechumenate."[628] Marriage preparation is a significant opportunity to learn more about the Church, especially the teachings of the Church on marriage and family life. For some, marriage preparation marks their first experience of church life in many years. "Regardless of why they come, the Church and its ministers need to welcome them as Christ welcomes them, with understanding, love, and acceptance, challenging them with the gospel message, and giving them hope that a lifelong commitment is possible."[629]

Preparation for the Baptism of their children is also an important opportunity to evangelize young adults and draw them closer to Christ and the Church. Effective baptismal preparation programs offer parents a chance to continue their formation in the Catholic faith and ordinarily include a more developed catechesis on the Sacrament of Baptism and on the Church's teachings on marriage and family life.

The distance some young adults feel from the Church can often be bridged by an adaptation of and approach to the language (mentality, sensibility, tastes, style, and vocabulary) employed in catechesis for them.[630] Retreat experiences are often very effective ways to bring young adults to Christ and the Church. If young adults have been away from the Church, the Gospel message should be specifically addressed to them in imaginative ways that encourage their return. Parish and diocesan programs of evangelization and outreach should actively seek out young adults, enthusiastically welcome them, and facilitate their homecoming. In addition, young adults

---

628 FC, no. 66.
629 USCCB, *Sons and Daughters of the Light: A Pastoral Plan for Ministry with Young Adults* (Washington, D.C.: USCCB, 1997), 30.
630 Cf. GDC, no. 185.

should be encouraged to articulate any questions, difficulties, or concerns that they have that may contribute to their distance from the Church.

The most effective catechesis for young adults is integrated into a comprehensive program of pastoral care that understands the concerns of young adults and candidly addresses the questions they ask and the problems they face. The goals of such a comprehensive program of young adult ministry are as follows:

- To connect young adults with Jesus Christ through spiritual formation/direction, religious education/formation, and vocation discernment
- To connect young adults with the Church through evangelizing outreach, formation of the faith community, and pastoral care
- To connect young adults with the mission of the Church in the world through forming a Christian conscience, educating and working for justice, and developing leaders for the present and the future
- To connect young adults with a peer community through developing peer leadership and identifying a young adult team for the purpose of forming faith communities of peers[631]

In catechesis with young adults, several important themes need to be emphasized: the formation of conscience, education for love, vocational discernment, Christian involvement in society, missionary responsibility in the world, the relationship between faith and reason, the existence and meaning of God, the problem of evil, the Church, the objective moral order in relation to personal subjectivity, the relationship between man and woman, and the social doctrine of the Church.[632]

It is important that the Church find attractive ways to let young adults know that Christ loves them and needs them and that they are vital members of the body of Christ, the Church. Young adults are the hope of the Church.[633] In a letter to the youth of the world, Pope John Paul II said, "The Church looks to the youth, indeed the Church in a special way looks

631   Cf. *Sons and Daughters of the Light*, 28-41.
632   Cf. GDC, no. 185.
633   Cf. CL, no. 46.

at herself in the youth, in all of you and in each of you. It has been so from the beginning, from apostolic times."[634]

D. Catechesis of Adolescents

Significant physical and emotional changes characterize the period of pre-adolescence and adolescence. While home and family remain the more powerful forces in the development of pre-adolescents and adolescents, their peer groups begin to exercise increasing influence on attitudes, values, and behavior. They learn to live the Christian faith by observing the good example of others whom they admire and trust.

Catechesis for pre-adolescents and adolescents should take into account their physical, social, and psychological conditions. Since adolescence is the age of hero worship, it is helpful to present the words and example of Jesus as well as the lives and deeds of the saints in ways that appeal to young people. Such catechesis should present Christ as the Son of God, friend, guide, and model who can be not only admired but also imitated. It should also present the basic content of his Revelation.

Since their minds are increasing in capability, catechesis for adolescents should make clear the rational bases for faith, the inner coherence of the truths of the faith, and their relation to one another. It should also help adolescents to articulate the beliefs and teachings of the Church and to apply them to their lives. The study of Sacred Scripture, the Church, the sacraments, and the principles of Christian morality—both personal and social—should characterize the catechesis of adolescents. Since they are better able to experience faith as a deeper relationship with God than are younger children, prayer and service to others in the name of Christ become more meaningful to them. This is an opportune developmental time to stress their baptismal commitment to evangelization. Because the example of adults is so important to them, their participation in the Mass, the sacraments, and other rituals alongside adults incorporates them further into the life of the Church. They may be invited to take a more active part in planning and celebrating liturgical experiences, especially the Eucharist. They should be given frequent and regular opportunities to receive the Sacrament of Penance and Reconciliation. Catechesis for

---

634   John Paul II, *Apostolic Letter to Youth* (*Dilecti Amici*) (Vatican City, 1985), no. 15, http://www.vatican.va /holy_father/john_paul_ii/apost_letters/documents/hf_jp-ii_apl_31031985_dilecti-amici_en.html (accessed on August 29, 2003).

Christian initiation, catechesis on special themes, group activity, membership in youth associations, the personal accompaniment of young people, retreats, and spiritual direction are useful approaches for the effective catechesis of adolescents. Adolescence is a time to learn how to pray vocal and liturgical prayers, to read and meditate upon the Sacred Scripture texts, and to evangelize their peers and invite them into the Catholic Church. Adolescence is also a time for developing ecumenical relationships, since it is an age when friendships are especially important and inquiry into the faith and traditions of others is lively.

A special concern in the catechesis of adolescents is catechesis for the Sacrament of Confirmation. In many dioceses in the United States, adolescence is the period in which the Sacrament of Confirmation is received and the process of Christian initiation is completed. The Church must make every effort through a revised and revitalized catechesis to ensure that adolescents do not view their preparation for and reception of the Sacrament of Confirmation as the end of their formal catechesis. They must be encouraged to continue to participate in catechetical programs, the celebration of Sunday Eucharist, and the practice of Christian living. As fully initiated Christians, they must be given the opportunity to serve the community in a variety of liturgical ministries.

A special challenge in the catechesis of adolescents is catechesis for Christian vocations. The catechesis of young people "prepares [them] for the important Christian commitments of adult life."[635] The foundation for accepting the call of Christ to marriage, chaste single life, priesthood, consecrated life, or lay ecclesial ministry is laid within the family and nurtured throughout childhood. Careful and serious consideration of these Christian vocations becomes even more important in adolescence. Parents, pastors, teachers, and catechists should help adolescents to address the vocational question directly and study the possibilities thoroughly. They should provide the best examples of each of the distinctively Christian vocations to young people and be willing to become personally involved with them as they struggle with their choice. They should encourage adolescents to listen carefully to the voice of the Holy Spirit within them and to respond generously to God's call to service in the Church and in the world.

---

635   CT, no. 39.

The most effective catechetical programs for adolescents are integrated into a comprehensive program of pastoral ministry for youth that includes catechesis, community life, evangelization, justice and service, leadership development, pastoral care, and prayer and worship.[636] Such programs aim to empower young people to live as disciples of Jesus Christ in our world today; to draw young people to responsible participation in the life, mission, and work of the Catholic faith community; and to foster the total personal and spiritual growth of each young person.[637]

The ministry of catechesis with adolescents has several distinct features that give direction to catechetical programming. Specifically, catechesis with adolescents

- Teaches the core content of the Catholic faith as presented in the *Catechism of the Catholic Church*—the profession of faith, celebration of the Christian mystery, life in Christ, and Christian prayer—in order to provide a solid foundation for continued growth in faith
- Recognizes that faith development is lifelong and therefore provides developmentally appropriate content and processes around key themes of Catholic faith that respond to the age-appropriate needs, interests, and concerns of younger and older adolescents
- Integrates knowledge of the Catholic faith with liturgical and prayer experiences and the development of practical skills for living the Catholic faith in today's world
- Utilizes the life experiences of adolescents, fostering a shared dialogue between the life of the adolescent—with his or her joys, struggles, questions, concerns, and hopes—and the wisdom of the Catholic Church
- Engages adolescents in the learning process by incorporating a variety of learning methods and activities through which adolescents can explore and learn important religious concepts of the Scriptures and Catholic faith—a variety of learning approaches, including music and media, keeps interest alive among adolescents and responds to their different learning styles

636   Cf. *Renewing the Vision*, 26.
637   Cf. *Renewing the Vision*, 9-17.

- Involves group participation in an environment that is characterized by warmth, trust, acceptance, and care, so that young people can hear and respond to God's call (fostering the freedom to search and question, to express one's own point of view, and to respond in faith to that call)
- Provides for real-life application of learning by helping adolescents to apply their learning to living more faithfully as Catholic adolescents—considering the next steps that they will take and the obstacles that they will face
- Promotes family faith development through parish and school programs by providing parent education programs and resources, incorporating a family perspective in catechetical programming, and providing parent-adolescent and intergenerational catechetical programming
- Promotes Christian attitudes toward human sexuality
- Recognizes and celebrates multicultural diversity within the Church's unity by including stories, songs, dances, feasts, values, rituals, saints, and heroes from the rich heritage of various cultures
- Incorporates a variety of program approaches, including parish and school programs; small-group programs; home-based programs, activities, and resources; one-on-one and mentoring programs; and independent or self-directed programs or activities
- Explicitly invites young people to explore the possibility of a personal call to ministry and the beauty of the total gift of self for the sake of the kingdom[638] based on a prayerful reflection within the celebration of sacraments (e.g., Holy Eucharist, Penance and Reconciliation)

E. Catechesis of Infants and Children

1. Catechesis Within the Family

While the catechesis offered within the family is ordinarily informal, unstructured, and spontaneous, it is no less crucial for the development

---

638   Cf. *Renewing the Vision*, 29-30.

of the child's faith. "In a certain sense nothing replaces family catechesis, especially for its positive and receptive environment, for the example of adults, and for its first explicit experience and practice of the faith."[639] The catechesis of infants and young children nourishes the beginnings of the life of faith.

"God's love is communicated to infants and young children primarily through parents."[640] Parents have shared the gift of human life with their children and, through Baptism, have enriched them with a share in God's own life. They have the duty to nourish it. Their faith, their attitude toward other human beings, and their trust in a loving God strongly influence the development of the child's faith. Parents are catechists precisely because they are parents. Their role in the formation of Christian values in their children is irreplaceable. They "should speak naturally and simply about God and their faith, as they do about other matters they want their children to understand and appreciate."[641]

Parents are also the most effective catechists of prayer for their young children. They know what their children are capable of understanding and can easily teach their children basic prayers and the fundamental attitude of prayer. By praying frequently with their children at special moments during the day and especially by praying with them at the Sunday Eucharist, parents introduce children into the prayer life of the Church. By incorporating prayer into everyday family experiences, parents teach their children by example. Their witness encourages their children to call upon God as their Father who loves and protects them; to look to Jesus, their Savior and brother, who leads them to the Father; and to acknowledge the presence of the Holy Spirit, who dwells within their hearts.

Children ordinarily enjoy listening to their parents read to them and tell them stories. Reading stories from Sacred Scripture combines both these simple activities. Just as children learn their family histories through stories told by their parents, they learn about the Catholic faith as their parents introduce them to the person of Jesus and the beauty of the word of God and tell them the story of Mary, the Mother of God, as well as of the lives of the saints.

---

639 GDC, no. 178.
640 *National Catechetical Directory*, no. 177.
641 *National Catechetical Directory*, no. 177.

2. Structured Catechesis

Catechetical programs for children in daycare and preschool seek to foster their growth in a wider faith community. They should always be suited to the age, circumstances, and learning capacity of young children and be designed to reinforce the primary human and Christian values present in the family. They should provide opportunities to participate in simple celebrations that deepen the child's sense of wonder. These opportunities provide a natural human foundation for the supernatural life of faith where children can develop a sense of trust, freedom, selflessness, and joyful participation. Catechetical programs can be employed to predispose young children to experiences of spontaneous and formal prayer, prayerful silence, and simple acts of worship. Children can learn to pray with and for fellow Christians and their churches. Ordinarily, parents and other adults who have received appropriate training in Sacred Scripture, theology, early childhood development, and catechetical methodology should, under the direction of the pastor, organize and present catechetical programs for young children. Catechesis that involves the whole family is a particularly effective method of catechesis for young children because it helps parents to become more confident in sharing their faith with their children and encouraging their children's emerging faith.

When children begin school, they enter a world wider than the family. The school environment provides greater opportunities for children's intellectual, affective, and behavioral development. This means that parents, pastors, catechists, and teachers need to cooperate closely to ensure that the catechesis offered children is truly an ecclesial catechesis that is consistent with Christian values lived in the family. Pastors have a serious obligation to assist parents and educators in their mission to hand on the faith to future generations. "This is an excellent occasion for adult catechesis."[642]

School-age children should receive formal and systematic catechesis in a parish-based catechetical program, a Catholic school, or a program of home-based catechesis in which the content of the faith and the experience of Christian life is presented authentically and completely. Catechesis for school-age children "is an initial catechesis but not a fragmentary one, since it will have to reveal, although in an elementary way, all the

---

642   GDC, no. 179.

principal mysteries of faith and their effects on the child's moral and religious life."[643] Having introduced them to the person of Jesus Christ within the family, catechesis for school-age children presents his teachings, his ministry, and the major events of his life. Children can begin to appreciate the parables of Jesus and capture glimpses of the Kingdom of God; they can learn more formal prayers; and they can commit brief passages of Sacred Scripture to memory. Sacramental catechesis for school-age children "gives meaning to the sacraments . . . and it communicates to the child the joy of being a witness to Christ in ordinary life."[644] Specifically, catechesis for the Sacraments of Penance and Reconciliation and of the Eucharist is ordinarily provided in these early years of schooling.

For a variety of reasons, some children are prevented from receiving catechesis at home, in a Catholic school, or in a parish-sponsored catechetical program. They do not receive adequate support within their families for the development of their faith. Some children are not even baptized; many more have not completed their sacramental initiation into the life of the Church. In such cases, "it is the responsibility of the Christian community to address this situation by providing generous, competent and realistic aid, by seeking dialogue with the families, by proposing appropriate forms of education and by providing catechesis which is proportionate to the concrete possibilities and needs of these children."[645]

The most important task of the catechesis of children is to provide, through the witness of adults, an environment in which young people can grow in faith. Several pastoral directives should guide the catechists of children:

- Be able to understand children, communicate with them, listen to them with respect, be sensitive to their circumstances, and be aware of their current values.
- Recognize that children have a dignity of their own and that they are important not only for what they will do in the future, but for who they are now.
- Encourage them to know and respect other cultural, religious, racial, and ethnic groups, and use catechetical materials that are

---

643   CT, no. 37.
644   CT, no. 37.
645   GDC, no. 180.

adapted to accommodate cultural, racial, and ethnic pluralism; the concerns of particular groups; and persons with special needs.

- Understand that the child's comprehension and other powers develop gradually, and present religious truths in greater depth and propose more mature challenges as the capacity for understanding and growth in faith increases.
- Provide experiences in which they can live faith and apply the message of salvation to real-life situations; encourage the use of imagination, as well as intelligence and memory.
- Provide experiences that link Liturgy and catechesis and promote appreciation for the community celebration of the Eucharist.
- Stimulate not only exterior but interior activity—a prayerful response from the heart.
- Foster a sense of community that is an important part of education for social life.

Catechists for older children should

- Assist them in the praxis of observing, exploring, interpreting, and evaluating their experiences; in learning to ascribe a Christian meaning to their lives; and in learning to act according to the norms of faith and love—the presence in today's society of many conflicting values makes it all the more important to help young people to interiorize authentic values
- Emphasize that growth in faith includes growth in the desire for a deeper, more mature knowledge of the truths of faith
- Present private prayer as a means of "individual reflection and personal communication with God"[646]

49. CATECHESIS FOR PERSONS WITH DISABILITIES

"We are a single flock under the care of a single shepherd. There can be no separate Church for persons with disabilities."[647] Persons with disabilities, especially children, are particularly beloved of the Lord and are integral

---

646 *National Catechetical Directory*, no. 181.
647 *Welcome and Justice for Persons with Disabilities*, no. 1.

members of the Christian community. They include those with cognitive disabilities, those with developmental disabilities, those with learning disabilities, the emotionally disturbed, persons with physical disabilities, the hard of hearing, the deaf, the visually impaired, the blind, and others. All persons with disabilities have the capacity to proclaim the Gospel and to be living witnesses to its truth within the community of faith and offer valuable gifts. Their involvement enriches every aspect of Church life. They are not just the recipients of catechesis—they are also its agents. Bishops have invited qualified persons with disabilities to ordination, to consecrated life, and to full-time, professional service in the Church.[648]

All persons with disabilities or special needs should be welcomed in the Church. Every person, however limited, is capable of growth in holiness. "The love of the Father for the weakest of his children and the continuous presence of Jesus and His Spirit give assurance that every person, however limited, is capable of growth in holiness."[649] Some persons with disabilities live in isolating conditions that make it difficult for them to participate in catechetical experiences. "Since provision of access to religious functions is a pastoral duty,"[650] parishes should make that much more effort to include those who may feel excluded.

Just as with each of God's human creations, each person with a disability has catechetical needs that the Christian community must recognize and meet. All baptized persons with disabilities have a right to adequate catechesis and deserve the means to develop a relationship with God.

Persons with disabilities should be integrated into ordinary catechetical programs as much as possible. Catechetical goals and objectives should be set for special students included in parish catechesis. They should not be segregated for specialized catechesis unless their disabilities make it impossible for them to participate in the basic catechetical program. Catechesis for persons with disabilities is most effective when it is carried out within the general pastoral care of the community. As much as possible, persons with disabilities themselves should guide catechetical personnel in adapting curricula to their particular needs. Those who care for them or work with them can also be of considerable help. Catholic

---

648 Cf. *Welcome and Justice for Persons with Disabilities.*

649 GDC, no. 189.

650 *Welcome and Justice for Persons with Disabilities,* no. 6.

elementary and secondary school teachers should also be given inservice training in how to make schools and classrooms more accessible to students with disabilities and how to integrate them most effectively into programs of regular education.[651] The whole community of faith needs to be aware of the presence of persons with special needs within it and be involved in their catechesis.

Catechesis for some persons with disabilities, however, requires more personalization. In these situations, the involvement of their families is indispensable: "The central importance of family members in the lives of all persons with disabilities, regardless of age, must never be underestimated. They lovingly foster the spiritual, mental, and physical development of the disabled person and are the primary teachers of religion and morality";[652] "no family is ever really prepared for the birth of a disabled child."[653] The Church's pastoral response in such situations is to learn about the disability, offer support to the family, and welcome the child.[654] "Ministers working in the apostolate for the disabled should treat them as a uniquely valuable resource for understanding the various needs of those they serve."[655] However, parishes should not assume that the parent of a child with a disability will serve as primary catechist. The level of parent participation should be tailored to meet the needs of the parent, the child with a disability, and other students. The setting should also be considered.

The following are guidelines for providing catechesis for persons with special needs.

- Catechesis for persons with disabilities must be adapted in content and method to their particular situations.
- Specialized catechists should help them interpret the meaning of their lives and give witness to Christ's presence in the local community in ways they can understand and appreciate.
- "Great care should be taken to avoid further isolation of persons with disabilities through these programs which, as far as possible, should be integrated with the normal catechetical activities of the parish."[656]

---

651   Cf. *Pastoral Statement of U.S. Catholic Bishops on Persons with Disabilities*, no. 30.
652   *Pastoral Statement of U.S. Catholic Bishops on Persons with Disabilities*, no. 16.
653   *Pastoral Statement of U.S. Catholic Bishops on Persons with Disabilities*, no. 15.
654   Cf. *Welcome and Justice for Persons with Disabilities*.
655   *Pastoral Statement of U.S. Catholic Bishops on Persons with Disabilities*, no. 16.
656   *Pastoral Statement of U.S. Catholic Bishops on Persons with Disabilities*, no. 25.

- Catechetical efforts should be promoted by diocesan staffs and parish committees that include persons with disabilities.[657]

Although providing such services is challenging to parishes and dioceses, the Church owes persons with disabilities her best efforts in order to ensure that they are able to hear the Gospel of Christ, receive the sacraments, and grow in their faith in the fullest and richest manner possible. Dioceses and parishes should share resources and personnel and collaborate in sponsoring catechetical programs for persons with disabilities. They need to provide adequate funding for the preparation and sponsorship of such programs. "Costs must never be the controlling consideration limiting the welcome offered to those among us with disabilities."[658]

50. CATECHESIS IN SPECIAL SITUATIONS

The community of the baptized comprises many different groups of believers, each of whom have the right to a sound and adequate catechesis. Some of the groups of persons in special situations for whom catechetical programs might be developed in certain circumstances include (but are not limited to) groups of professional people, workers, artists, scientists, the marginalized (e.g., immigrants, refugees, migrants, the chronically ill, drug addicts, prisoners, school dropouts, the illiterate), the socially and economically disadvantaged, college students, young adults, military personnel, unwed parents, married couples (with or without children), couples in mixed marriages, the divorced, the divorced and remarried, the widowed, homosexual persons, and so forth. Catechetical programs for these groups can be adapted to the specific needs of those being catechized in language that can be easily understood, "while always maintaining fidelity to the message which catechesis transmits."[659]

The most effective catechesis for persons in special situations is integrated into a comprehensive pastoral ministry for and with them. As much as possible, dioceses and parishes should provide catechesis suited to the

---

657   Cf. *Welcome and Justice for Persons with Disabilities*, no. 2
658   *Welcome and Justice for Persons with Disabilities*, no. 6.
659   GDC, no. 191; cf. CT, no. 59.

special needs of every group. This catechesis should be developed in consultation with those for whom it is intended. Catechesis for persons in special situations presents the whole content of the Christian message and the demands of the Gospel. It aims to help them respond to God's uniquely personal love for them within the context of their special situation.

51. CATECHESIS IN THE CONTEXT OF ECUMENICAL AND INTERRELIGIOUS DIALOGUE

A. The Unity of the Church

The Church is one. She is one because the source of her unity is the Trinity of Persons in one God: Father, Son, and Holy Spirit. She is one because her founder, Jesus Christ, reconciled all persons to the Father through the sacrifice of the cross. She is one because the Holy Spirit gathers the faithful into communion and joins them in the Body of Christ. Charity is the fundamental bond of the Church's unity that is expressed in the profession of one faith received from the apostles, the common celebration of the sacraments, and apostolic succession. This one Church is characterized by a great diversity that comes from the variety of God's gifts given to the Church and the diversity of those who receive them. This diversity, however, does not detract from the Church's essential unity. Rather, it is a dimension of her catholicity. "Within the unity of the People of God, a multiplicity of peoples and cultures is gathered together."[660]

Christ himself bestowed the gift of unity on the Church from the very beginning. And St. Paul exhorted the Christians at Ephesus "to preserve the unity of the spirit through the bond of peace."[661] Nevertheless there have been serious wounds to the unity of the Church through the centuries. In our age the Church must continue to "pray and work to maintain, reinforce, and perfect the unity that Christ wills for her."[662]

---

660   CCC, no. 814.
661   Eph 4:3.
662   CCC, no. 820.

B. The Principles of Ecumenical Catechesis

The Holy Spirit is calling every Christian community to strive for unity among all Christians and to foster ecumenical initiatives. "Catechesis, therefore, is always called to assume an 'ecumenical dimension' everywhere."[663] Thus, it should aim to form a genuine ecumenical attitude in those being catechized, to foster ecumenism. It does so in a variety of ways.

First, the Catholic Church brings to the ecumenical movement a gift of her own self-understanding, with the truth and gifts of grace given her by Christ.[664] In order to engage in authentic ecumenical work, Catholics must know their own Church and be able to give an account of her teaching and her discipline. It is essential that they be aware of the Catholic principles of ecumenism.[665]

Second, catechesis in the context of ecumenical dialogue engenders and nourishes an authentic desire for unity. It should inspire serious efforts, including self-purification and self-renewal, to remove obstacles to unity. It should include dialogue and prayer, both public and private.

Third, this catechesis desires to present the whole doctrine of the Church clearly and unambiguously, with due regard to the hierarchy of truths. This should be done in a considerate manner that honestly presents the differences but avoids placing obstacles to further dialogue.

Fourth, catechesis seeks to present the teachings of other churches, ecclesial communities, and religions correctly and honestly. It explains "the divisions that do exist [between and among Christians] and the steps that are being taken to overcome them."[666] It avoids words, judgments, and actions that misrepresent other Christians. This will help Catholics deepen their understanding of their own faith and develop genuine respect for the teachings of other ecclesial communities while also bearing witness to the Church's commitment to seek the unity of all Christians.

Finally, catechesis "prepares Catholic children and young people, as well as adults, for living in contact with [those who are not Catholics], affirming their Catholic identity while respecting the faith of others."[667]

---

663 GDC, no. 197.
664 Cf. UR, no. 4.
665 Cf. *Directory for the Application of Principles and Norms on Ecumenism*, no. 24.
666 *Directory for the Application of Principles and Norms on Ecumenism*, no. 190.
667 CT, no. 32.

C. The Ecumenical Formation of Catechists

While ecumenical formation is necessary for all the Christian faithful, cat-echists need specialized training in ecumenism. Catholic catechists must have a clear awareness of basic Catholic principles of ecumenism: namely, that the Church founded by Jesus Christ "subsists in the Catholic Church"[668] and that the unity Christ bestowed on his Church from the beginning "subsists in the Catholic Church as something she can never lose,"[669] while something of the Church can be found in the other churches and ecclesial communities, depending on what they have preserved of the revealed truth and gifts of grace given by Christ to his Church. They are in "some, though imperfect, communion with the Catholic Church."[670] Maintaining these basic Catholic principles of ecumenism can be very challenging in the modern-day situation, in which "the Church's constant missionary proclamation is endangered today by relativistic theories which seek to justify religious pluralism, not only de facto but also de iure (or in principle)" and which result in a popular attitude "in which Christian rev-elation and the mystery of Jesus Christ and the Church lose their charac-ter of absolute truth and salvific universality."[671]

The Directory for the Application of Principles and Norms on Ecumenism includes, among the primary means of such formation, hearing and study-ing the word of God, preaching, catechesis, prayer, Liturgy, and the spiri-tual life. It also provides a fundamental rationale and detailed plan for the ecumenical formation of those engaged in pastoral work.[672] Some key ele-ments in the ecumenical formation of catechists are as follows:

- Careful study of Sacred Scripture and the Church's living Tradition
- Familiarity with the biblical foundations of ecumenism
- Familiarity with Catholic principles of ecumenism
- Knowledge of the history of ecumenism
- Training in ecumenical collaboration and dialogue

---

668   CCC, no. 816, citing LG, no. 8.
669   UR, no. 4.
670   UR, no. 3.
671   Congregation for the Doctrine of the Faith, On the Unicity and Salvific Universality of Jesus Christ and the Church (Dominus Iesus) (DI) (Vatican City, 2000), no. 4, http://www.vatican.va/roman_curia/congregations/cfaith/documents/rc_con_cfaith_doc_20000806_dominus-iesus_en.html (accessed August 29, 2003).
672   Cf. Directory for the Application of Principles and Norms on Ecumenism, nos. 70-91.

- Participation in visits to other churches, informal exchanges, joint study days, and common prayer
- Experience in ecumenical collaboration and dialogue
- Familiarity with fundamental ecumenical issues[673]

D. Catechesis in Relation to Jews

Special care should be given to catechesis in relation to the Jewish religion. "The Jews and Judaism should not occupy an occasional and marginal place in catechesis: their presence there is essential and should be organically integrated."[674] It should uncover the ancient link between the Church and the Jewish people, the first to hear the word of God. Catechesis that presents precise, objective, and accurate teaching on the Jews and Judaism helps Christians to appreciate and love the Jews, who were chosen by God to prepare for the coming of Christ. In particular, an objective of catechesis should be to overcome every form of anti-Semitism.[675]

Unfortunately, many Christians do not have a fundamental understanding of the history and traditions of Judaism. Painful ignorance that substitutes caricatures and stereotypes for accurate information persists among many. "Religious teaching, catechesis and preaching should be a preparation not only for objectivity, justice and tolerance but also for understanding and dialogue. Our two traditions are so related that they cannot ignore each other. Mutual knowledge must be encouraged at every level."[676]

God's Mercy Endures Forever: Guidelines on the Presentation of Jews and Judaism in Catholic Preaching contains general principles on presenting the Jews and Judaism in homilies by Catholic priests. Several of these principles can be adapted for catechists. For example, catechists are encouraged to

- Affirm the value of the whole Bible, both Old and New Testaments, and recognize the special meaning of the Old Testament for the Jewish people, its original audience

---

673 Cf. USCCB Secretariat for Ecumenical and Interreligious Affairs, *Ecumenical Formation of Pastoral Workers* (Washington, D.C.: USCCB, 1998), 7-19.

674 Vatican Commission for Religious Relations with the Jews, *Notes on the Correct Way to Present the Jews and Judaism in Preaching and Catechesis in the Roman Catholic Church* (1985), no. I, 2, in *Catholic Jewish Relations: Documents from the Holy See* (London: Catholic Truth Society, 1999).

675 Cf. NA, no. 4.

676 *Notes on the Correct Way to Present the Jews and Judaism in Preaching and Catechesis in the Roman Catholic Church*, no. 27.

- Show both the independence and the interconnectedness of the Old Testament and the New Testament
- Emphasize the Jewishness of Jesus and his teachings
- Respect the continuing existence of God's covenant with the Jewish people and their faithful response, despite centuries of suffering, to God's call
- Show that Christians and Jews together look to the Ten Commandments as a foundation of morality[677]

E. Catechesis in Relation to Other Non-Christian Religions

Catechesis in relation to other non-Christian religions also has distinctive characteristics. Especially in a religiously pluralistic society, such catechesis should deepen and strengthen the identity of Catholics who encounter adherents to other religions and at the same time help them grow in respect for those believers and their religions.[678]

Because society is so pluralistic, "it is necessary above all to reassert the definitive and complete character of the revelation of Jesus Christ."[679] It must always be taught clearly that Jesus Christ is the unique and universal Savior of the human family and that his Church is the universal sacrament of salvation. It is "in him, in whom God reconciled all things to himself, [that all peoples] find the fullness of their religious life."[680] The Church considers the goodness and truth found in the other faiths "to be a preparation for the Gospel and given by him who enlightens all men that they may at length have life."[681]

Catholics need to be familiar with the history of Islam, especially the conflicts between Christians and Muslims. The Church urges both Catholics and Muslims to work sincerely for mutual understanding and to preserve as well as to promote together for the benefit of all mankind social justice and moral welfare, as well as peace and freedom.[682] In the United

---

677 Cf. USCCB Bishops' Committee on the Liturgy, *God's Mercy Endures Forever: Guidelines on the Presentation of Jews and Judaism in Catholic Preaching* (Washington, D.C.: USCCB, 1988), no. 31.
678 Cf. GDC, no. 200.
679 DI, no. 5.
680 NA, no. 2.
681 LG, no. 16.
682 Cf. NA, no. 3.

States, the growing number of immigrants who prefer the Islamic faith makes imperative efforts to try to understand elements of their belief, as well as dialogue and cooperation between Catholics and Muslims.

For the task of promoting respectful relationships with all non-Christian religions, fervent Catholic communities and well-formed catechists are indispensable. In these situations catechists are encouraged to

- Present, when called for, an accurate account of the essential elements of traditional non-Christian religious beliefs, as perceived by their adherents in the light of their own religious experience
- Develop an appreciation of the insights of the adherents of other religions and their contributions to humanity
- "Promote joint projects in the cause of justice and peace"[683]
- Foster a missionary spirit among those being catechized
- Motivate them to bear lively witness to the faith and to participate actively in the Church's efforts to evangelize the world

In the United States, a climate of religious disillusionment and relativism has spawned a proliferation of new religious and spiritual movements, sects, and cults. Some derive from Christian traditions, some from Far Eastern, non-Christian traditions, and others from unknown or obscure origins. While much of their doctrine and many of their practices are contradictory to the Christian faith, they have a certain appeal. Catechesis in relation to these New Age[684] movements should accurately describe the beliefs and practices of adherents to these movements and carefully contrast them with Catholic beliefs and practices. It should help the Catholic faithful deepen their knowledge of Sacred Scripture, awaken a vibrant experience of prayer in them, understand the teachings of the Church thoroughly, and articulate those teachings clearly. It should educate them to accept responsibility for the Catholic faith and to defend it vigorously against error and misunderstanding.

The multiplication of these new religious movements, sects, and cults reveals a hunger among many to find some source of transcendent meaning in their lives. Those who join these movements form a particularly

---

683   *National Catechetical Directory*, no. 79.
684   Cf. Pontifical Council for Culture, *Jesus Christ: The Bearer of the Water of Life: A Christian Reflection on the New Age* (Vatican City, 2003), http://www.vatican.va/roman_curia/pontifical_ councils/interelg/ documents/rc_pc_interelg_doc_20030203_new-age_en.html (accessed on August 29, 2003).

important group for the Church to evangelize. They should hear the Gospel boldly proclaimed, for it contains the answers to the deepest questions of human longing. "The Church has an immense spiritual patrimony to offer mankind, a heritage in Christ, who called himself "the way, and the truth, and the life."[685]

52. CONCLUSION

Crowds of people from every walk of life came to the seashore to listen to Jesus proclaim the coming of the kingdom. The message of salvation in Jesus Christ is intended for all people despite their social, cultural, racial, ethnic, or economic differences. The Church's catechesis presents the universal truth of the Gospel to every stratum of human society in a wide variety of catechetical settings, with the resolute intention to transform all of society and renew the face of the earth. It adapts the Good News to the circumstances of all those who seek Christ in every part of the world while maintaining the unity of faith among all. In this catechesis, the Church recognizes and celebrates the diversity within the community of faith, affirms the fundamental equality of every person, and acknowledges the need for charity, mutual respect, and justice among all groups in a pluralistic society in ushering in the Kingdom of God.

This chapter has described the principles, guidelines, and criteria for presenting the Gospel in many diverse settings. The next chapter describes the roles and responsibilities of those who bear the word of God from one generation to the next.

---

685 RM, no. 38.

CHAPTER 8

Those Who Catechize

I planted, Apollos watered, but God caused
the growth. Therefore, neither the one who plants nor
the one who waters is anything, but only
God, who causes the growth. (1 Cor 3:6-7)

53. INTRODUCTION

Faith is a gift from God. In his Providence, God has chosen to use human instruments to ensure the growth of the faith received in Baptism. Under the prayerful intercession of the Virgin Mary, who was herself both a disciple and a catechist, members of the Church community are called not only to grow in knowledge of the faith but, at the same time, to pass on that faith to others. Like St. Paul, the evangelist and Apostle, catechists exemplify the manner in which we cooperate with God's grace to ensure the growth of faith and remind us that it is God who causes the growth.

All members of the community of believers in Jesus Christ participate in the Church's catechetical mission. Some are called to more specific catechetical roles. Parents, parish catechists, teachers, Catholic school principals, parish catechetical leaders for adults and children, youth ministry leaders, those who work in diocesan and national catechetical offices, deacons, consecrated religious, priests, and bishops are all catechists with distinctive roles. From the earliest days of the Church, immediately following the apostles' acceptance of Christ's missionary mandate, catechists have made and continue to make "an outstanding and absolutely necessary contribution to the spread of the faith and the Church by their great work."[686]

---

686 AG, no. 17.

Esteemed members of the Church's apostolate, they perform "a fundamental evangelical service."[687]

This chapter describes the roles and responsibilities of all who participate in the Church's catechetical mission. It also provides the principles, guidelines, and criteria for their formation as catechists.

54. DIFFERING ROLES OF THOSE WHO CATECHIZE

A. The Bishop and Diocesan Staff: A Shared Responsibility

Within the variety of ministries and services performed by the particular Church in its efforts to evangelize, catechesis occupies a place of particular importance. "Catechesis is a responsibility of the entire Christian community."[688] All members of the community share the duty to bear witness to the faith. Catechesis is a collaborative effort within the diocese, under the direction of the local apostle, the bishop, who is specifically responsible for the transmission of the Faith in the particular Church entrusted to him. Assisting the bishop in his catechetical responsibility are his priests, deacons, religious, and laity, each acting in a collaborative fashion according to their roles within the Church.

Since the proclamation and transmission of the Gospel is central to the episcopal ministry, the bishop has primary responsibility for catechesis in the diocese. Catechesis is a fundamental part of a bishop's prophetic ministry. Through their catechetical ministry, bishops transmit the faith to be professed and lived to those within the local Church.

Bishops are "beyond all others the ones primarily responsible for catechesis, the catechists par excellence."[689] As chief catechist in the diocese, the bishop is responsible for the total catechetical mission of the local church. Catechesis is one of the fundamental tasks of the bishop's ministry. First of all, the bishop is a catechist himself; he is a "herald of the faith."[690]

---

687   John Paul II, *Address to Catechists* (April 30, 1992).
688   GDC, no. 220.
689   CT, no. 63.
690   LG, no. 25.

By the power of the Holy Spirit, "bishops have been constituted true and authentic teachers."[691] This derives from the individual bishop's relationship with the whole Church, whose faith he articulates. In his diocese, the bishop "has a unique and authoritative role in teaching the faith of the Catholic Church in the particular church that is given to his care."[692] In his own preaching and teaching, the bishop transmits the teachings of Christ— the teachings of the entire Church. By his profound conviction of the importance of catechesis for the Christian life of his diocese, the bishop should bring about and maintain "a real passion for catechesis."[693]

In addition to devoting himself personally to the proclamation of the Gospel and the ministry of catechesis, the bishop is also to supervise the catechetical mission in the diocese. He is to ensure that the ministry of catechesis receives the support of competent personnel, effective means, and adequate financial resources. He is to make certain that the texts and other instruments used in catechesis transmit the Catholic faith completely and authentically. He is to ensure "that catechists are adequately prepared for their task, being well-instructed in the doctrine of the Church and possessing both a practical and theoretical knowledge of the laws of psychology and of educational method."[694] He is also to adopt a catechetical plan that is integrated into the overall diocesan pastoral plan and coordinated with the United States Conference of Catholic Bishops.

Speaking to his brother bishops, Pope John Paul II said,

> Let the concern to foster active and effective catechesis yield to no other care whatever in any way. This concern will lead you to transmit personally to your faithful the doctrine of life. But it should also lead you to take on in your diocese, in accordance with the plans of the Episcopal Conference to which you belong, the chief management of catechesis, while at the same time surrounding yourselves with competent and trustworthy assistants.[695]

---

691   CD, no. 2.
692   USCCB, *The Teaching Ministry of the Diocesan Bishop: A Pastoral Reflection* (Washington, D.C.: USCCB, 1992), 6.
693   CT, no. 63.
694   CD, no. 14; cf. CIC, c. 780.
695   CT, no. 63.

The bishop does not, therefore, work alone. He works with his priests and through those whom he appoints to assist him in his diocesan catechetical department. He should designate a highly skilled and professional diocesan director of catechesis and should commission as many truly competent diocesan catechetical staff persons as are needed to ensure that all who have a right to catechesis in the diocese have a realistic opportunity to receive it. In his designation of others as teachers and catechists, the bishop should vigilantly ensure that they proclaim the authentic Gospel of Jesus Christ and hand on the complete and accurate deposit of faith.

B. Pastors and Parish Leadership

1. Pastors

Pastors have specific responsibilities that derive from their particular catechetical role. "All believers have a right to catechesis; all pastors have the duty to provide it."[696] Pastors are the bishop's closest collaborators in ensuring that the goals of the diocesan catechetical mission are achieved:

> Attentive to the norms established by the diocesan bishop, the pastor is to take care in a special way:
> 1°   That suitable catechesis is imparted for the celebration of the sacraments;
> 2°   That through catechetical instruction imparted for an appropriate period of time children [and youth] are prepared properly for the first reception of the sacraments of penance and the Most Holy Eucharist and for the sacrament of confirmation;
> 3°   That having received first communion [and Confirmation], these children [and youth] are enriched more fully and deeply through catechetical formation;
> 4°   That catechetical formation is given also to those who are physically or mentally impeded, insofar as their condition permits;

---

696   CT, no. 64.

5° That the faith of youth and adults is strengthened, enlightened, and developed through various means and endeavors.[697]

The pastor should also ensure that

- Catechesis is emphasized in a way that provides age-appropriate opportunities for adults, youth, and children
- A total parish plan for catechesis is developed and implemented in consultation with the parish council and parish catechetical leadership
- Catechesis for adults of all ages is a priority—adult formation should be provided in such a way that parishioners would recognize it as the parish's primary catechetical mission
- The catechesis of youth and young adults is situated within a comprehensive plan for youth ministry in the parish
- Catechists at all levels are well formed and trained for this task
- Catechetical formation is available for all language groups
- The baptismal catechumenate is a vital component in the organization of catechesis in the parish
- The catechumenate is an essential process in the parish, one that serves as the inspiration for all catechesis

Pastors should also work with parents, school and catechetical personnel, and appropriate boards and commissions in the parish to plan and carry out the catechetical mission in the local parish. The pastor has the primary responsibility to ensure that the catechetical needs, goals, and priorities of the parish are identified, articulated, and met. In parishes with no resident pastor, pastoral administrators have the same obligation.

2. Priests

Priests share the teaching role of their bishops and are the immediate collaborators with them in the proclamation of the Gospel. The special role in the diocesan catechetical mission that they exercise arises directly from the Sacrament of Holy Orders, which constitutes priests as educators in the

---

697 CIC, c. 777; cf. CCEO, c. 619.

faith.[698] Since a priest "must be the *catechist of catechists*, forming . . . a veritable community of disciples of the Lord,"[699] in his preaching and teaching and in the sacramental ministry of the Church, the priest transmits the Gospel of Christ, encourages conversion to him, fosters the life of faith and ongoing formation in faith, and inspires the prayer of the community of faith. They are leaders who offer support for all those involved in catechesis. In his parish, the priest has the responsibility of forming the Christian community and ensuring that the faithful are properly formed and reach true Christian maturity.[700] Priests help to foster the ministry of catechists and assist them in carrying out their responsibilities by collaborating with catechetical leaders to provide catechists with formation and by supporting them, above all by their prayers. The parish priest plays an active role in the catechetical programs and is available to celebrate the sacraments with classes or groups. In addition, the Church expects priests "to neglect nothing with a view to a well-organized and well-oriented catechetical effort."[701]

Parochial vicars, in giving support to a pastor's catechetical responsibilities, are especially called to

- Foster a sense of common responsibility for catechesis in the parish and a recognition and appreciation for catechists and their mission
- Ensure that parish catechetical programs are systematic and complete
- Encourage those faithful who have the necessary qualities to be catechists among them
- Integrate catechesis with evangelization and foster the link between catechesis, sacraments, and Liturgy
- Ensure the connection between parish and diocesan catechetical efforts[702]

Priests are absolutely essential contributors to an effective catechetical program. Their zealous leadership is essential to parish catechesis. In

---

698 Cf. Second Vatican Council, *Decree on the Ministry and Life of Priests* (*Presbyterorum Ordinis*) (PO) (1965), no. 6.

699 Congregation for the Clergy, *Directory on the Ministry and Life of Priests* (Washington, D.C.: USCCB, 1994), no. 47.

700 Cf. CIC, c. 773; cf. CCEO, c. 617.

701 CT, no. 64.

702 Cf. CIC, cc. 776-777; cf. CCEO, cc. 624 §1, 619.

order to maintain and enrich their ministry as catechists, priests are to give careful attention to their own catechetical formation and continue their education and spiritual formation after ordination.

Frequently, candidates for the priesthood are being given catechetical responsibilities in the parishes in which they serve a pastoral internship. Seminarians need a clear understanding of the nature, goals, and methods of catechesis as well as the roles they will have in the catechetical programs of the parishes and institutions to which they will be assigned as priests. They should learn the processes of human growth and development and faith formation so that they will be able to adapt the Gospel message to the age and ability of those they catechize. They should also have an understanding of the catechetical ministry of the Church and training in the organization and supervision of parish catechetical programs. They should be sensitive to the diversity of cultures, and those who are not native-born should have the opportunity to learn the culture of the United States.

3. Deacons

"Deacons [also are] to serve the people of God in the ministry of the word in communion with the bishop and his *presbyterium*."[703] In this sense they participate in the Church's catechetical ministry as preachers and teachers. The deacon is called "to read the sacred scripture to the faithful [and] to instruct and exhort the people."[704] The formation of permanent deacons should include studies in theology, Liturgy, Sacred Scripture, catechesis, and communication skills.[705] With proper catechetical training, which includes supervised catechetical experience, deacons may serve as especially effective parish and diocesan catechetical leaders.

4. Women and Men in Consecrated Life

By virtue of their vocation, those in consecrated life catechize by the witness of their consecration and by their apostolic work. Women and men religious offer a public witness to their singular commitment to the mission

---

703   CIC, c. 757.
704   LG, no. 29.
705   Cf. Congregation for Catholic Education, *Basic Norms for the Formation of Permanent Deacons* (Washington, D.C.: USCCB, 1998), no. 9.

of the Church in their consecrated life. This witness strengthens the cate-chetical mission immeasurably. The catechesis offered by consecrated per-sons comes within the context of lives lived with extraordinary dedication to community life and an uncommon commitment to the Beatitudes. As a result, their catechesis has distinctive character.

While the Church is blessed with many lay women and men who con-tribute effectively in the work of catechesis, the contributions of those in consecrated life are unique and cannot be supplied by either priests or laity. Those contributions derive from their profession of the evangelical counsels and the special charisms of their particular communities. Some religious institutes for men and women were founded for the specific pur-pose of providing catechetical formation to children, young people, and adults. Throughout the history of the Church, many men and women reli-gious have committed themselves to the catechetical ministry. The history of catechesis in the United States is a chronicle of the critical leadership and dedication of men and women religious in the Church's catechetical mission. To continue this leadership and dedication, Pope John Paul II has asked that "religious communities dedicate as much as possible of what ability and means that they have to the specific work of catechesis."[706] With appropriate training, women and men in consecrated life are partic-ularly suited to serve as parish or diocesan catechetical leaders.

5. Parish Catechetical Leaders

The single most critical factor in an effective parish catechetical program is the leadership of a professionally trained parish catechetical leader. Depending on the size and scope of the parish catechetical program, parishes should allocate their resources so that they are able to acquire the services of a competent and qualified catechetical leader (or someone in the process of becoming qualified and competent) or to share those serv-ices with another parish. Depending on the scope of responsibilities, the position is usually titled "parish director of catechesis or religious educa-tion," "parish coordinator of catechesis or religious education," or "minis-ter of catechesis or religious education." Ordinarily, under the direction of the pastor, the main responsibilities of this position are as follows:

---

706   CT, no. 65.

- Overall direction of the parish catechetical programs for adults, youth, and children
- Planning, implementation, and evaluation of the parish catechetical program
- Recruitment, formation, ongoing development, and evaluation of catechists
- Implementation of diocesan and parish catechetical policies and guidelines, including the areas of catechist certification and supervision and administrative policies related to negligence, sexual abuse, sexual harassment, and the safety and protection of minors[707]
- Collaboration with the pastor, other parish ministers, and appropriate committees, boards, and councils
- Assistance in liturgical planning
- Attention to their own personal, spiritual, and professional development

Dioceses and parishes should actively seek to identify potential parish catechetical leaders and, with the help of Catholic colleges and universities and organizations, provide them with opportunities to develop the competence and skills necessary for effective leadership and thorough knowledge of the faith. Only fully initiated, practicing Catholics who fully adhere to the Church's teaching in faith and morals and who are models of Christian virtue and courageous witnesses to the Catholic faith should be designated as parish catechetical leaders. Preparation for service as a parish catechetical leader should include advanced studies in theology, Scripture, Liturgy, catechesis and catechetical methodology, educational psychology and theory, and administration, as well as practical catechetical experience with adults, youth, and children. A comprehensive knowledge of the *General Directory for Catechesis* and the *Catechism of the Catholic Church* is essential. In accord with diocesan policies, pastors who employ parish catechetical leaders should formulate a clear and specific agreement with them that lists the responsibilities of the position and elements of equitable compensation. Parish catechetical leaders should be full members of the parish pastoral staff and attend all its meetings.

---

707 Cf. USCCB, *Promise to Protect, Pledge to Heal* (Washington, D.C.: USCCB, 2003)..

The functions of such positions vary from parish to parish, but parish catechetical leaders are not simply administrators or general pastoral ministers. The need for systematic training and study should not be minimized. They are catechists first. They should continue their personal, spiritual, and professional development and participate in diocesan programs of inservice training and formation, catechetical institutes, conventions, retreats, and accredited programs.

6. Youth Ministers

A comprehensive youth ministry program, whether it is based in a single parish or represents the cooperative efforts of several parishes, includes the dimension of structured or formal catechesis. Coordinators of youth ministry, therefore, should have theological formation as well as competence and experience in catechesis. They should be able to lead and guide young people to grow in the knowledge of the Catholic faith, in the practice of that faith in light of the principles of Christian morality and social justice, in the celebration of the sacraments, and in the development of their spiritual lives. Coordinators of youth ministry should be practicing Catholics who live the Gospel in all aspects of their lives. They should be models of Christian living for the young people they serve and have the ability to speak credibly about their personal experience of the gift of faith. Within their comprehensive responsibilities, coordinators of youth ministry have specific catechetical responsibilities[708] that should always be fulfilled in collaboration with pastors and parish catechetical leaders.

Training for youth ministry should be as comprehensive as the responsibilities are and should employ all the principles of sound adult faith formation. Adequate training in the Church's mission of evangelization and catechesis in general and youth catechesis in particular should be a minimum requirement for all youth ministers. Dioceses with the help of Catholic universities and organizations should provide that training for their youth ministers and, if possible, develop certification programs in which all the dimensions of youth ministry can be developed over a period of time. Whether coordinators of youth ministry work full-time or part-time, they should be provided compensation and benefits appropriate to their efforts.

---

708   See Chapter 7 of this *Directory*.

7. Campus Ministers

By virtue of their Baptism, all the faithful on school campuses share in the proclamation of the Gospel within the academic community and are called to live exemplary Christian lives. Catholic faculty, staff, and administration have a special opportunity and responsibility to build up the Church on campus. But the Church also has a presence on campus that is specifically dedicated to give vigorous Christian witness within the academic world and to prepare students to bring the light of the Gospel into the ordinary situations of everyday life. That apostolic service is provided by campus ministers.

Campus ministers are professionally trained, are duly appointed by the bishop, and are sent "to form the faith community so that it can be a genuine sign and instrument of the kingdom."[709] In order to represent the Church on campus, campus ministry must have an adequate number of personnel. Theologically qualified and professionally competent priests, women and men in consecrated life, and lay persons may serve as campus ministers. Among their tasks are the following functions:

- To form a vibrant community of faith on campus
- To help students to discern the vocation for which God has created them
- To ensure that the sacraments are available to students
- To provide catechetical opportunities, such as Bible study groups
- To educate for the call to service and to create or identify opportunities for such service
- To identify, call forth, and coordinate the diverse gifts of the Spirit within the faith community on campus
- To educate all the baptized to appreciate their own call to service
- To respond, as much as possible, to the individual needs of the students, including their religious, ethnic, and cultural situations
- To recruit Catholic administrators, faculty, staff, and students to assist them in building a community of faith on campus
- To create an environment that encourages initiative and involvement

---

709 USCCB, *Empowered by the Spirit: Campus Ministry Faces the Future* (Washington, D.C.: USCCB, 1986), no. 24.

- To attend to their own personal, professional and spiritual development
- To maintain close relationships with neighboring parishes and the diocese[710]

The university campus provides campus ministers with a prime opportunity for catechesis. Some college students today, like some other young adults, often have a limited understanding of the basics of Catholic teaching. The college years are a time of both challenge and opportunity. Many desire to grow in their knowledge and practice of the faith and are eager to develop an adult faith, whereas others adopt an improper notion of freedom that leads them to neglect or reject Christian moral norms. Students' Catholic faith may be challenged by professors or peers from other religions. It is the role of the campus minister to strengthen their knowledge of the faith, especially through apologetics.

Many students themselves are suitable candidates to become catechists for the Church. They want to know the faith and to be able to hand it on to others. While they are already in the academic environment, courses of study should be initiated in campus ministry to provide theological education, spiritual formation, and practical experience to prepare them to serve parishes as catechists when they graduate.

Campus ministry programs should also serve the administration of the colleges and universities in which they function. In collaboration with the other members of the community of faith on campus, campus ministers should work for responsible governance and evaluate the institution's programs, policies, and research in the light of Catholic social doctrine.

8. Catechists

The apostolic work of the catechist springs from the Sacrament of Baptism through which all believers come to share in the prophetic ministry of Christ and the evangelizing mission of the Church. It is strengthened by the Sacrament of Confirmation. The call to the ministry of catechist is a vocation, an interior call,[711] the voice of the Holy Spirit. Catechists need to be practicing Catholics who participate fully in the communal worship

---

710   Cf. *Empowered by the Spirit*, nos. 24-32.
711   Cf. GDC, nos. 224, 225, 231, 233.

and life of the Church and who have been prepared for their apostolate by appropriate catechetical training. Their commissioning by the Church is a participation in the divine calling to teach as Jesus did. Their personal relationship with Jesus Christ energizes their service to the Church and provides the continuing motivation, vitality, and force of their catechetical activity. Christ invites all catechists to follow him as a teacher of the faith and a witness to the truth of the faith.

Like all the faithful, catechists are called to holiness. Because of their ministry and mission, however, the call to holiness has a particular urgency. The spiritual life of a catechist should be characterized by

- A love of God—Father, Son, and Holy Spirit—and of Christ's Church, our Holy Father, and God's holy people
- A coherence and authenticity of life that is characterized by their faithful practice of the faith in a spirit of faith, charity, hope, courage, and joy
- Personal prayer and dedication to the evangelizing mission of the Church
- A missionary zeal by which they are fully convinced of the truth of the Catholic faith and enthusiastically proclaim it
- Active participation in their local parish community, especially by attendance at Sunday Eucharist
- A devotion to Mary, the first disciple and the model of catechists, and to the Most Holy Eucharist, the source of nourishment for catechists[712]

Lay catechists have a special solidarity with those whom they catechize and a particular sensitivity to their needs. They live in the same world as those they catechize, and they share the same demands of living in the world as do those they teach. Their proclamation of the Gospel, their personal testimony, and their living witness to the transcendent values of the Christian life can be particularly effective because they know the ordinary experiences of everyday life so well and are able to incarnate the Gospel in those ordinary circumstances.

Catechists must be attentive to adapt their method of catechesis to the needs of particular groups they serve. Catechists serve a wide variety

---

712 Cf. Congregation for the Evangelization of Peoples, *Guide for Catechists* (Washington, D.C.: USCCB, 1993), nos. 7-10.

of persons, and the message of the Gospel must be proclaimed in such a way that they can understand it, and that it is applied to their life situation. Those who are in need of catechesis include those who do not have the constant presence of a priest; families; adults, young adults, children, and adolescents; those preparing to receive sacraments; those with special needs; immigrants, migrants, refugees, and people on the move; those in campus ministry programs; Catholic school children; members of movements and associations; those in hospitals and the military; those in prisons. The Church has a serious responsibility to identify the groups in need of specialized catechesis and to provide training and formation for those who respond to the Holy Spirit's call to be a catechist to these groups.

Catechists are to identify and create "suitable conditions which are necessary for the Christian message to be sought, accepted, and more profoundly investigated"[713] for each of the various groups they serve. It is clear that, in order to present the Catholic faith in its fullness and in a way that is attractive to each group, those who catechize need preparation and ongoing formation specific to the conditions of those to whom they proclaim the Gospel message. To this end, catechist formation programs cooperatively developed by parishes and dioceses must ensure that catechists receive assistance in developing their knowledge of the faith and the Gospel message as well as "the dimension of *savoir-faire*, of knowing how to transmit the message, so that it is an act of communication."[714] Faith is the result of the initiative of God's grace and the cooperation of human freedom. Catechists should humbly acknowledge, with St. Paul, "I planted, Apollos watered, but God caused the growth."[715]

9. Catholic Schools

"The Catholic school forms part of the saving mission of the Church, especially for education in the faith."[716] It is "not simply an institution which offers academic instruction of high quality, but, even more important, is an effective vehicle of total Christian formation."[717]

---

713   *General Catechetical Directory*, no. 71.
714   GDC, no. 238.
715   1 Cor 3:6.
716   Sacred Congregation for Catholic Education, *The Catholic School* (1977), no. 9.
717   USCCB, *Teach Them* (Washington, D.C.: USCCB, 1976), p. 5.

9a. Principals

Under the direction of the pastor or the duly elected or appointed school board, the principal of the Catholic school plays a crucial role in achieving the catechetical objectives of the parish. The Catholic school is a center for evangelization; thus, its catechetical program is essential to its distinctly Catholic identity and character. It is "an active apostolate."[718] Therefore, the principal of a Catholic school must be a practicing Catholic in good standing who understands and accepts the teachings of the Church and the moral demands of the Gospel. As a catechetical leader in the Catholic school, the principal is called to

- Recognize that all members of the faculty and staff "are an integral part of the process of religious education"[719]
- Recruit teachers who are practicing Catholics, who can understand and accept the teachings of the Catholic Church and the moral demands of the Gospel, and who can contribute to the achievement of the school's Catholic identity and apostolic goals
- Supervise, through observation and evaluation, the performance of each religion teacher
- Provide opportunities for ongoing catechesis for faculty members
- Design a curriculum that supports the school's catechetical goals and, if the school is associated with a parish, the parish's catechetical goals
- Develop goals for the implementation of an overall catechetical plan for the school, and periodically evaluate progress toward the goals
- Foster a distinctively Christian community among the faculty, students, and parents
- Provide, alongside the pastor, for the spiritual growth of the faculty
- Collaborate with parish, area, and diocesan personnel in planning and implementing programs of total parish catechesis[720]

---

718 Second Vatican Council, *Declaration on Christian Education* (*Gravissimum educationis*), no. 8.
719 *Teach Them*, p. 7.
720 Cf. *National Catechetical Directory*, no. 215.

9b. Catechesis in the Catholic School

Catechetical instruction in the Catholic school should be based on the *Catechism of the Catholic Church* and thoroughly integrated into the curriculum and objectives of the school. It should have its proper place in the order of each day alongside other lessons. It should be coordinated with the catechetical plan of the parish or parishes to which it is connected. The Catholic school "can and must play its specific role in the work of catechesis. Since its educational goals are rooted in Christian principles, the school as a whole is inserted into the evangelical function of the Church. It assists in and promotes faith education."[721]

9c. Religion Teachers

The Catholic school's effectiveness as a community of faith and a center for evangelization and catechesis depends to a large extent on its teachers of religion. Who they are, what they say, and what they do should be integrated harmoniously if they are to be genuine educators in the faith. "The role of the religion teacher is of first importance."[722] Religion teachers in Catholic schools not only teach the Catholic faith as an academic subject but also bear witness to the truth of what they teach.

> The religion teacher is the key, the vital component, if the educational goals of the school are to be achieved. But the effectiveness of religious instruction is closely tied to the personal witness given by the teacher; this witness is what brings the content of the lessons to life. Teachers of religion, therefore, must be men and women endowed with many gifts, both natural and supernatural, who are also capable of giving witness to these gifts.[723]

Religion teachers in Catholic schools have the same responsibilities and perform many of the same functions of parish catechists. Therefore,

---

721 Congregation for Catholic Education, *The Religious Dimension of Education in a Catholic School* (Washington, D.C.: USCCB, 1988), no. 69.

722 Sacred Congregation for Catholic Education, *Lay Catholics in Schools: Witnesses to Faith* (1982), no. 59, http://www.vatican.va/roman_curia/congregations/ccatheduc/documents/rc_con_ccatheduc_doc_19821015_lay-catholics_en.html (accessed on August 29, 2003).

723 *The Religious Dimension of Education in a Catholic School*, no. 96.

they should be practicing Catholics with a thorough knowledge of the Christian message and the ability to communicate it completely, faithfully, and enthusiastically; they should also meet diocesan standards for certification as a catechist.

9d. All Teachers

The distinctive Catholic identity and mission of the Catholic school also depend on the efforts and example of the whole faculty. "The integration of culture and faith is mediated by the other integration of faith and life in the person of the teacher. The nobility of the task to which teachers are called demands that, in imitation of Christ, the only Teacher, they reveal the Christian message not only by word but also by every gesture of their behavior."[724] All teachers in Catholic schools share in the catechetical ministry. "All members of the faculty, at least by their example, are an integral part of the process of religious education. . . . Teachers' life style and character are as important as their professional credentials."[725] Their daily witness to the meaning of mature faith and Christian living has a profound effect on the education and formation of their students.[726] While some situations might entail compelling reasons for members of another faith tradition to teach in a Catholic school, as much as possible, all teachers in a Catholic school should be practicing Catholics.

The Catholic school affords a particularly favorable setting for catechesis with its daily opportunity for proclaiming and living the Gospel message; for learning and appreciating the teachings of our Church; for acquiring a deep understanding, reverence, and love of the Liturgy; for building community; for prayer; for proper formation of conscience; for the development of virtue; and for participating in Christian service. In addition, Catholic schools strive to relate all of the sciences to salvation and sanctification. Students are shown how Jesus illumines all of life—science, mathematics, history, business, biology, and so forth. For these reasons, whenever possible, parents should send their children to a Catholic school.

---

724   *The Catholic School*, no. 43.
725   *Teach Them*, p. 7.
726   Cf. *Teach Them*, p. 3.

10. Others Who Catechize

Within a diocese or a parish are many others whose major responsibility is not specifically catechetical in nature, but who nevertheless catechize as part of their overall effort. In fact an important catechetical dimension is inherent in most aspects of the Church's mission. In addition to the many roles within the Church that are predominantly catechetical, those who are responsible, either on the diocesan or parish level, for evangelization, mission, charitable works, stewardship, peace and justice, Liturgy, youth ministry, young adult ministry, the catechumenate, ministry in higher education, seminary education, communications, ministry for persons with disabilities, family ministry, prison ministry, chaplaincies, and respect-life advocacy all hand on the Gospel message and contribute significantly to the success of diocesan or parish catechetical endeavors. Frequent communication, cooperation, and collaboration between and among all those involved in the Church's central mission of evangelization and catechesis should characterize the efforts of all those committed to proclaim the Gospel message.

C. Parents and Families

Parents are the most influential agents of catechesis for their children.[727] They have a unique responsibility for the education of their children; they are the first educators, or catechists. They catechize primarily by the witness of their Christian lives and by their love for the faith. One way that parents communicate Christian values and attitudes to their children is by loving each other within the context of a Christian marriage and their love for Christ and his Church. Their participation in the life of the parish—above all in the Sunday Eucharist—their willingness to evangelize and serve others, and their dedication to daily prayer demonstrate the authenticity of their profession of faith.

While a number of parents make the choice to educate and catechize their children at home, in general, parents or guardians are catechists for their children precisely because they are parents or guardians, not because they have developed any specialized skills. The catechesis given by parents with the family "precedes, accompanies and enriches all other

---

727   Cf. CCC, nos. 2222-2226.

forms of catechesis."[728] When children are baptized, parents accept the responsibility to bring up their children in the practice of the faith and to see to it that the divine life that God gives them is kept safe from the poison of sin, to grow always stronger in their hearts.[729] At the same time, the Church promises to help parents foster their children's faith and assists them specifically in their role as catechists of their children, whether they assume complete responsibility themselves or look to the parish school or religious education program for help and support.

Parish life itself is an aid to parents because it is here, at the Eucharistic banquet, that they are nourished by Christ himself. The vibrancy of the parish community, the beauty of worship, and the example of generous love and service of parishioners strengthens parents in the faith.

Adult catechesis, designed especially for parents, also helps them nourish their own faith, as well as that of their children. Such programs help parents to understand important issues in their own lives and the lives of their children, such as the preparation for reception of the sacraments or the questions raised by particular moral concerns in the light of the Catholic faith. This enables them to practice the faith in their everyday lives. These programs that prepare parents whose children will be receiving sacraments should encourage parents to ensure that their children receive formal catechetical instruction in programs sponsored by the parish.

55. PREPARATION AND ONGOING FORMATION OF CATECHISTS

A. The Ministry of Catechesis

Men and women from a wide variety of backgrounds are called to share in the Church's catechetical mission. Most are volunteers. They bring a wide variety of talents and abilities to their task. They have widely divergent levels of experience and competence in catechesis. Programs of formation should be designed to help them acquire the knowledge and skills they need to hand on the faith to those entrusted to their care and assist them in living as disciples in Christ.

---

728   CT, no. 68.
729   Cf. *Rite of Baptism of Children*, no. 56.

B. Discernment of the Call to Catechize

The Church entrusts the ministry of catechesis to exemplary followers of Christ with unquestioned personal integrity and moral character:

> Positive qualities in candidates should be: faith that manifests itself in their piety and daily life; love for the Church and communion with its pastors; apostolic spirit and missionary zeal; love for their brothers and sisters and a willingness to give generous service; sufficient education; the respect of the community; the human, moral and technical qualities necessary for the work of a catechist, such as dynamism, good relations with others, etc.[730]

The candidate should rise from within the community of faith, be invited to consider becoming a catechist, be known to the pastor, and prayerfully consider becoming a catechist. The suggestion that anyone can be a catechist should be scrupulously avoided in all communication involving the recruitment of catechists. In consultation with the parish catechetical leader, the pastor should assist the candidate in the discernment of the vocation to be a catechist. Only after the candidate has given careful and prayerful consideration to the responsibilities connected with being a catechist should the pastor formally invite the person to begin initial catechist formation. When this occurs, some form of commissioning ceremony should be planned that expresses the Church's call, recognizes the catechist's generous response, and confidently sends the catechist out to proclaim the Gospel of Jesus Christ. Ideally, each year all catechists, both veterans and newly invited, should be commissioned on Catechetical Sunday (the third Sunday in September) in order to renew their charge and encourage the support of the faith community for catechetical ministry.

C. Need for Formation

Like all Christians, catechists are called to continual conversion and growth in their faith and, for this reason, are called to ongoing spiritual formation. The catechist should continue his or her own spiritual formation through frequent reception of the sacraments, especially the Sacraments of

---

730   *Guide for Catechists*, no. 18.

the Holy Eucharist and Penance and Reconciliation, through spiritual direction, and through continued study of the faith. The catechist should also be provided with opportunities for spiritual growth such as retreats, conferences, etc. In addition to spiritual formation, the catechist is also in need of pedagogical formation, especially as society, teaching methods, and culture change.

D. Initial Formation of Catechists

Initial formation of catechists most profitably precedes the beginning of their ministry and can employ different methodologies. Whether the training is done at a diocesan catechetical center or in the parish, it should be adapted as much as possible to the specific needs of the individual catechist. Because the catechist has been invited by the pastor to begin initial formation, it is assumed that the individual is personally known to the pastor and the pastoral staff, especially the parish catechetical leader. Under no circumstances should the initial formation of new catechists "be improvised or left to the initiative of the candidates themselves."[731] The initial formation of new catechists should

- Help them develop an understanding of the nature and goals of catechesis
- Familiarize them with the resources available to them
- State that the catechist needs to be a Catholic who is a model of Christian virtue and a courageous witness to the Catholic faith
- Provide thorough formation in the knowledge and understanding of our Catholic faith and practice, making the catechist aware of the social, cultural, ethnic, demographic, and religious circumstances of the people he or she will serve, so that the catechist can bring the Gospel message to them
- Encourage and foster among new catechists the importance of ongoing study, especially within Scripture and the *Catechism*
- Guide the new catechist in a deeper daily practice of prayer
- Respect the new catechist's time constraints without compromising the full formation necessary

---

731 *Guide for Catechists*, no. 28.

- Develop the human, spiritual, and apostolic qualities of the new catechist
- Promote a continuous dialogue of prayer between the new catechist and God as well as open communication between the catechist, those providing the formation, and the local church
- Encourage new catechists to consider seeking out a spiritual director as ideal to growth in ministry
- Remain within the context of the community of faith where all authentic apostolic education occurs[732]

Formation programs for catechists should also include a basic presentation of the social sciences, since they provide an awareness of the sociocultural contexts in which those being catechized live and by which they are strongly influenced. Catechist formation is to include study of the human sciences, especially psychology, education, and communication. In this study the autonomy of the social sciences should be respected, and their values and limitations should be discerned. However, the social sciences should not be seen as ends in themselves. In the formation of catechists, social sciences are always at the service of evangelization.

E. Ongoing Formation of Catechists

Since effective catechesis depends on virtuous and skilled catechists, their ongoing formation should enhance the human, spiritual, and apostolic qualities and catechetical skills they bring to their ministry. The pastoral care of catechists is an essential aspect of the diocese's overall catechetical plan. "Diocesan pastoral programs must give absolute priority to the *formation of lay catechists*."[733] Encouragement in the ministry of catechesis, the provision of competent and professional directors and coordinators of catechesis, the recruitment of catechists, the balanced distribution of catechists, the provision of training in both the diocese and parish, the adequate formation of catechists, attention to the personal and spiritual needs of the catechist, and the coordination of catechetical efforts and adequate funding[734] are all the responsibility of diocesan offices. With due consider-

---

732   Cf. *Guide for Catechists*, no. 28.
733   GDC, no. 234.
734   Cf. GDC, no. 233.

ation to the lives of catechists and their ability to respond, great importance should be attached to the following objectives.

The ongoing formation of catechists is to include all aspects of the catechist's life. On the human level, formation is to

- Help them to develop natural virtues and necessary knowledge: honesty; integrity; enthusiasm; perseverance; knowledge of social, cultural, and ethnic conditions; ability to communicate; willingness to work with others; ability to dialogue with those of other Christian communities and other religions; leadership ability; good judgment; openness of mind; flexibility; sensitivity; and hopefulness
- Include reflection on real-life human situations so that catechists will be able to relate the various aspects of the Christian message to the concrete experiences of their lives

On the spiritual level, the catechists' ongoing formation is to

- Help them develop their spiritual lives—their communion of faith and love with the person of Jesus Christ—by promoting, as much as possible, an intense sacramental and prayer life, especially through frequent reception of the Eucharist and the Sacrament of Penance and Reconciliation, recitation of Morning and Evening Prayer in union with the whole Church, daily meditation, Marian devotion, participation in prayer groups, days of renewal, and spiritual retreats
- Encourage them to seek a spiritual director
- Help them see the development of their spiritual lives as essentially bound to the life of the Church

On the intellectual level, their ongoing formation is to

- Help them develop their understanding of the Church's doctrine and be firmly rooted in Sacred Scripture and Tradition
- Present the various elements of the Christian faith "in a well structured way and in harmony with each other by means of an organic vision that respects the 'hierarchy of truths'"[735]

---

735   GDC, no. 241.

- Reflect the Christ-centered and ecclesial nature of catechesis and equip them to lead those being catechized into the mystery of Christ, his life, his role in salvation history, and his transforming presence in the sacraments
- Equip them to transmit the authentic faith of the Church by adapting the message of Christ "to all cultures, ages, and situations"[736]
- Depend on the *General Directory for Catechesis* and the *Catechism of the Catholic Church* as the sure norm for teaching the faith
- Help them mature in their own faith and enable them to offer a convincing explanation for their faith and hope

Because catechists are witnesses to Jesus Christ in the Church and in the world, their ongoing formation is to

- Help them develop an apostolic zeal
- Encourage them to become evangelizers
- Equip them to proclaim the truth of Jesus Christ boldly and enthusiastically
- Help them to introduce those whom they catechize into the mystery of salvation and the religious, liturgical, moral, and community life of the Body of Christ
- Show them how to build a community of faith
- Encourage them to devote themselves to the missionary apostolate
- Encourage them to carry out their apostolic activity in communion with the local and universal Church

In order to integrate these dimensions of their role, ongoing formation for catechists is to

- Help them to harmonize the human, spiritual, doctrinal, and apostolic dimensions of their apostolate
- Keep them abreast of the life of the Church—its needs, new documents, and so on—and of changing social, cultural, ethnic, and religious circumstances
- Help them overcome discouragement and burnout

---

736   GDC, no. 236.

Since catechists nurture the faith that was implanted by the Holy Spirit in those being catechized, their formation should also include training in catechetical methodology. Catechists do not merely instruct their students about Christ; they lead them to him. Consequently, their formation should be inspired by God's own original methodology of faith: his gradual Revelation of the truth that is Christ. Their formation should help them grow in their capacity as genuine teachers of that truth, keenly aware of both the authentic Gospel message and the circumstances of those for whom the message is intended. It should help them to develop their own style of handing on the faith "by adapting the general principles of catechetical pedagogy to [their] own personalit[ies]."[737]

In concrete terms, catechist formation should help catechists to organize and direct educational activities. It should provide assistance in catechetical planning, goal setting, the presentation of catechetical lessons, and the evaluation of those lessons. And it should help them decide which techniques of group dynamics to use and when. Their training should help them to make effective use of the resources available for catechesis, especially the use of media, and to adapt materials to the age, capacity, and culture of those they seek to reach. The pedagogy for catechist formation should model the pedagogy proper to the catechetical process.[738] Catechist formation should provide specialized training for catechists of persons with disabilities. In all catechist formation, "the goal or ideal is that catechists should be the protagonists of their own learning by being creative in formation and not by just applying external rules."[739]

F. Possible Settings for Catechist Formation

The formation of catechists takes place most effectively within the community of faith under the direction of the local pastor. The parish is where "catechists test their own vocation and continually nourish their own apostolic awareness."[740] Parish-centered programs for catechists remind them that their calling as catechists comes from the Church, that they are

---

737   GDC, no. 244.
738   Cf. GDC, no. 237.
739   GDC, no. 245.
740   GDC, no. 246.

sent by the Church, and that they hand on the faith of the Church. Such programs attend to the progressive growth of catechists as believers and witnesses through the normal course of parish educational and liturgical life as well as through specialized programs of catechist development. They provide opportunities to meet with other catechists for lesson preparation and evaluation. They provide catechists with courses in catechesis and opportunities for retreats, special liturgical experiences, and systematic doctrinal study based on the *Catechism of the Catholic Church*.

Some opportunities for catechist formation are more appropriately provided by the diocese. Institutes, workshops, and seminars for those with responsibility for catechesis in parishes, schools, clusters of parishes, deaneries, or vicariates should be provided at the diocesan or interdiocesan level. Dioceses are well advised to develop comprehensive catechist formation programs that lead to a more formal certification. Some dioceses have worked closely with Catholic colleges and universities to set up training and certification programs for catechists and catechetical leaders. The availability of expert faculty, access to the latest research, and scholarship assistance are just some of the ways the collaboration between dioceses and institutes of higher learning can be fruitful. These opportunities for further professional development ordinarily offer more than basic catechetical formation and engage parish catechetical leaders in the study and research of specialized topics important to those who exercise leadership in catechesis.

Most Catholic colleges and universities in the country have departments of theology; some offer graduate degrees in various disciplines within Catholic theology. Only a few, however, have departments of catechetics, and still fewer offer graduate degrees in catechetics. Dioceses and Catholic colleges and universities are encouraged to collaborate in the establishment of institutes for the advanced study of pastoral catechesis in order to provide comprehensive training and formation for priests, religious, and laity who have responsibility for catechesis at the diocesan or national level. Seminaries can likewise be valuable partners with dioceses in providing opportunities for the ongoing formation of catechetical leaders.

Especially in dioceses without a Catholic college or university in close proximity, certification programs often make productive use of distance learning models. Such programs have the advantage of offering systematic and organic formation over a period of several years. In them, trained specialists are able to present the totality of the Christian message, a thorough knowledge of the sociocultural situation, and sound catechetical methodology to catechists from all parts of the diocese. Through its Commission on Certification and Accreditation, the United States Conference of Catholic Bishops affirms and verifies the quality and validity of such programs.

56. CONCLUSION

This presentation of the various catechetical roles within the Church sets forth both the personal qualities of catechists and the training and skills they require. The foundation for these qualities and skills of catechesis must be a solid spiritual life rooted in the sacraments. The catechist's spiritual life enables him or her to know that he or she is God's instrument in the mission to "make disciples of all nations."[741] Catechists water the seed planted by evangelists, but God gives the growth. Their life in the Holy Spirit renews them continually as members of the community of believers and in their specific identity as catechists. This life in the Holy Spirit—nourished by prayer, the celebration of the Eucharist, and the building of community—makes their catechesis ring true in the hearts and minds of those to whom they are sent. No number of attractive personal qualities, no amount of skill and training, and no level of scholarship or erudition can replace the power of God's word communicated through a life lived in the Spirit.

Because catechesis is always an act of the Church, it takes place in the many settings that make up the Church's life at all levels: family, parish, diocese, and nation. The next chapter will provide guidance for organizing catechetical ministry at these various levels and settings.

---

741 Mt 28:19.

CHAPTER 9

Organizing
Catechetical Ministry

And he gave some as apostles, others as prophets, others as
evangelists, others as pastors and teachers, to equip the holy
ones for the work of ministry, for building up the body of
Christ, until we all attain to the unity of faith and
knowledge of the Son of God, to mature manhood,
to the extent of the full stature of Christ. (Eph 4:11-13)

57. INTRODUCTION

In commissioning the apostles to go, make disciples, and teach,[742] Christ
sent them to create a new civilization of love, a whole new way of being and
living. This new life in Christ is exemplified by the unity of the Church, in
which the many gifts of Christ are expressed in different ministries in order
to make the community more Christlike. These ministries equip the
Church for her mission and contribute to the growth of the Body of Christ.
But even more importantly, the differentiated ministries are ordered to the
unity of faith, to the knowledge of Christ, and to a fully developed adulthood whose model is the firstborn of the new creation, Jesus Christ.

Neither catechesis nor evangelization is possible without the action of
God working through his Spirit.[743] But the Church also depends on effective organizational structures to achieve her goals for catechesis set forth
in this directory. Such structures aim to provide practical opportunities for

---

742   Cf. Mt 28:19-20.
743   Cf. EN, no. 75.

the entire Christian community to grow in faith. Sound organizational structures can ensure that the Gospel will be proclaimed in its entirety and with fidelity. The witness to the faith given by individuals who are living according to Christian beliefs and virtues proclaims the Gospel of Christ clearly and persuasively to a world in need of transformation and hope.

This chapter describes the diversity and complementarity of responsibilities, as well as the need for coordination among all those involved in catechetical ministry. It gives principles and guidance for organizing catechesis.

58. GENERAL PRINCIPLES AND GUIDANCE

Several organizational principles are important to catechetical organization.

- Organization for catechesis at the parish, diocesan, or national levels should be part of an overall pastoral plan that flows from the Church's comprehensive mission. All levels of organization should respect the competence of the other levels. Urgent demands on limited resources require close collaboration and mutual regard for appropriate authority.
- Organization for catechesis is person-centered. Moreover, it supports and respects the Christian family as the basic community in which the faith is nurtured. It encourages those who are catechized to participate in determining the organizational structures.
- The responsibility for catechesis is shared by each member of the Church. Each of the faithful has a duty to live and foster the faith according to one's particular role and individual ability.
- Those involved in organization for catechesis should develop a clear statement to explain the principles and goals of catechesis, the measure of accountability and the provision for the communication of information.
- Organization for catechesis should ensure the equitable distribution of services, resources, and opportunities. Parishes in need should have opportunities equal to those of more affluent parishes.
- Organizational structures for catechesis should flow directly from specific catechetical needs, as these change over time, and aim to achieve the stated catechetical goals.[744]

---

744   Cf. *National Catechetical Directory*, no. 221.

Planning is an essential part of catechetical organization. Catechetical planning should include

- A clear understanding of the fundamental mission of the Church and the major objectives to advance that mission
- Analysis of the social, cultural, ethnic, and religious situation in the diocese
- Assessment of catechetical needs and available resources
- Identification of long- and short-range goals
- Identification and prioritization of concrete strategies to reach those goals
- Establishment of a budget based on stewardship principles that ensure priorities are named as a process for allocating resources
- Preparation of a primary working instrument or plan for the catechetical mission of the diocese
- Establishment of favorable conditions for carrying out the strategies
- Periodic review and evaluation
- Restatement of goals and strategies as necessary[745]

Evaluation is also an essential part of catechetical organization. Catechetical programs should be evaluated on a regular basis in light of the stated goals and objectives of the program. The program goals and objectives should also be evaluated regularly in light of catechetical needs and available resources. The norms and guidelines set forth in this *Directory*[746] provide criteria for the evaluation of catechetical programs.

The rapid changes in society and culture, new discoveries of the social sciences, technological advances, and the Church's continued growth call for continued study to view these changes from a catechetical perspective. Through its departments and secretariats, the United States Conference of Catholic Bishops wishes to work in close collaboration with the Catholic colleges, universities, learned societies, and research centers in the country to develop research instruments and disseminate the results of catechetical research to diocesan offices and other interested groups. The implications of this research should be shared with catechetical leaders and catechists so that they may proclaim the message of Jesus Christ realistically and confidently as it applies to our changing world.

745　Cf. *National Catechetical Directory*, no. 222.
746　See Chapter 10 of this *Directory*.

59. DIOCESAN STRUCTURES

"Through the Gospel and the Eucharist, [the diocese] constitutes one particular church in which the one, holy, catholic and apostolic Church of Christ is truly present and active."[747] "In all the ministries and services which the particular Church performs to carry out its mission of evangelization, catechesis occupies a position of importance."[748] "The organization of catechetical pastoral care has as its reference point the Bishop and the Diocese."[749]

A. The Bishop

The bishop, as local apostle and chief teacher of the faith in his diocese, is entrusted with the "management of catechesis"[750] in his particular Church. He should

- "Ensure *effective priority* for an active and fruitful catechesis in his Church"[751]
- Put "into operation the necessary personnel, means and equipment, and also financial resources"[752]
- Establish an "*articulated, coherent and global* program . . . integrated into the diocesan pastoral plan"[753]
- "Ensure that catechetical goals and priorities are established by the Christian community, that the necessary structures exist, and that appropriate programs are designed, carried out, and evaluated"[754]
- "Issue norms for catechetics, . . . make provision that suitable instruments for catechesis are available, even by preparing a catechism if it seems opportune, and . . . foster and coordinate catechetical endeavors"[755]

---

747   CD, no. 11.
748   GDC, no. 219.
749   GDC, no. 265.
750   CT, no. 63.
751   GDC, no. 223.
752   CT, no. 63.
753   GDC, no. 223.
754   *National Catechetical Directory*, no. 218.
755   CIC, c. 775 §1; cf. CCEO, c. 621 §1.

- Be "responsible for choosing qualified leaders for the catechetical ministry . . . [and] for seeing to it that all involved in [catechesis] receive continuing catechetical formation"[756]

B. The Diocese

In fulfilling his duties as pastor and chief catechist of the diocese, the bishop may consult with several councils: namely, the diocesan presbyteral, pastoral, and finance councils.[757] These councils assist the bishop in establishing the pastoral plan for the diocese. A key component in the diocesan pastoral plan is the diocesan catechetical plan. These councils and diocesan catechetical leaders work with the bishop to identify the educational and catechetical goals for the diocesan church and to determine the diocesan catechetical plan for achieving those goals.

The diocesan catechetical commission, committee, or board "has the responsibility of developing policy, thus giving unified leadership to the various concerns reflected in the total catechetical ministry."[758] It should be broadly representative of all the people of the diocese and include members from the various cultural, racial, and ethnic groups and geographic regions of the diocese. Its members should be practicing Catholics who are active in catechesis, education, or related pastoral fields or who possess an expertise that would be beneficial to the catechetical commission, such as parents, youth, or persons with disabilities. The chief tasks of the diocesan catechetical commission, committee, or board are as follows:

- To collaborate closely with the diocesan catechetical office
- To identify, define, and set priorities among the catechetical objectives related to the goals specified by the diocesan pastoral council
- To suggest programs and activities to achieve those goals
- To consult with the other consultative bodies on strategies for the implementation of those programs and activities
- To evaluate itself and its performance on a regular basis[759]

---

756 *National Catechetical Directory*, no. 218.
757 Cf. USCCB, *United in Service: Reflections on the Presbyteral Council* (Washington, D.C.: USCCB, 1992), chapter three.
758 *National Catechetical Directory*, no. 238.
759 Cf. *National Catechetical Directory*, no. 238.

C. The Diocesan Catechetical Office

The bishop directs catechesis through the diocesan offices responsible for catechetical activities. Ordinarily, several diocesan offices and agencies share responsibility for the diocesan catechetical mission. Chief among these is the diocesan catechetical office. "The diocesan catechetical office (*Officium Catechisticum*) is 'the means which the Bishop as head of the community and teacher of doctrine utilizes to direct and moderate all the catechetical activities of the diocese.'"[760]

Catechesis is so basic to the life of every diocesan church that "no diocese can be without its own Catechetical Office."[761] The diocesan catechetical office was instituted in every diocese by the decree *Provido Sane* in 1935.[762] In 1971 the *General Catechetical Directory* affirmed that "the Catechetical Office, therefore, which is part of the diocesan curia, is the means which the bishop as head of the community and teacher of doctrine utilizes to direct and moderate all the catechetical activities of the diocese."[763] The *National Catechetical Directory* of 1979 reaffirmed this statement and offered several models for diocesan administrative structures.[764] The *General Directory for Catechesis* of 1997 confirmed what has become a common practice[765] and referred to the bishop's responsibility to foster and coordinate catechetical endeavors, as set forth in the *Code of Canon Law*.[766]

The size, needs, administrative structure, and resources of a diocese will determine the most effective means to direct the catechetical mission of the diocese.[767] While catechetical needs and priorities vary from diocese to diocese, diocesan catechetical offices should perform the following specific functions:

- Keep the diocesan Church mindful of its mission to evangelize
- Analyze the catechetical needs of the diocese

---

760 GDC, no. 265, quoting *General Catechetical Directory*, no. 126.
761 *General Catechetical Directory*, no. 126.
762 Cf. *Acta Apostolicae Sedis* 27 (1935), 151.
763 *General Catechetical Directory*, no. 126.
764 Cf. *National Catechetical Directory*, no. 238.
765 Cf. GDC, no. 265.
766 Cf. CIC, c. 775 §1; cf. CCEO, c. 621 §1.
767 For additional information on effective structures for diocesan educational and catechetical offices and the identification, recruitment, selection and retention of diocesan educational and catechetical leaders see *Those Who Hear You Hear Me: A Resource for Bishops and Diocesan Educational/Catechetical Leaders* (Washington, D.C.: USCCB, 1995).

- Integrate catechesis within the schools and parishes with the diocese's total plan for Catholic education and prepare parish catechetical personnel to do the same
- Collaborate with appropriate individuals, groups, offices, and agencies in the development of the diocesan catechetical plan
- Develop diocesan catechetical policies in consultation with others responsible for the catechetical mission of the diocese
- Collaborate with the liturgical office especially for catechumenal and initiatory catechesis
- Develop a diocesan curriculum guide based on the *General Directory for Catechesis*, the *National Directory for Catechesis*, and the *Catechism of the Catholic Church*
- Provide guidelines for the organization of lifelong parish catechesis, of the baptismal catechumenate, and of other programs of sacramental preparation
- Evaluate and recommend catechetical textbooks, materials, and other resources
- Provide assistance in the evaluation of parish catechetical programs, using instruments that measure cognitive, affective, and behavioral objectives
- Provide access to catechetical resources, including textbooks and instructional aids that have been found to be in conformity with the *Catechism of the Catholic Church* by the Ad Hoc Committee to Oversee the Use of the *Catechism of the Catholic Church*
- Provide consultation on catechetical matters to the parishes, especially by site visits
- Research and propose catechetical models that can be adapted to the needs of particular areas, parishes, or schools
- Provide personnel and resources to meet the needs of persons with disabilities
- Work with Catholic colleges and universities to establish theologically and academically sound programs of preparation for parish catechetical leaders
- Develop processes for the recruitment, approval, orientation, placement, ongoing formation, evaluation, and retention of parish catechetical leaders
- Establish norms for the accreditation and certification of parish catechetical leaders, including parish directors or coordinators of religious education and Catholic school principals

- Conduct regular surveys to determine the number of adults, youth, children, preschoolers, persons with disabilities, and so forth who are receiving formal catechetical instruction; the availability of training and continuing education of personnel; the kinds of programs in use and their effectiveness; the number of hours of instruction being given; the service and worship components of programs; and costs
- Develop a compensation plan for parish catechetical leaders
- Assist parishes in the selection, initial formation, ongoing formation, and retention of catechists
- Establish permanent centers for catechetical formation, or cooperate with Catholic colleges or universities in setting up such programs
- Encourage and motivate catechists through diocesan and parish commissioning rites, recognition ceremonies, catechetical awards, and ongoing affirmation
- Keep catechetical personnel informed concerning important church documents and recommendations that pertain to catechesis

"The Diocesan Catechetical Office should have sufficient professional personnel to serve as resources to parishes, areas, or regions in relation to all aspects of catechesis."[768] Since the diocesan director of catechesis is the official delegate of the bishop for catechetical matters, the bishop should appoint a competent director who represents him faithfully. The diocesan director of catechesis should be an exemplary Catholic with advanced academic training in theology, catechetics, or a related field; proven experience in parish catechesis; excellent communication and leadership skills; and the ability to collaborate effectively. The diocesan director of catechesis will meet regularly with the bishop on catechetical matters.

Other diocesan catechetical personnel should also be exemplary Catholics who have appropriate academic credentials and demonstrated competence in theology, catechetics, or related fields. They should have previous experience as catechetical leaders in parishes or schools. They should receive compensation that appropriately reflects their education and experience. They should also be provided opportunities for professional development and spiritual formation appropriate to their level of

768 *National Catechetical Directory*, no. 238.

responsibility. Diocesan catechetical personnel should frequently come together for prayer and regularly participate in the Eucharist in order to express their solidarity in Jesus Christ, to foster the community of faith among them, to grow in their ministry of proclaiming the Gospel message, and to rededicate themselves to the service of God and his holy people.

D. Coordination of Catechesis

Catechesis is the centerpiece of a diocese's evangelizing activities and is closely linked with all other forms of education in the faith. Effective coordination of catechesis within a diocese ensures a unified and coherent presentation of the faith.

Since catechesis is an integral part of so many diocesan efforts to proclaim the Gospel, the diocesan catechetical office should collaborate with other diocesan offices and agents that have a catechetical dimension, most especially the Catholic school office. A critical component of the ministry of the Catholic school office is the service it provides to Catholic school personnel who have catechetical responsibilities. The superintendent of Catholic schools is a diocesan catechetical leader who should have "an ability to articulate the role of the Catholic school and its programs so it functions effectively within the diocesan mission statement, planning, and decision making."[769] The superintendent should provide leadership, advocacy, and support for the catechetical dimension of the overall mission of the diocesan office of Catholic schools. Since "instruction in religious truths and values is an integral part of the school program,"[770] Catholic school office personnel should ensure that inservice training, consultation services, and opportunities for ongoing formation in catechesis is provided for Catholic school teachers, especially those who have catechetical responsibilities.

Other offices and agencies with whom the diocesan catechetical office should collaborate ordinarily include the diocesan office for evangelization, the liturgy office, the office for religious education for persons with disabilities, the youth ministry office, the program of priestly formation, the office for the continuing education for the clergy, the Catholic missions office, the ecumenical and interfaith affairs office, the family life

---

769   *Those Who Hear You Hear Me*, 22.
770   USCCB, *To Teach as Jesus Did* (Washington, D.C.: USCCB, 1973), no. 103.

office, the social justice office, ministry in higher education, Catholic Charities, and the office for communications. This need for collaboration is not only a practical concern that ensures a well-coordinated catechesis, but also a profoundly theological one since catechesis intends to communicate the unity of the faith.

A diocese should give special consideration to drawing its resources together to offer a "single, coherent, process of Christian initiation for *children, adolescents* and *young people*" that is closely linked to the sacraments of initiation.[771] Collaboration among the catechetical, liturgical, youth, and young adult offices in this regard is indispensable. The diocese should also offer a process for adult Christians "who need to deepen their faith in order to complete the Christian initiation begun at Baptism."[772] These and all other collaborative catechetical efforts should not be organized as if they were "separate watertight compartments" without any communication between them.[773]

60. THE PARISH COMMUNITY

A parish is a community of the Christian faithful established within a diocese. The pastoral care of a parish is entrusted to a pastor under the authority of the diocesan bishop. The parish is "the primary experience of the Church"[774] for most Catholics. It is where the faithful gather for the celebration of the sacraments and the proclamation of the word of God, and where they are enabled to live distinctively Christian lives of charity and service in their family, economic, and civic situations. It is "the living and permanent environment for growth in the faith."[775] The parish energizes the faithful to carry out Christ's mission by providing spiritual, moral, and material support for the regular and continuing catechetical development of the parishioners.

The parish is the preeminent place for the catechesis of adults, youth, and children. "Knowledge of the faith, liturgical life, the following of Christ are all a gift of the Spirit which are received in prayer, and similarly a duty of spiritual and moral study and witness. Neither aspect may be

---

771   GDC, no. 274.
772   GDC, no. 274.
773   CT, no. 45.
774   OHWB, no. 114.
775   GDC, no. 158.

neglected."[776] Pastors have the duty to provide catechesis; parishioners have the reciprocal duty to participate in and support the catechetical activities of the parish. Parish catechetical efforts should be in harmony with the catechetical goals and objectives of the diocese.

A. Parish Catechetical Plan

Like the diocese, every parish needs to develop a coherent catechetical plan that integrates the various components of the overall program and provides opportunities for all parishioners to hear the Gospel message, celebrate it in prayer and Liturgy, and live it in their daily lives. That plan should reflect the priority of adult catechesis,[777] take into account the needs of everyone in the parish, and provide special accommodation for cultural, racial, and ethnic groups, persons with disabilities, the neglected, and those unable to represent their own rights and interests. It should develop goals and objectives specific to the parish community and include the regular assessment of progress toward the achievement of those goals and objectives. It should devise a schedule of catechetical activities that encourages adults to participate but does not conflict with the calendars of local public and parochial schools. The parish catechetical plan should be adequately financed and staffed by professionally trained catechetical leaders so that the teachings of the Church are readily accessible to all the Christian faithful in the parish. "The quality of any form of pastoral activity is placed at risk if it does not rely on truly competent and trained personnel."[778]

B. Parish Catechetical
Commission or Committee

If the pastor so chooses, he may establish a commission to assist him with his catechetical responsibilities. No single model of a representative commission, however, will be suited to every parish. Different circumstances in parishes require different organizational forms. In parishes that have established parish pastoral councils, the catechetical commission can be

---

776 GDC, no. 87.
777 Cf. OHWB, no. 13.
778 GDC, no. 234.

a committee of the parish pastoral council. Otherwise, it can take the form of a separate standing committee or some other entity. No matter what organizational form is chosen, the various educational and catechetical components of a parish program of evangelization and pastoral care should be developed in harmony with one another and with the total program of pastoral care planned by the parish. Whether elected or appointed, the members of the parish catechetical commission or committee should represent the diversity in age, ability, and the cultural, racial, ethnic, social, and economic conditions present in the parish. They should receive appropriate training and pastoral formation that help them understand the Church's universal mission, the overall goals of the parish, and the catechetical priorities within that pastoral plan.

Parish catechetical efforts should be coordinated with those of neighboring parishes, clusters of parishes, deaneries, and regions. As much as possible, parishes should share resources and avoid the duplication of catechetical services, especially so that the catechetical needs of poor or otherwise disadvantaged groups can be met.

61. SOME PASTORAL EFFORTS

The most effective catechetical initiatives are rooted in the vibrant Christian life of a parish community. The parish organizes its catechetical priorities to ensure that all segments of the parish have a realistic opportunity to grow in their understanding and practice of the Catholic faith. A comprehensive parish-based catechesis harmonizes the catechesis of adults, families, parents, youth, children in the parish catechetical program and Catholic school, children in the parish baptismal catechumenate, and small Christian communities.

At the same time, comprehensive organization for catechesis must include extra-parochial or inter-parochial efforts. Beyond the single parish, or as a cooperative venture among neighboring parishes, catechesis should be offered to children and youth in Catholic elementary and secondary schools that are not connected to a single parish. Organized catechetical programs for persons with disabilities should be provided on the most effective level: parochial, regional, or diocesan. On the diocesan level, seminarians, college students, and those involved in ministry in higher education should have the opportunity for basic and continuing catechetical training and formation. In addition, other groups of people in other settings, such as daycare centers, nursing homes, and professional organizations, should be incorporated into the diocesan, regional, or parochial organization for catechesis.

Careful consideration should also be given to the possibility of combining catechetical programs in smaller parishes, particularly if they share a single pastor or are planning to do so in the future. Smaller parishes are encouraged to share the services of a competent and qualified catechetical leader to ensure that the catechetical programs in the smaller parishes nevertheless have the benefit of sound catechetical planning, organization, and direction.

A. Parish-Based
Organization for Catechesis

1. Catechetical Programs for Adults

Effective organization for adult catechesis depends in great measure on the quality and structure of parish life. Pastors are responsible for ensuring that realistic catechetical opportunities for adults of all ages are readily available to them as part of the total parish catechetical plan. The pastor should clearly demonstrate his personal commitment to lifelong learning and growth in the Christian faith. He should model mature adult faith for his parishioners and make adult catechesis a priority in the parish. If the parish has a pastoral staff, he should make certain that each member of the staff shares his commitment to adult catechesis. Along with the other pastoral leaders in the parish, the pastor should establish parish policies and procedures that give priority to adult catechesis, provide adequate financial resources, provide space and time for adult catechesis, and encourage adults to participate in the catechetical programs offered.[779] Bishops and pastors need to match the rhetoric of the universal Church, the U.S. Church, and our diocesan Churches with personnel and budget adequate for this task.

While the pastor may never abdicate his responsibility, he may choose to designate an adult catechetical leader in the parish whose primary responsibility is to implement parish policies and procedures for adult catechesis. This person could be the parish director of religious education,

---

779   Cf. OHWB, nos. 127-134.

another member of the parish staff, or another person prepared for leadership in adult catechesis. Whether the parish adult catechetical leader is an employee or volunteer, he or she should be qualified and competent, be familiar with the Church's major catechetical documents, and have the time, energy, and commitment for leadership in adult catechesis. The position of the adult catechetical leader should be clearly visible within the parish organizational structure. In order to ensure a unified parish catechetical program, the adult catechetical leader should collaborate closely with the parish director of religious education and report to the person who is most directly responsible for total parish catechesis.[780]

In addition to an adult catechetical leader, the parish should have a team of parishioners committed to and responsible for adult catechesis. This adult catechetical team could take the form of an adult catechesis commission or committee. It should be made up of representatives from all major parish demographic and cultural groups. The role of the adult catechetical team is to plan, implement, and evaluate adult catechesis in the parish. The team functions under the direction of the pastor, the adult faith formation leader, and the supervision of the parish director of religious education and in harmony with the persons, parish commissions, or committees responsible for other aspects of parish catechesis.[781]

Parishes should provide catechists specifically trained to hand the faith on to adults—engaging them in dialogue and reflection on the Gospel and teachings of the Church. "Catechists of adults need to be people of faith with an evangelizing spirit, a zeal for God's kingdom, and a commitment to lifelong formation."[782] They should be able to accompany other adults on their journey of faith, to draw them more deeply into the Christian life, to guide them in Christian prayer, and to help them relate the truths of the Catholic faith to the circumstances of their everyday lives.[783] "There is a primary need for catechists who know how to work with families, persons, or groups with particular needs," such as those preparing for marriage, persons with disabilities, those who are poor or marginalized, and "those in irregular situations."[784]

Specific guidelines regarding adult catechesis can be found in Chapter 7.

---

780 Cf. OHWB, nos. 135-141.
781 Cf. OHWB, nos. 142-148.
782 OHWB, no. 150.
783 Cf. OHWB, nos. 149-153.
784 *Adult Catechesis in the Christian Community*, no. 74.

2. Family-Centered Catechetical Programs

Many parishes offer family-centered catechetical programs within the total parish catechetical plan. All forms of organized family catechesis should flow from and lead back to the parish. Special attention needs to be given to the catechetical needs of interchurch families.[785] Catechesis can help strengthen the family bond of interchurch families through hospitality, including everyone in activities and encouraging them to celebrate what is held in common.

Within family-centered catechetical programs are opportunities for parents to catechize their children directly, for spouses to catechize each other, and for children to catechize one another and their parents. Family catechesis should include prayerful celebration within the family that is closely linked to the liturgical celebration of the parish. It should include opportunities for Christian service within the family and the neighborhood, which at the same time disposes the family members to render service in the name of Christ to the whole human family.

3. Home-Based Catechesis

As the primary educators of their children, parents have the right and the duty to choose the kind of educational environment that they determine best suits their children's educational needs. Therefore, home schooling is a viable option for the general education of children.

If Catholic parents choose to provide catechesis for the children in their home, that catechesis must be both complete and authentic. The bishop of the diocese, the pastor of the parish, the parents, and the children all have God-given responsibilities that must be respected in considering home-based catechesis. The home-based catechesis of children is a cooperative effort between the children, their parents, parish leadership, and the diocesan bishop. Parents who choose to be not only the primary educators of their children but also their catechists must adhere to all guidelines for catechists as outlined by the diocesan bishop.

Parents who choose to catechize their children at home should not feel alone in this task. They are part of the parish's total catechetical effort and should be welcomed in all parish catechetical program activities. Pastors in collaboration with parish catechetical leaders should provide the support,

---

785 Cf. *Directory for the Application of Principles and Norms on Ecumenism*, no. 151.

encouragement, and direction that parents need in order to ensure that they teach their children what the Church intends to be taught by providing parents with copies of the appropriate sections of the diocesan curriculum. Parents who would like to provide catechesis at home should make themselves known to the local pastor and consult with him or his delegate to ensure that the catechesis provided in the home is the catechesis of the Church. Dialogue between the pastor and the parents is essential to the complete and authentic catechesis of children in their homes.

All parents have an obligation to involve their children in the life and mission of the Church. Since their children are being initiated into the life of the Church, which is fundamentally realized in the local parish, parents who provide catechesis for their children in their homes should participate fully in the life of the local parish. They should celebrate the Sunday Eucharist in the local parish, involve themselves in its charitable works, and attend appropriate training and formation sessions the parish or diocese provides. Since the celebration of the sacraments continually integrates children into the Body of Christ, preparing children for reception of the sacraments should always be undertaken in collaboration with the local pastor and catechetical leader. These children should be encouraged to participate in non-instructional, preparatory activities of the parish peer group preparing for the sacrament. Parents who provide catechesis for their children in their homes can use those catechetical materials that have been approved by the diocesan bishop.

4. Catechetical Programs for Children

All parishes are to provide catechesis for children of all ages, whether they attend Catholic or public schools or are schooled at home. For those children who attend public schools, the parish should provide a comprehensive and systematic program of instruction and formation in the different dimensions of the Christian faith. For those children who attend a Catholic school, the comprehensive and systematic program of instruction and formation in the Christian faith should be clearly visible and at the same time be well integrated in the school's overall curriculum. These programs are intended not to supplant the role of parents as the primary educators of their children, but rather to support and enhance it. In fact, parental involvement in all parish catechetical programs for children is essential. General guidelines for the catechesis of children may be found in Chapter 7.

Catechesis should include education and formation in the inherent dignity of every person, in the Church's mission *ad gentes*, and in the development of a social conscience. It should provide opportunities to receive the sacraments and to participate in Christian service projects and missionary activities. It should foster in the students knowledge of and familiarity with the various vocations in the Church and encourage them to pray to know and embrace the vocation to which God has called them—priesthood, the consecrated life, the dedicated single life, or the married life.

All involved in parish catechetical ministry should foster the development of a Christian community among themselves and those being catechized. They should understand the state of continuous change in which children live, what they are exposed to, their different levels of belief or unbelief, and their searching, questioning, and doubting.[786] They should frequently celebrate the Eucharist, the Sacrament of Penance and Reconciliation, and other sacramental experiences together in order to express and strengthen their Catholic faith.

4a. Parish Catechetical Programs

Catechetical programs for children who attend public schools should be offered for preschool children as well as for children in the primary, intermediate, and junior and senior high grades. These programs should be coordinated with one another and integrated into the total parish catechetical plan. They should be adequately staffed with a parish director of catechesis who has been approved by the diocese, with other qualified and competent catechetical leaders, and with properly formed catechists. Since catechetical programs for children are among the top priorities of every Catholic parish, these programs should be allocated a sufficient amount of parish funds to achieve their goals. The Church "is bidden to offer catechesis her best resources in people and energy, without sparing effort, toil or material means, in order to organize it better and to train qualified personnel."[787]

Effective organization of parish catechetical programs for children should also include enthusiastic evangelization and recruitment efforts in order to reach families whose children do not participate in parish cate-

---

786   Cf. GDC, no. 75.
787   CT, no. 15.

chetical programs. Those responsible for parish catechetical programs for children should use every means available to remind parents of the importance of providing catechesis for their children and to invite them to place their children in parish programs that are designed to assist them in their responsibility. Public service announcements on radio, television, and the Internet; posters in supermarkets and gas stations; and warm personal invitations can be employed to reach out to parents who may be on the margins of the Church and have little or no understanding of either their duty to provide their children adequate catechesis or the Church's ability to assist them. Specific guidelines regarding children's catechesis can be found in Chapter 7.

4b. Catholic Schools

Catholic schools are vital to the Church's mission of evangelization and catechesis. They exist in order to educate the whole person: mind, body, and soul. They present the totality of the Catholic faith. Whether Catholic schools are part of a parish structure or are regional, diocesan, or private, growth in the Catholic faith for the children and young people who attend them is essential to their identity and purpose.

A parochial school is an integral part of the total parish catechetical plan. It is an evangelizing community within the larger evangelizing community that is the parish. A parochial school depends on the parish of which it is a part to provide the ecclesial vision for its particular participation in the Church's mission. As one of the components of the total catechetical effort of the parish, the parochial school should be in harmony with and complement the other catechetical programs offered by the parish. Similarly regional, diocesan, and private Catholic schools not affiliated with a specific parish should work in close collaboration with neighboring parishes.

The Catholic school should strive to integrate the Catholic faith into every aspect of its life. It seeks to relate all human culture to the news of salvation, so that the life of faith will illuminate the knowledge that students gradually gain of the world, of life, and of mankind.[788] In Catholic schools, children and young people can "experience learning and living fully integrated in the light of faith."[789]

---

788 Cf. GE, no. 8.
789 *To Teach as Jesus Did*, no. 103.

The Catholic school should have a clearly defined religion curriculum with specific goals and objectives that are in harmony with the parish catechetical plan and with the diocesan catechetical priorities. The principal and teachers should ensure that a specific part of each day is dedicated to religious instruction. It should be clear to the whole school community of parents, faculty and staff, students and parishioners that the teaching of the truths of the faith occupies a high priority within the school. In addition to classroom, grade-level, and all-school liturgical and prayer experiences, a generous amount of time should be allotted to religious instruction. The integration of religious truth and values with the rest of life is a hallmark of education in Catholic schools. This process should also be given adequate time in the curriculum and receive the proper guidance of skilled teachers. The Catholic school "must present the Christian message and the Christian event with the same seriousness and the same depth with which other disciplines present their knowledge."[790]

In many dioceses throughout the United States, Catholic schools have been beacons of hope for those who are poor in the goods of this world. The Church has made an enormous commitment in human and financial resources to make and keep Catholic schools accessible and affordable for disadvantaged families and children, especially in the impoverished areas of many urban centers. The parents and families of these children have also made heroic sacrifices to send their children to Catholic schools and keep them there as long as possible. Many of these children and their families are not Catholic, but the Church is determined to serve the human and social needs of the poor and to provide them a distinctively Catholic education, which includes a thorough and faithful catechesis. Many of these Catholic schools are genuine centers of evangelization that effectively proclaim the Gospel to those who have never heard it before as well as to those who have heard it but have not been moved by it to transform their lives. Unfortunately, too many Catholic schools have had to close due to lack of sufficient funds and enrollment. Dioceses should continue to make every effort to keep Catholic schools open, accessible, and affordable, especially for the poor.

---

790   GDC, no. 73.

5. Youth Catechesis

Of all the stages of human development, adolescence is the most difficult to define. Different cultural, racial, and ethnic factors mean that some children enter adolescence earlier than others, some periods of adolescence are longer than others, and some adolescents mature earlier than others. In general, youth catechesis is directed to adolescents from about the age of eleven or twelve years to about the age of eighteen or nineteen. In each of these situations, however, adolescent catechesis is most effective when situated within a comprehensive program of youth ministry that includes social, liturgical, and catechetical components as well as opportunities for service. "If we are to succeed, we must offer young people a *spiritually challenging* and *world-shaping vision* that meets their hunger for the chance to *participate in a worthy adventure*."[791] Whether the young people attend Catholic or public high schools, they should be welcomed into the parish program of youth ministry.

The organization of catechesis for young people should be guided by their need to hear the Gospel proclaimed, to pray and to celebrate the Holy Mass, to form a Christian community, to live the Christian life, and to serve the needs of others. It should "provide concrete ways by which the demands, excitement, and adventure of being a disciple of Jesus Christ can be personally experienced by adolescents."[792] Catechesis for young people should speak to their minds, their hearts, and their souls to enkindle faith in Jesus Christ, zeal for his Gospel, and enthusiasm for Christian living. Those who plan parish catechetical programs for young people should make special efforts to reach out to those Catholic junior high and high school students in the parish who do not regularly participate in the life of the parish. Guidelines for the catechesis of youth may be found in Chapter 7.

The pastor should be personally involved in the catechesis of the young people in his parish and provide support and encouragement for those more directly involved in handing on the faith to them. He should demonstrate the priority of youth catechesis in the parish by selecting and adequately compensating a qualified and competent person to coordinate parish youth catechesis. An adequate number of catechists specially trained to work with young people and a budget sufficient to provide a

---

791   *Renewing the Vision*, 10.
792   *Renewing the Vision*, 10-11.

comprehensive, systematic, and attractive program are essential for an effective parish catechetical program for young people.

6. The Baptismal Catechumenate

The baptismal catechumenate is a vital component in the organization of catechesis in the parish. Because it provides a gradual process for new members to be initiated into the life and practice of the Catholic faith, it should be the cornerstone of the parish catechetical plan. The baptismal catechumenate is especially suited to the spiritual journey of adults because they freely choose to cooperate with God's grace and with the action of the Church as they proceed through the period of inquiry and maturation. It is "a typical *locus* of catechesis, instituted by the Church to prepare adults, who desire to become Christians and to receive the Sacraments of Christian initiation."[793] More specific information and guidelines regarding the baptismal catechumenate may be found in Chapter 5.

In the period of the catechumenate, the faithful should make the message of Christ known by actively participating, especially in the liturgical life of the parish, and by welcoming catechumens into the parish community, into personal conversations, and into their own homes. During the liturgical celebrations that mark the stages of Christian initiation, the faithful should make every effort to be present and take an active part. On the day of election, the faithful should be willing to give testimony about the catechumens. During the period of purification and enlightenment, the faithful should participate in the rites of the scrutinies and presentations and give the elect the good example of their own continual conversion to Christ. At the Easter Vigil, the faithful should proudly and publicly renew their own baptismal promises. And during the period immediately following the Baptism of the elect, the faithful should attend the Sunday Masses of the Easter season prepared especially for the neophytes and make them feel at home in the community of the baptized.[794]

Some members of the Christian faithful exercise particular roles in the baptismal catechumenate. Sponsors present the candidates for acceptance as catechumens. Godparents accompany the candidates on the day of election, at the celebration of the sacraments of initiation, and during the

---

793   GDC, no. 256.
794   Cf. RCIA, no. 9.

period of post-baptismal catechesis, or mystagogy. Catechists provide catechumens, according to their particular needs and abilities, with instruction and formation in the faith and in the obligations of the Christian life.

Either in person or through his delegate, the diocesan bishop establishes, regulates, and promotes the program of pastoral formation for all those involved in the baptismal catechumenate. He also formally admits the candidates to their election and to the sacraments of initiation.

Priests should provide a welcoming environment for those searching for Christ to find a home in the parish. They are to provide pastoral and personal care for the catechumens. As much as possible, they ensure the pastoral priority of the baptismal catechumenate in the parish catechetical plan. "With the help of deacons and catechists, they are to provide instruction for the catechumens; they are also to approve the choice of godparents and willingly listen to and help them; they are to be diligent in the correct celebration and adaptation of the rites throughout the entire course of Christian initiation."[795] Deacons are to be ready to assist at all stages of the baptismal catechumenate.

The catechetical plan of the parish also needs to include the process of initiation for candidates for full communion who are already baptized. The content and rites of such a process should take account of the particular circumstances, experience, knowledge, and Christian practice of each individual.[796]

7. Small Christian Communities

Many parishes include small Christian communities, which arise because the faithful want to "live the Church's life more intensely, or from the desire and quest for a more human dimension such as larger ecclesial communities can only offer with difficulty."[797] Small Christian communities are important centers for the cultivation of both Christian virtues and human values. They often provide opportunities for the faithful to experience a more intense communion. To be authentic, however, "every community must live in union with the particular and the universal Church, in heartfelt communion with the Church's Pastors and the Magisterium, with a

---

795   RCIA, no. 13.
796   Cf. *Directory for the Application of Principles and Norms on Ecumenism*, no. 99-100.
797   EN, no. 58.

commitment to missionary outreach and without yielding to isolationism or ideological exploitation."[798]

Because small Christian communities provide a particularly fruitful climate for adult catechesis, the catechesis offered in them should be integrated with the other elements of the parish catechetical plan, be supervised by the pastor of the parish, and be in harmony with the catechesis of the universal Church. Catechetical leaders and catechists within small Christian communities should meet the same standards for their respective responsibilities that are set by the diocese for other parish catechetical leaders and catechists. Catechetical materials used in small Christian communities should be approved by the diocese. The goal of all of the Church's evangelical and catechetical activity is to deepen the experience of the Christian life for those to whom the Gospel is proclaimed. This should be especially true of the catechesis provided within small Christian communities.

B. Organization for Catechesis Outside the Parish

While the parish remains the primary setting for catechesis, the organization of the Church's catechetical mission encompasses several structures that are beyond the boundaries of a single parish. For example, some Catholic schools are not connected to one parish. Whether a Catholic school is inter-parochial, regional, diocesan, or private, education in the faith is central to its mission. In all these situations, each Catholic school should work in close collaboration with parishes from which its students come. In every case, the catechetical instruction and formation of the students and faculty should be undertaken in collaboration with the local pastors and with the oversight of the diocesan bishop. Catechetical resources and materials used in these non-parochial settings should be approved by the diocese.

In addition to these examples of structured catechetical programs, the Church's organization for catechesis includes catechetical programs for persons with disabilities and catechetical programs in seminaries, in colleges and universities, in campus ministry, and in several special structures, as are detailed later in this section.

---

798   RM, no. 51.

1. Catechesis for Persons with Disabilities

Organization for catechesis for persons with disabilities should begin with (1) a careful determination of the number of Catholic persons in the community who have disabilities, and (2) a thorough assessment of their catechetical needs. A parish often has more Catholic persons with disabilities than is generally known. Every parish should seek out its parishioners with cognitive, emotional, and physical disabilities, support them with love and concern, and ensure that they have ready access to a catechetical program suited to their needs and abilities. Many persons with disabilities are self-sufficient; others reside with their families, and still others live in institutions and group homes in the parish and are unable to come to the parish church and participate in parish activities. Special efforts must be made to welcome all persons with disabilities into the life of the parish, especially its sacramental life. Bringing Holy Communion to persons with disabilities, making pastoral visits, and using various means of communication to keep them informed of parish life are just a few of the many ways to ensure their inclusion.[799]

The pastor or pastors of the parishes in which catechetical programs for persons with disabilities are being offered should delegate a person to coordinate the individual programs for each category of persons with disabilities. They should share their resources to support the programs and to maximize their effectiveness and efficiency. Those involved in catechetical programs for persons with disabilities should receive appropriate training for their particular responsibilities and have opportunities for continuing education and spiritual development. All those who provide catechetical programs for persons with disabilities should take great care to avoid isolating them through these programs, which—as much as possible—should be integrated with the other catechetical activities of the parish, region, or diocese. Families of some persons with disabilities are their primary catechists and thus should also receive special pastoral consideration and direction so that they can cooperate in the catechetical program with confidence and competence. Further guidelines for the catechesis of persons with disabilities may be found in Chapter 7.

---

799 Cf. *Guidelines for the Celebration of the Sacraments with Persons with Disabilities*, 4.

2. Catechetical Preparation in Seminaries

Priests are vital catechetical leaders by virtue of their ordination. They exercise pivotal roles in the catechetical programs of the parishes and institutions to which they are assigned. In addition, they are often called upon to provide training and formation for catechists. It follows that seminarians need a thorough understanding of the nature, mission, goals, and scope of catechesis as well as the multiplicity of catechetical responsibilities that will be theirs as priests.

The Second Vatican Council's *Decree on Priestly Formation* underscores the importance of catechetical training for seminarians. "A sacred minister's learning ought to be sacred in the sense of being derived from a sacred source and directed to a sacred purpose."[800] In harmony with the aforementioned document, the document *Program of Priestly Formation* indicates that "in addition to the principles of biblical interpretation, catechesis, and communications theory, seminarians should also learn those practical skills needed to communicate the Gospel in an effective and appropriate manner."[801]

The catechetical preparation of seminarians should be carried out in collaboration with the personnel of the diocesan offices that have responsibility for catechesis and should recommend or require seminarians to take a course or courses in catechetics, to participate in a supervised catechetical internship, and to have personal pastoral experience as a catechist. Seminarians are encouraged to attend catechetical workshops, conferences, and congresses.

3. Catechetical Preparation in Catholic Colleges and Universities

It is vitally important that Catholic institutions of higher education initiate and maintain strong programs in both theology and catechetics. Catholics who teach Catholic theology in Catholic colleges and universities have the responsibility to seek the *mandatum* from the diocesan bishop.[802] As centers

---

800 PO, no. 19.

801 USCCB, *Program of Priestly Formation*, 4th ed. (Washington, D.C.: USCCB, 1993), no. 377.

802 Cf. John Paul II, *Ex corde Ecclesiae* (ECE) (Washington, D.C.: USCCB, 1990); USCCB, *The Application of Ex corde Ecclesiae for the United States* (Washington, D.C.: USCCB, 1999); and USCCB, *Guidelines Concerning the Academic Mandatum in Catholic Universities* (Washington, D.C.: USCCB, 2001).

of authentic Catholic theology, Catholic colleges and universities should, as much as possible, provide undergraduate and graduate programs in Catholic theology, catechesis, and related fields for those preparing for professional careers in catechetical ministry.

Undergraduate programs in Catholic universities should provide degree programs in catechetics, Sacred Scripture, and systematic theology; "the requirements for such degrees should be as demanding as those for any other academic discipline."[803] As much as possible, members of the undergraduate faculty should be available to the parishes and institutions of the diocese as important resource persons in theology and catechetics.

Graduate programs should provide advanced degree programs and post-degree experiences for catechetical leaders who are preparing for professional careers in catechetical ministry. They should serve as centers for catechetical research and should collaborate with diocesan personnel to establish academic qualifications for professional leadership. "They should be interdisciplinary, offering advanced courses in theology, scripture, Liturgy, catechetics, communications, parish administration, and related sacred and human sciences."[804] The theologies, liturgies, and forms of spirituality of the Eastern Churches should not be neglected in these programs, since knowledge of them enriches the student's understanding of the universal Church.

Catholic universities should also provide opportunities for individual courses, certificate programs, institutes, workshops, seminars, and conferences in catechetics. Graduate and undergraduate faculty and administration should collaborate closely with diocesan catechetical personnel not just in the diocese in which the Catholic college or university is located, but also with those in neighboring dioceses. Together they can decide on a core curriculum for those wishing to prepare for service as catechetical leaders, catechists, Catholic school principals or religion teachers. They can work together to provide scholarship funds in order to encourage and facilitate theological study by the economically disadvantaged, those from diverse cultures, and those intending to work with persons with disabilities. They can also collaborate in providing programs for continuing adult faith formation.

---

803 *National Catechetical Directory*, no. 242.
804 *National Catechetical Directory*, no. 242.

4. Organization for Catechesis in Ministry in Higher Education

The Catholic university is a primary place where faith, culture, and reason intersect. As an integral part of its educational mission, the Church has fostered the development of the academic life and has affirmed the university as a place of learning which seeks the truth. The Church respects the legitimate autonomy of the academic community and sees the university as partner in building a better society in which all people have the opportunity to realize their full potential. Fruitful cooperation between the Church and the university continues to be a cornerstone of a civil society that seeks the common good.

The Church's support for higher education has been shown not only in the establishment of Catholic colleges and universities, but also in the development and maintenance of a dynamic presence at secular and private institutions. That presence is campus ministry. "Campus ministry can be defined as the public presence and service through which properly prepared baptized persons are empowered by the Spirit to use their talents and gifts on behalf of the Church in order to be a sign and instrument of the kingdom in the academic worlds."[805]

Whatever forms it takes, campus ministry brings the Catholics within the university community together for prayer, worship, study, and opportunities for service so that they can grow in and fully live the Catholic faith. Goals of campus ministry on university campuses include the following:

- To form students to become theologically educated and to thus prepare them to serve as catechists, liturgists, social justice advocates, and teachers in Catholic schools
- To promote theological study and reflection on the religious nature of the human person so that intellectual, moral, and spiritual growth can proceed together
- To sustain a Christian community on campus, with the pastoral care and liturgical worship it requires
- To integrate its apostolic ministry with other ministries of the local community and the diocese

---

805 *Empowered by the Spirit*, no. 21.

- To prepare students to be evangelizers who are able to bring the light of the Gospel to the culture through their Christian witness and personal morality
- To help students to discern their vocation within the life of the Church[806]

On the diocesan level, campus ministry needs the support and guidance of a diocesan director of campus ministry who is appointed by the bishop. "The director can help facilitate their personal growth, call for a proper accountability, and possible diocesan-wide programming. As the diocesan bishop's representative, the director encourages the interaction among campus ministers in the diocese who serve on public, Catholic, and other private campuses."[807]

Campus ministry is a vital component of the diocesan evangelical and catechetical mission; as such, it should be integrated into the diocesan organization and plan; and it should work in close collaboration with the parishes from which the students come and the youth ministry programs in which they have participated. The diocesan bishop should ensure that pastoral care is provided at non-Catholic colleges and universities and should appoint, as much as possible, qualified personnel as campus ministers. He should try to provide adequate funding for their operation and ensure payment of just salaries in order to attract and retain campus ministers with experience and academic qualifications. It would be helpful to work with benefactors and administrators in order to fund chairs of Catholic thought at secular institutions. If that is not possible, he might consider hiring campus ministers with doctoral degrees who can teach occasional courses in philosophy, ethics, or religious studies on the secular campus.

In general, all campus ministry is characterized by innovative programming and a diversity in organization, style, and approach. Our statement *Empowered by the Spirit* contains excellent specific recommendations regarding the aspects of campus ministry, as well as strategies to achieve those aspects.[808]

---

806   Cf. *To Teach as Jesus Did*, no. 67.
807   *Empowered by the Spirit*, no. 32.
808   Cf. *Empowered by the Spirit*, nos. 34-102.

5. Other Catechetical Structures

Because all the baptized have a right to catechesis, parishes, dioceses, and other church structures are to provide realistic opportunities to receive instruction and formation in the faith for those in special groups and settings. Early childhood education, daycare, and after-school programs offered by the Church, whether or not they take place in Catholic schools, should include a catechetical dimension. Convalescent and nursing homes, residential facilities for persons with physical, mental, or emotional disabilities, and schools for the deaf or blind should include specialized catechetical programs for the residents. Catholic chaplains assigned by the bishop to these centers and facilities should ensure that specially trained catechists are available to bring the Good News of salvation in Jesus Christ to the particular groups in ways suited to their needs and abilities. Those catechists should work closely with the chaplains to design a program of catechesis that integrates the content of the Christian message with the liturgical, moral, and prayer life of the Church. Diocesan and parish catechetical staff should assist these catechists and chaplains as much as possible and provide the vital link between the catechetical plan of the residential facility or center and the catechetical plan of the diocese.

A number of movements and associations in the United States emphasize a particular grace, charism, or apostolic work in the Church. They bring men and women together who seek to pray, to worship, to work for social justice, and to grow in the faith. Ordinarily their purpose is "to help the disciples of Jesus Christ to fulfill their lay mission in the world and in the Church."[809] They often provide opportunities for religious devotion and apostolic service. Formation of the faithful involved in these associations and movements should develop the fundamental aspects of the Christian life and always include catechesis. That catechesis should be true to the proper nature of catechesis and include the presentation of fundamental Catholic doctrine, the celebration of Catholic worship, and the encouragement of Catholic witness. Such catechesis will facilitate the achievement of the objectives of the various associations and movements. "Education in the spirituality proper to a particular movement or association enriches the Church and is a natural continuation of the basic formation received by all Christians."[810]

---

809   GDC, no. 261.
810   GDC, no. 262.

Since membership in associations and movements is not an alternative to parish life, the leaders of these movements and associations should encourage their adherents and members to participate actively in their parishes. The leaders of movements, associations, groups, and societies should always make the bishop aware of their presence in the diocese. Local pastors should become actively involved with them. And the diocesan catechetical staff should assist them as much as possible to ensure that the Christian message is presented completely and authentically in the catechesis of the members of associations and movements.

Hospitals, professional groups, police and fire departments, fraternities and sororities, and prisons provide opportune settings especially for adult catechesis. As much as possible, the bishop should assign chaplains to such groups so that the opportunities for catechesis can be properly developed and supervised. Diocesan catechetical personnel should maintain contact with the chaplains so that the catechesis offered in these situations can be integrated with the diocesan catechetical plan.

62. REGIONAL COOPERATION AND NATIONAL ASSOCIATIONS

Regional and interdiocesan cooperation in catechesis has several important benefits. It brings together proximate geographical regions of the Church that often share common pastoral concerns. It provides the opportunity to develop and coordinate regional responses to those concerns. It provides a forum in which dioceses can combine catechetical resources and assist one another. It helps to broaden and deepen the insights of those involved in regional consultation. And, when necessary, it offers the Church the advantage of speaking in a common voice across diocesan boundaries.

Bishops should determine the advisability and set the parameters of such regional cooperation; and diocesan catechetical personnel, parish catechetical leaders, catechists, and parents should be involved. Such planned coordination promotes mutual assistance and fosters the development of regional organizations and associations that can provide catechetical services and disseminate information through regional catechetical conferences, congresses, and institutes or through catechetical societies that are not available in a single diocese. Given the significance of public policy decisions for the effective operation of diocesan educational and catechetical plans, there should be a close relationship between diocesan educational and catechetical personnel and their respective state Catholic conference.

In addition, several independent national organizations and associations provide catechetical services and information to their members. Diocesan and parish catechetical personnel should be aware of these national associations and organizations and the services offered so that they make use of their assistance and resources as needed.

63. THE SERVICE OF THE UNITED STATES CONFERENCE OF CATHOLIC BISHOPS

The *Code of Canon Law* indicates that "the conference of bishops can establish a catechetical office whose primary function is to assist individual dioceses in catechetical matters."[811] The *General Catechetical Directory* states that a conference of bishops should have a permanent structure to promote catechetics on the national level. The United States Conference of Catholic Bishops has established a standing Committee on Catechesis within its permanent structure and has provided personnel and adequate resources for its effective operation. The Committee on Catechesis and its staff have a twofold task:

- "To serve the catechetical needs of the country as a whole. The effort here would extend to publications of national importance, national congresses, relations with the mass media, and generally all those works and projects which are beyond the powers of individual dioceses and regions
- "To serve dioceses and regions by publicizing catechetical ideas and undertakings, by coordinating action, and by giving assistance to those dioceses that are less advanced in catechetical matters"[812]

In addition, the bishops' national catechetical office may coordinate its efforts with other catechetical institutes or cooperate with catechetical activities at the international level if the episcopal conference so determines.

---

811   CIC, c. 775 §3; cf. CCEO, c. 622.
812   *General Catechetical Directory*, no. 128.

64. THE SERVICE OF THE HOLY SEE

The Successor of Peter has the primary responsibility to proclaim and transmit the Gospel of Jesus Christ to the ends of the earth. The pope exercises this ministry principally through his teaching office. In issues regarding catechesis, he "acts in an immediate and particular way through the Congregation for [the] Clergy, which assists 'the Roman Pontiff in the exercise of his supreme pastoral office.'"[813]

The Congregation for the Clergy has several catechetical functions:

- To promote the religious education of the Christian faithful of all ages and conditions
- To issue timely norms so that catechetical lessons be conducted according to a proper program
- To maintain a watchful attention to the suitable delivery of catechetical instruction
- To grant, with the assent of the Congregation of the Doctrine of the Faith, the prescribed approbation of the Holy See for catechisms and other writings pertaining to catechetical instruction
- To be available to catechetical offices and international initiatives on religious education, coordinate their activities, and, where necessary, lend assistance[814]

65. CONCLUSION

The Church is faithful to her deepest identity when she brings all her considerable resources to bear on proclaiming the Christian message completely and authentically to all the nations. The presentation of the Gospel requires the best efforts of the Church at every level and the tireless dedication of the entire community of the faithful. Apostles, prophets, evangelists, pastors, and teachers prepare the baptized for the work of ministry, for building up the Body of Christ, so that the Church reaches unity of faith, knowledge of the Son of God, and mature adulthood in the fullness of Jesus Christ.[815]

---

813   GDC, no. 270.
814   GDC, no. 271.
815   Cf. Eph 4:11-14.

National, regional, diocesan, and parish catechetical structures embody Christ's apostolic commission to go, make disciples, baptize, and teach in practical forms, functions, organizations, policies, and procedures. They are essential if the Church is to be faithful to her mission in the world.

This chapter has described the shared but differentiated responsibilities within the Church's catechetical mission. It provided the fundamental priniciples for the organization of the ministry of catechesis. The next chapter addresses catechetical resources.

CHAPTER 10

Resources for Catechesis

Every scribe who has been instructed in the kingdom of heaven is like the head of a household who brings from his storeroom both the new and the old. (Mt 13:52)

66. INTRODUCTION

Called by the Holy Spirit, inspired by the dynamism of Christ's compelling mission, and sent by the Church, catechists make Christ and his Church known, loved, and followed by faithful disciples and by those who do not yet know him. They bring the word of God to adults, young people, and children in a variety of settings in thousands of parishes and institutions throughout the United States. By the grace of God, in their very persons they make the Gospel incarnate in different cultures and introduce the different cultures into the community of the faithful. They facilitate the encounter God initiates with every person. The heart of the catechist speaks the word of God to the heart of the one being catechized. Into their hearts, by the power of the Holy Spirit, the Father and the Son will come to make their dwelling.[816]

The service of catechists to God and to the Church is truly irreplaceable. No catechetical materials, resources, or tools—no matter how excellent—can replace the catechist. Dioceses and parishes must provide high-quality catechist formation programs that present the faith in a comprehensive, systematic, and sequential manner. But sound catechetical resources, "both new and old," in the hands of faithful and skilled catechists can be powerful instruments in the proclamation of the Gospel and in fostering growth in faith. Catechetical resources are many and varied.

---

816   Cf. Jn 14:23.

They include Sacred Scripture, the Church's official documents and catechisms, catechetical textbooks and other instructional materials, multimedia resources, and the various means of telecommunications technology.

This chapter provides principles, guidelines, and criteria for those
developing and producing catechetical resources, as well as for those who
are charged with selecting, evaluating, and using them in various catechetical settings.

67. RESOURCES IN GENERAL

A. Sacred Scripture

Sacred Scripture, the word of God written under the inspiration of the
Holy Spirit, has a preeminent position in the life of the Church and especially in the ministry of evangelization and catechesis. The earliest forms
of Christian catechesis made regular use of the Old Testament and the
personal witness of the apostles and disciples that would become the New
Testament. Much of the catechesis in the Patristic period took the form
of commentary on the word of God contained in Sacred Scripture.
Through all the ages of the Church, study of Sacred Scripture has been
the cornerstone of catechesis. The Second Vatican Council advised that
catechesis, as one form of the ministry of the word, should be nurtured
and should thrive in holiness through the word of Scripture.[817] Catechesis
should take Sacred Scripture as its inspiration, its fundamental curriculum, and its end because it strengthens faith, nourishes the soul, and nurtures the spiritual life. "Scripture provides the starting point, foundation,
and norm of catechetical teaching."[818]

Catechesis should assume the thought and perspective of Sacred
Scripture and make frequent, direct use of the biblical texts themselves.
"The presentation of the gospels should be done in such a way as to elicit
an encounter with Christ, who provides the key to the whole biblical
revelation and communicates the call of God that summons each one
to respond."[819]

---

817   Cf. DV, no. 10.
818   *The Interpretation of the Bible in the Church*, 39.
819   *The Interpretation of the Bible in the Church*, 39.

Sacred Scripture is also the primary source in the explanation of the word of God that is a central function of catechesis. Catechesis rooted in Sacred Scripture should

- "Initiate a person in a correct understanding and fruitful reading of the Bible"[820]
- Be "an authentic introduction to *lectio divina*, that is, to a reading of the Sacred Scriptures done in accordance to the Spirit who dwells in the Church"[821]
- "Bring about the discovery of the divine truth it contains and evoke as generous a response as is possible to the message God addresses through his word to the whole human race"[822]
- "Proceed from the historical context of divine revelation so as to present persons and events of the Old and New Testaments in the light of God's overall plan"[823]
- "Make particular use of stories, both those of the New Testament and those of the Old"[824]
- "Single out the Decalogue"[825]
- "Make use of the prophetic oracles, the wisdom teaching, and the great discourses in the gospels such as the Sermon on the Mount"[826]

B. *Catechism of the Catholic Church*

The *Catechism of the Catholic Church* is the authoritative contemporary expression of the living Tradition of the Church and a basic source of wisdom for all catechetical activity. It is a re-presentation of the deposit of faith in today's world in the light of more than two thousand years of lived Christian experience. Catechetical leaders and catechists can find in the *Catechism* an important summary of the teachings of the Church. It is normative for the composition of all catechetical materials and resources used in catechesis. All who are responsible for instruction in the Christian faith and formation in the Christian life can see in the *Catechism* a

---

820 *Message to the People of God* (October 27, 1977).
821 *Message to the People of God* (October 27, 1977).
822 *The Interpretation of the Bible in the Church*, 39.
823 *The Interpretation of the Bible in the Church*, 39.
824 *The Interpretation of the Bible in the Church*, 39.
825 *The Interpretation of the Bible in the Church*, 39.
826 *The Interpretation of the Bible in the Church*, 39.

reliable guide for their efforts. They can look to it for a systematic and authentic presentation of the teaching of the Church.[827] In summary, the *Catechism of the Catholic Church* is a basic resource for all catechetical activity, whether offered informally by parents in their homes or formally by professional catechists in organized catechetical programs.

C. Local Catechisms

"Among the aids available to catechesis, catechisms excel all others."[828] Episcopal conferences are encouraged to prepare local catechisms that are faithful to the essential content of Revelation, employ sound catechetical methodologies, and are adapted to social, cultural, ethnic, and religious situations of those for whom they are intended.[829] One of the primary aims of the *Catechism of the Catholic Church* is to assist the bishops and the Christian faithful in the preparation of local catechisms.[830]

The *Catechism of the Catholic Church* "does not set out to provide the adaptation of doctrinal presentations and catechetical methods required by the differences of culture, age, spiritual maturity, and social and ecclesial condition among all those to whom it is addressed."[831] Those "indispensable adaptations"[832] are precisely the responsibility of local catechisms. Local catechisms "take into account various situations and cultures, while carefully preserving the unity of faith and catholic doctrine."[833] Local catechisms are prepared or approved by diocesan bishops for use in their diocese or by the United States Conference of Catholic Bishops for use in the dioceses of the United States. Consequently, local catechisms, along with the *Catechism of the Catholic Church*, are the most reliable catechetical resources and should be the primary references for the development of other catechetical resources.

Local catechisms, moreover, are invaluable instruments of catechesis because they communicate the universal truths of the faith in ways that relate to the individual human person immersed in a particular cultural

---

827   Cf. *The Interpretation of the Bible in the Church*, 39.

828   GDC, no. 284.

829   Cf. CT, no. 50.

830   Cf. FD, no. 3.

831   CCC, no. 24.

832   CCC, no. 24.

833   FD, no. 3.

context. They present the synthesis of faith with reference to the particular culture of the people to whom the catechesis is directed. "This kind of adaptation and preaching of the revealed word must ever be the law of all evangelization."[834]

A local catechism may be prepared by an individual bishop for use within his diocese and published by him in accord with the norms of the Church.[835] Catechisms published by the conference of bishops for their territory require the prior approval of the Holy See.[836]

68. CATECHETICAL TEXTBOOKS AND OTHER INSTRUCTIONAL MATERIALS

A. Catechetical Textbooks

Catechetical textbooks are among the tools for learning placed directly in the hands of catechumens and those being catechized. In the United States, catechetical textbooks for children and young people are ordinarily part of an integrated series that has been prepared for a number of grade levels, usually preschool or kindergarten through sixth or eighth grade. In addition, high school texts address core components of the faith in a variety of formats. Catechetical materials for adults most often take the form of adult catechisms or resources for the baptismal catechumenate, for parish renewal, and for small Christian communities. All catechetical textbooks should

- Present the authentic message of Christ and his Church, adapted to the capacity of the learners and in language that can be understood by them
- Be faithful to the Sacred Scripture
- Highlight the essential truths of the faith, giving proper emphasis to particular truths in accord with their importance within the hierarchy of truths
- Be in conformity with the *Catechism of the Catholic Church*
- Be approved by the local bishop

---

834   GS, no. 44.
835   Cf. CIC, c. 775 §1; GDC, no. 266d.
836   Cf. CIC, c. 775 §2; GDC, nos. 270, 271, 284, 285.

- Give to those who use them a better knowledge of the mysteries of Christ
- Promote a true conversion to Jesus Christ
- Inspire and encourage those who use them to live the Christian life more faithfully
- Be culturally appropriate and reflect the real-life situations of those who use them
- Promote charity, appreciation, and respect for persons of all racial, ethnic, social, and religious backgrounds
- Present other ecclesial communities and religions accurately
- Employ a variety of sound catechetical methodologies based on the results of responsible catechetical research
- Include appropriate examples of Christian prayer and opportunities for liturgical experiences and incorporate the use of Sacred Scripture as a text for study along with other catechetical textbooks
- Offer short passages of Sacred Scripture that can easily be learned by heart
- Contain opportunities to review and measure progress in learning
- Be visually attractive, engage the students, and incorporate a variety of examples of Christian art
- Include graphics that represent the various regional, cultural, economic, and religious characteristics of the people who will be using them
- Engage the intellect, emotion, imagination, and creativity of the students

Increasing numbers of Catholics need catechetical materials in languages other than English. These materials are most effectively developed by native speakers of those languages who know the respective cultures and who also have catechetical expertise. It is ordinarily not sufficient merely to translate catechetical materials prepared for English speakers into the languages of those being catechized.

Wherever appropriate, special materials for use in the catechesis of persons with disabilities should be developed by professionals in the respective fields of special education in collaboration with those familiar with the languages and cultures of the persons with the specific disabilities.

Catechist and teacher manuals are essential components of any sound catechetical textbook series. Fundamentally, they should communicate to catechists and teachers what they themselves are expected to communicate to the students. Catechists and teachers manuals should contain "an explanation of the message of salvation (constant references must be made to the sources, and a clear distinction must be kept between those things which pertain to the faith and to the doctrine that must be held, and those things which are mere opinions of theologians); psychological and pedagogical advice; suggestions about methods."[837]

B. Other Instructional Materials

Other instructional materials include catechetical guides for program leaders and catechists, parent education materials, resources for the baptismal catechumenate and marriage, and other sacramental preparation materials.

Supplementary educational resources for program leaders provide a helpful overview of the catechetical plan and practical suggestions for achieving its objectives. Supplementary materials for catechists should enrich their knowledge of the curriculum and strengthen their ability to adapt individual program objectives to the capacity of the students.

Catechetical textbook series should also include materials specifically designed to assist parents in their roles as the primary catechists of their children. Those materials should be geared directly to the parents and provide them with both the information and the practical tools to reinforce the objectives of the catechesis their children are receiving.

It is important that resources prepared specifically for sacramental preparation be well integrated into a basic catechetical textbook series and include materials for students, catechists, and parents. Textbooks are to prepare students for Confession and are to include the directive that this sacrament be received prior to First Holy Communion. They should present the sacraments as effective signs of God's grace that incorporate the Christian into the Paschal Mystery of Jesus Christ as it is remembered and celebrated in his Church. The content of these texts should include what has been previously articulated in Chapter 5, "Guidelines in a Worshiping Community."[838] Practical suggestions for parents to engage their children in preparation for their reception of the sacraments and for their continual participation in the sacramental life of the Church should be included. This is also true for background materials that set forth the

---

837 *General Catechetical Directory*, no. 121.
838 Cf. Section 35-C of this *Directory*, "Catechetical Guidelines for Celebration of the Sacraments."

Church's principles for ecumenical formation and the results of specific dialogues between the Church and other ecclesial communities.

Catechetical materials designed for use by those in the baptismal catechumenate and those preparing for full communion with the Catholic Church should present the structure of the initiation of adults, its offices and ministries, the time and place of initiation, and the possible adaptations of the Roman ritual as set forth in the *Rite of Christian Initiation of Adults.*

All these instructional materials should be in evident harmony with the *Catechism of the Catholic Church* and be artistically sensitive, technically up to date, theologically authentic, ecumenically accurate, and methodologically sound.

69. COMMUNICATIONS TECHNOLOGY AND CATECHESIS

A. The Impact of Communications Media in Catechesis

Television has such a dominant impact on the education and formation of children that it has sometimes been referred to as "the other parent." Adults, too, spend more time watching television now than at any other time in history. Consequently, "the use of media is now essential in evangelization and catechesis."[839]

While the developments in communication technology present challenges and potential problems for catechetical leaders and catechists, they also present many promising opportunities to proclaim the message of Jesus Christ in engaging new ways to vast numbers of people who might otherwise never hear it. They provide a new and more effective forum for proclaiming the Gospel to all nations and all people. For example, real-time captioning for the deaf as well as audio description, large print, and Braille for the blind make the Gospel more accessible to persons with those disabilities than ever before.

The communications media are useful catechetical tools, but those who use them must be aware that they have the power to shape the environment and that they are therefore multidimensional catechetical

---

[839] AN, no. 11.

resources. Media create a new culture with new languages, customs, laws, and techniques and proceed from new fundamental assumptions that often dispute or contradict the more conventional basic premises in anthropology, psychology, and ethics. They raise profound questions about the distinction between the medium and the message: the "how" and "what" of communications. In fact, the communications media are themselves suitable subject matter for catechesis.

Among the contemporary means of communication are the electronic media (television, radio, films, audio- and videocassettes, DVDs, compact discs, and an entire range of other audiovisual aids); the print media (newspapers, magazines, books, pamphlets, and parish bulletins); and computer-related media (the Internet, CD-ROMs, distance-learning materials, and interactive software programs).

In some instances, communication technology changes so rapidly that before an individual medium and its inherent implications can be properly understood, it is already obsolete. This can confuse catechists and make them hesitant to employ contemporary media in catechesis. It will be helpful for diocesan catechetical and communications personnel to explore each individual medium of communication for its catechetical potential so that they may better assist catechists in developing the specific skills needed for the effective use of these media in proclaiming the Gospel.

Contemporary communications media do not merely transmit information; they generate visual, audible, emotional, and, in some cases, entirely virtual experiences for individuals and communities. Well-planned catechesis must employ these media so that the message of Jesus Christ can be effectively communicated in the real circumstances and culture of those who seek him.

B. Instruments of Catechesis

Each individual medium of communication can and should be employed as an instrument of catechetical formation by those who have the training and formation to do so.[840] The *Code of Canon Law* urges the bishops "to endeavor to make use"[841] of contemporary means of communication.

---

840   EA, no. 72.
841   CIC, c. 822 §1; cf. CCEO, c. 651.

1. Electronic Media

Electronic media, such as radio and television, can be very effective instruments of catechesis because they can be used to present the teachings of Christ and the Church directly to the listener or viewer. The broadcast media can be particularly helpful in communicating the Gospel message to the elderly, the sick, and shut-ins, as well as to people in isolated or rural areas. The broadcast media offer fruitful opportunities for ecumenical and interfaith cooperation as well.

Diocesan and parish catechetical leaders should be aware of the obligations of the broadcast media, especially cable television stations, to provide public service airtime free of charge to eligible groups. They should work with diocesan communications personnel to explore the possibility of applying for airtime to present catechetical programs or to make spot announcements. In some cases, dioceses should pool their resources to improve the quality and frequency of catechetical programming through the broadcast media. The USCCB Committee on Communications and its Department of Communications can facilitate such collaboration and are valuable sources of information on the electronic media and their use as instruments of catechesis.

The United States Conference of Catholic Bishops has established norms for those who make presentations on Christian doctrine on radio and television programs:[842]

> For expressions of faith and moral teaching to be authentic, they must be in harmony with the doctrine and practice of the Catholic Church. Bishops, who teach with unique authority and who are the guardians of church teaching and practice, are obliged to see that these expressions are indeed faithful to church teaching.[843]

Today, most people, especially the young, expect to learn through sophisticated audiovisual media resources. Catechetical programs should incorporate the use of these media resources in their overall catechetical plans. While catechists are not expected to be media specialists, it is essen-

---

842   Cf. USCCB, *Protocol for Catholic Media Programming and Media Outlets* (Washington, D.C.: USCCB, 2000), http://www.usccb.org/comm./protocol.htm (accessed on June 12, 2003).

843   *Protocol for Catholic Media Programming and Media Outlets*, 1.

tial that they receive some training in the use of the media and develop an understanding of the implications of media in their catechesis. Catechists should be given the criteria and skills with which to evaluate the media and to grow in their awareness of the culture that the media creates. That training should include the specific characteristics of the different media, the ability to distinguish between reality and virtual reality, ways to identify the primary and secondary messages communicated in the media, and opportunities to learn how to operate the equipment. Dioceses or regions should establish media centers to assist catechetical leaders and catechists in developing the skills necessary to use multimedia resources most effectively. These media centers should incorporate the latest technological developments in the creation of communication networks, information hubs, resource centers, and libraries of media materials that can be easily and inexpensively distributed throughout the diocese or region.

2. Print Media

While the electronic media reach millions of people with instantaneous communication, the print media of many different kinds continue to be read in nearly every home and workplace in the United States. The Catholic press remains an important instrument of evangelization and catechesis for the Church in the United States. Catholic newspapers, magazines, journals, books, pamphlets, and parish bulletins can be very useful catechetical tools, especially in the catechesis of adults. Editors and publishers should provide print media that meet high standards of journalistic excellence. Their publications should faithfully present the teachings of the Church to all readers and especially help Catholics to evaluate their experiences in the light of the Gospel. The Catholic print media should foster the growth in faith of their readers and promote a community of faith among them. Special efforts should be made in Catholic publications to reach minority cultural, racial, and ethnic groups in their own languages in ways that reflect their cultural values and concerns. Editors and publishers of Catholic print media should collaborate with national and diocesan catechetical leaders in order to maximize the effective use of the Catholic press for catechetical purposes.

Catechetical leaders at all levels should work closely with members of the Catholic press to develop a comprehensive approach for the consistent coverage of catechesis and provide leads, information, stories, and photographs of newsworthy aspects of catechesis. When appropriate, catechetical leaders and catechists should collaborate with the Catholic press as planners, consultants, and writers.

In conjunction with a diocesan communications office, catechetical leaders should also provide secular publications with information on catechetical matters and be prepared to meet with journalists and editors to help them understand the Church and its ministry of evangelization and catechesis. A willingness to answer inquiries from secular journalists and to provide them with suggestions for articles and feature stories on catechetical topics is necessary. Community-based newspapers may be especially interested in covering the catechetical activities of the parishes in which their readers live and worship.

3. Computer-Related Media

The age of the computer has opened up the whole new world of cyberspace. As with all communications media, all the dimensions of cyberspace can be used as effective catechetical instruments. The United States Conference of Catholic Bishops, most dioceses, Catholic colleges and universities (and their libraries), and many Catholic organizations have established easily accessible websites that contain massive amounts of information and links to countless other websites with even more specialized information. Catechists can hold lesson-planning sessions via instant messaging, send the outline of a catechetical lesson to a group of students by e-mail, present a catechetical lesson to a specially constituted newsgroup, and discuss the points of the lesson with them in a chat room. Catechetical leaders in a diocese can hold cluster meetings on regional catechetical concerns through audio or video teleconferencing via the Internet. Diocesan offices can communicate with parish catechetical leaders via e-mail; national catechetical organizations are able to conduct their business meetings or offer opportunities for the continuing education and formation of diocesan catechetical leaders by making use of web cameras.

In addition, the Internet offers many opportunities for the personal and spiritual development of catechists. Dozens of sites provide immediate access to many enriching resources: the daily readings from Sacred Scripture, the prayers of the Church, the liturgical books, the documents of the universal Church and the United States Conference of Catholic Bishops, the writings of the Fathers of the Church and other theological texts, liturgical sources, spiritual reading, Catholic magazines and newspapers, virtual tours of the great cathedrals of the world, close-up looks and expert commentaries on religious art and architecture, and sacred music—to name but a few.

On the other hand, cyberspace also contains many disturbing obstacles to the communication of the Gospel message. "Most parents are concerned about the easy access children have to pornography on the Internet or other potentially damaging information such as hate messages and information on getting and using weapons."[844] In addition, simply because information is available on the Internet does not make that information true or reliable—even if the website claims to be Catholic. The anonymity and lack of accountability in cyberspace requires a more sophisticated level of media literacy than has ever been needed in the past. Nevertheless, the Internet's potential to proclaim the Gospel of Jesus Christ, to invite potential disciples to follow him, and to welcome them into his Church has only been partially realized. It is only limited by the imagination of contemporary evangelists and catechists.

C. The Media as a Subject of Catechesis

A diocesan or parish catechetical plan should include instruction on the communications media. It should help people develop their knowledge and skills as viewers, listeners, readers, and users so that they might understand and evaluate the media in the light of the Gospel. It should enable them to become advocates for improving the communications media and for ensuring that it contributes to the dignity of the human person.

Television and the Internet now occupy so much time in the lives of the people of the United States that catechesis should focus especially on developing a critical understanding of these media. Television viewers and Internet users need to know who sponsors, plans, and produces the programs and websites. An awareness of the techniques used by advertisers and others to influence, persuade, and manipulate is critical, as is the ability to distinguish between the image presented and the reality or distortion of reality that it represents. It is necessary that viewers understand the profit motives of commercial television and the Internet.

---

844   USCCB, *Your Family and Cyberspace* (Washington, D.C.: USCCB, 2000), 3.

Catechesis should help television viewers and Internet users become familiar with the advantages and disadvantages of the Internet. It should help parents, for example, to educate themselves about the Internet, to select an internet service provider (ISP) that offers filtered access, and to guide their children in the appropriate uses of the Internet.

70. PREPARATION AND EVALUATION OF CATECHETICAL MATERIALS

A. Preparation

All catechetical textbooks and other materials are to be prepared according to the criteria and guidelines contained in this *National Directory for Catechesis*. Authors, editors, and publishers of catechetical resources should be guided in general by the *Catechism of the Catholic Church* and the *General Directory for Catechesis*. In particular, they should adhere to the guidelines for the preparation of catechetical resources set forth in 1990 by us in *Guidelines for Doctrinally Sound Catechetical Materials*. According to that document, two basic principles, four fundamental criteria, and sixty-nine practical guidelines govern the preparation of doctrinally sound catechetical materials, and seventeen guidelines govern the presentation of sound doctrine in catechetical materials.[845]

After the promulgation of the *Catechism of the Catholic Church* in 1992, we bishops of the United States issued a further refinement of *Guidelines for Doctrinally Sound Catechetical Materials* in the *Protocol for Assessing the Conformity of Catechetical Materials with the "Catechism of the Catholic Church."* The *Protocol* sets forth specific criteria and indicators that measure the conformity of catechetical works with the *Catechism of the Catholic Church*. Authors, editors, and publishers of catechetical materials should carefully follow these criteria and indicators as they prepare catechetical textbooks and other resources. The fundamental criteria that should guide the development of catechetical materials derive from the principles of authenticity and completeness.

In order for catechetical materials to be authentic, the following criteria should be observed.

---

845   Cf. *Guidelines for Doctrinally Sound Catechetical Materials*, 7-25.

- Catechetical materials must contain nothing contradictory to the *Catechism*.
- They should encourage and assist in the development of a common language of faith within the Church. They should promote a healthy and vital Catholic identity in such a way that the believer is encouraged to hear the message clearly, live it with conviction, and share it courageously with others.
- They should make clear the wider context of teaching from which the "In Brief" sections of the *Catechism* are drawn.
- Finally, they should evince the theological structure of the *Catechism*, which
    — Is organized around the creative and saving initiative of God the Father, the salvific mission of God the Son, and the sanctifying role of God the Holy Spirit
    — Is centered on the person, life, and mission of Jesus Christ
    — Presents the continuing presence and mission of Christ in and through the Church
    — Treats the sacraments within the Paschal Mystery
    — Presents the Christian moral life in the personal and social teachings of the Church as a new life in the Holy Spirit
    — Integrates the Church's distinctive teaching on the dignity of human life within a systematic and organic treatment of the Christian moral life
    — Treats human sexuality within the context of education in sexual morality, an arrangement that now supersedes the development of separate segments on education in human sexuality apart from the moral teaching
    — Presents the Church's teaching on social justice within the broader context of Christian moral education

In order for catechetical materials to be considered complete, the doctrines of the Church should be presented as an integrated whole; the presentation of the faith should have an intrinsic cohesiveness. Specifically, materials should

- Reflect the four pillars of the *Catechism*, including the articles of the Creed, the sacraments, the commandments, and the petitions of the Lord's Prayer

- Include an appropriate presentation of the teaching's foundation in Sacred Scripture
- Reflect in an appropriate manner the variety and multiplicity of the sources of the faith found in the *Catechism*: for example, the teachings from the Councils and the Eastern and Western Fathers, liturgical texts, and spiritual writings
- Show that God's love is revealed primarily in the Word made flesh, Jesus Christ
- Give proper importance to the biblical, anthropological, liturgical, moral, and spiritual, as well as to the ecumenical and missionary dimensions of the *Catechism*[846]

In addition to these criteria, the *Protocol* offers the specific doctrinal points that must be present in the catechetical materials if they are to be in conformity with the *Catechism of the Catholic Church*. The United States Conference of Catholic Bishops offers the service of the bishop members and staff of the Ad Hoc Committee to Oversee the Use of the *Catechism of the Catholic Church* to assist the publishers of catechetical materials in ensuring that their materials are in conformity with the *Catechism*.

The preparation of catechetical materials should also be based on sound principles of catechetical methodology. They must take into account the diverse cultural, racial, ethnic, and ecclesial conditions that characterize those who will use the catechetical materials. Authors, editors, and publishers of catechetical materials are encouraged to pay close attention to the needs of the particular groups that compose the Church in the United States. While no single catechetical series or text can address the many different cultural and social groups in the United States, all catechetical series and texts must acknowledge this diversity. Sound catechetical materials present the Church's teaching not only authentically and completely, but also in ways that engage the particular individuals and communities who use them.

The *Code of Canon Law* directs that "catechisms and other writings pertaining to catechetical instruction or their translations require the approval of the local ordinary" for their publication.[847] Before publication

---

846   Cf. USCCB, *Protocol for Assessing the Conformity of Catechetical Materials with the "Catechism of the Catholic Church"* (1998).

847   CIC, c. 827 §1; cf. CCEO, c. 658 §1.

of such materials, publishers must submit them to the proper local ordinary for ecclesiastical approval.

B. Evaluation

The determination of whether certain catechetical materials may be used in a particular diocese is the responsibility of the local bishop. It is his duty "to issue norms for catechetics, [and] to make provision that suitable instruments for catechesis are available. . . ."[848] Therefore, as part of his pastoral leadership in catechesis, the bishop should establish a process for the evaluation of catechetical materials proposed for use in his diocese. That process should assess both the doctrine presented in the catechetical materials and the methods employed in the presentation of the doctrine.

The process should be developed in light of the major catechetical documents of the universal Church and those of the United States Conference of Catholic Bishops. The process should also take into account the diverse communities for whom the catechetical materials are intended, the conditions in which they live, and the ways in which they learn. In addition, the process should incorporate serious consideration of the overall diocesan catechetical plan and the specific catechetical objectives set forth in that plan.

The bishop should call upon his diocesan catechetical staff to coordinate this evaluation process. It is advisable that knowledgeable and interested pastors, principals of Catholic schools, parish catechetical leaders, teachers, catechists, and parents representing the various cultural groups and geographic regions in the diocese be invited to serve on a catechetical material selection and evaluation commission, task force, or committee. That committee should, first of all, be familiar with the list of catechetical materials that the bishops' Ad Hoc Committee to Oversee the Use of the Catechism has found to be in conformity with the Catechism. They may also want to consult with appropriate staff of the United States Conference of Catholic Bishops and the personnel of the national catechetical and educational organizations.

If necessary, the diocesan catechetical textbook evaluation committee should devise an instrument of evaluation that measures the level of effectiveness of the catechetical materials used in the parishes and

---

848   CIC, c. 775 §1; cf. CCEO, c. 621.

Catholic schools of the diocese. It should also assess how the parish cat-echetical plan assists the diocese in achieving the goals of its overall cat-echetical plan. It should determine if the catechetical materials respect the cultural diversity of the diocese.

This instrument of evaluation should be developed directly from the official documents of the universal Church and those of the Catholic Church in the United States and be based on sound catechetical method-ology. It should measure both the knowledge of the content of the faith and the implications of that knowledge for living a Christian life. As much as possible, the committee should keep the publishers of the evalu-ated catechetical materials informed of the progress of the evaluation process, provide the results of the process, and outline the criteria by which those results were determined.

71. CONCLUSION

Jesus sent the seventy disciples ahead of him to the same towns and vil-lages he would later visit. Their only equipment for the journey was their trust in him. They were not to seek comfort along the way. They had only to deliver a single message: the kingdom of God is at hand.

But the seventy disciples returned rejoicing in the success of their mission, for they had exerted the healing power of Jesus' name over the demons and proclaimed the Good News of the Kingdom of God. "I have given you the power to 'tread on upon serpents' and scorpions and upon the full force of the enemy and nothing will harm you,"[849] Jesus said to them. Their effectiveness depended entirely on him. They healed in his name; they preached in his name; they bore witness to him.

While no material resources for catechesis can ever replace the per-sonal witness of the fully-formed catechist to the person of Jesus Christ, cat-echetical aids, both new and old, that are faithful to God's Revelation of the truth in Jesus Christ and suited to the particular needs of those being cate-chized can be very effective in the hands of skilled catechists. They should fuse fidelity to authentic doctrine with adaptation to specific circumstances.

---

849   Lk 10:19.

Conclusion

You will receive power when the holy Spirit
comes upon you, and you will be my witnesses in
Jerusalem, throughout Judea and Samaria, and
to the ends of the earth. (Acts 1:7-8)

72. A NEW MILLENNIUM,
A RENEWED PASSION FOR CATECHESIS

As the Church embarks upon a new millennium of life in Christ, the power of the Holy Spirit invigorates her universal mission to proclaim the name of Jesus Christ boldly and to bear witness to him courageously throughout the whole world. His promise to accompany his disciples "until the end of the age"[850] propels our journey in faith, gives us reason for the hope that is in us,[851] and ensures the fulfillment of our mission. The jubilee message to "open wide the doors to Christ"[852] and to "put out into the deep"[853] echoes down the next thousand years of Christianity with fresh enthusiasm as a summons to all the faithful to meet Christ.

This *National Directory for Catechesis* provides the fundamental theological and pastoral principles drawn from the Church's teaching and offers guidelines for the application of those principles within the catechetical mission of the Church in the United States. We bishops of the United States have developed this directory to be a source of inspiration for the new evangelization and for a renewed catechesis in the dioceses and parishes of this country. It is our hope that its publication fires a new energy and a fresh commitment that impels the disciples of this age to hold nothing back and to reinvest themselves in catechetical initiatives

---

850   Mt 28:20.
851   Cf. 1 Pt 3:15.
852   Cf. USCCB, *Open Wide the Doors to Christ: A Framework for Action to Implement* Tertio Millennio Adveniente (Washington, D.C.: USCCB, 1997).
853   John Paul II, *Novo Millennio Ineunte* (Vatican City, 2001), no. 1, http://www.vatican.va/holy_father/john_paul_ii/apost_letters (accessed on June 12, 2003).

that ensure the faithful and enthusiastic proclamation of the Gospel. The Church "is bidden to offer catechesis her best resources in people and energy, without sparing effort, toil or material means, in order to organize it better and to train qualified personnel. This is no mere human calculation; it is an attitude of faith."[854]

Consequently, no less than a burning conviction for the proclamation of the Good News can characterize the Church's commitment to catechesis. Like St. Paul, the catechists of the new millennium cry out, "Woe to me if I do not preach" the Gospel.[855] This passion reawakens in the hearts of the faithful the zeal to share their encounter with Christ. No one who meets Christ and no one who knows Christ can keep that knowledge secret. We must proclaim him openly and confidently testify to his transforming presence in our lives. This passion stirs in all the members of the Body of Christ a reinvigorated sense of mission akin to the enthusiasm of the first Christians. This passion reawakens and redirects the Church's apostolic outreach and fuels the initiatives of the new evangelization. Such genuine passion sets the hearts of catechists on fire with the love of Christ and the desire to lead others to his light.

The new millennium stretches out before the Church like a daring adventure. The very thought of it excites the heart and quickens the step. As pilgrims on the journey, we are not alone. We have the assurance of Christ's presence in us and with us. We are united in communion with all the baptized, a communion that is nourished at the table of God's Word and the table of the Eucharist. There is no reason to be afraid, for Christ has breathed his life-giving Spirit, the Teacher within, on his followers[856] and has given his own mother, the star of evangelization, to accompany us.[857]

73. THE HOLY SPIRIT, THE TEACHER WITHIN

"The Advocate, the holy Spirit that the Father will send in my name—he will teach you everything and remind you of all that [I] told you."[858] It is the Holy Spirit who sets the hearts of believers aflame. This action of the Holy

---

854   CT, no. 15.
855   1 Cor 9:16.
856   Cf. Jn 20:19.
857   Cf. Jn 19:27.
858   Jn 14:26.

Spirit enables us to live "in Christ" and transforms us into witnesses for Christ. "The Spirit is thus promised to the Church and to each Christian as a Teacher within, who, in the secret of conscience and the heart, makes one understand what one has heard but was not capable of grasping."[859]

The power of the Holy Spirit overshadowed the Virgin Mary and brought forth the incarnate Word of God. He descended on Christ at his Baptism, led him through the desert to his mission, and anointed him to preach the Good News. Only after Jesus gave his Holy Spirit to his disciples were they able to begin the Church's work of evangelization, a work that is simply not possible without the action of God working through his Holy Spirit.

The Holy Spirit prompts, inspires, and guides all the work of the Church. He is the "soul of the Church."[860] "If the Spirit of God has a pre-eminent place in the whole life of the Church, it is in her evangelizing mission that he is most active."[861] The Holy Spirit opens the minds of the non-believers to hear the word of God and the hearts of the faithful to understand the mystery of Christ and the Church:

> It must be said that the Holy Spirit is the principal agent of evangelization: it is he who impels each individual to proclaim the Gospel, and it is he who in the depths of consciences causes the word of salvation to be accepted and understood. But it can equally be said that he is the goal of evangelization: he alone stirs up the new creation, the new humanity of which evangelization is to be the result, with that unity in variety which evangelization wishes to achieve within the Christian community. Through the Holy Spirit the Gospel penetrates to the heart of the world, for it is he who causes people to discern the signs of the times—signs willed by God—which evangelization reveals and puts to use within history.[862]

The Holy Spirit gives the evangelizer the words with which to proclaim the Gospel and gives the catechist the faith in which to form disciples. The

---

859   CT, no. 72.
860   EN, no. 75.
861   EN, no. 75.
862   EN, no. 75.

Spirit is, therefore, "the principal catechist"[863] and the "principle inspiring all catechetical work and all who do this work."[864] The Advocate whom the Father will send in Christ's name—who will teach the disciples everything and remind them of all that Christ told them[865]—is "the Spirit of truth" who "will guide you to all truth."[866]

Only the interior Teacher can initiate and sustain the work of catechesis in the Church because only he can bring about growth in faith, direct Christian life toward maturity, encourage the baptized to bear witness to Christ, and transform believers into disciples. Catechists will only be effective to the degree that they entrust themselves to the Holy Spirit, enter into communion with him, and allow themselves to become his instruments.

This *National Directory for Catechesis* hopes to channel the energy and optimism of the new millennium toward the further renewal of catechesis. This renewal should lead those who seek Christ to put fear aside, to know Christ ever more deeply, and to bear courageous witness to him in an increasingly secular world. It aims to "transform humanity from within and make it new."[867] It will only reach this horizon insofar as it is a renewal in the Holy Spirit by the Holy Spirit.

74. MARY, STAR OF EVANGELIZATION

At this moment in history, the Church has unprecedented opportunities to bring the Gospel of Jesus Christ to all people and nations. By her vocation as the Virgin Mother of God, Mary is a singular model for the Church's mission of evangelization and catechesis.

Through the power of the Holy Spirit, she bore the only-begotten Son of God, his Word made flesh, into the world in a wholly unique and unrepeatable proclamation. She was her Son's first catechist. She formed him by her human knowledge of the Scriptures and of God's plan for the salvation of his people, by her habit of daily prayer to the Father, and by her resolute surrender to his will. Mary is "a living catechism [and] the mother and model of catechists."[868]

---

863   GDC, no. 288.
864   CT, no. 72.
865   Cf. Jn 14:26.
866   Jn 16:13.
867   EN, no. 18.
868   CT, no. 73.

Mary was not only Christ's first teacher but also Christ's first disciple. Within the intimacy of family life, Christ formed her in the knowledge of his divine Sonship and of his obedience to the will of his heavenly Father. Through her intercession with Christ during the wedding at Cana, "his disciples began to believe in him."[869] Traditionally the Church has understood that Mary was present with the other disciples in the upper room when "there appeared to them tongues as of fire, which parted and came to rest on each one of them. And they were all filled with the holy Spirit."[870]

As the "Virgin of Pentecost,"[871] Mary is truly the Mother of the Church. Through her union with Christ and her unique proclamation of his Gospel, she continually draws believers to the Church and participates in the sacrifice of her Son and in the Church's work of salvation. The faithful encounter Jesus through Mary. She is the certain path to Christ. "By her complete adherence to the Father's will, to his Son's redemptive work, and to every prompting of the Holy Spirit, the Virgin Mary is the Church's model of faith and charity."[872] She is an incomparable sign of hope for the Church. She is "the image and beginning of the Church as it is to be perfected in the world to come."[873] Her pilgrimage of faith leads the pilgrim People of God on their journey to encounter the Lord and finally into communion with the Father, the Son, and the Holy Spirit.

From the time of the first evangelization of this continent, the Virgin of Guadalupe has inspired the birth of the Church in the peoples throughout the Americas. They recognize in the *mestiza* face of the Virgin of Guadalupe "an impressive example of a perfectly inculturated evangelization."[874] She is rightfully honored as the patroness of all America.

For the Church in the United States of America, the Immaculate Conception of the Blessed Virgin Mary has been the beacon that has led the faithful to encounter their Lord. As the earliest missionaries boldly proclaimed the Gospel of Christ, they preached the Virgin Mary as its perfect realization. The many diverse peoples that compose the Church in the United States continue to look to Mary, the "Star of Evangelization,"[875] to illuminate their way toward communion with the Blessed Trinity. Under

---

869   Jn 2:11.
870   Acts 2:3-4.
871   CT, no. 73.
872   CCC, no. 967.
873   LG, no. 68.
874   EA, no. 11.
875   EN, no. 82.

her title "Immaculate Conception," Mary is rightfully honored as the patroness of the United States.

May the Virgin Mary, "whose intercession was once responsible for strengthening the faith of the first disciples," obtain for the Church in the United States "the outpouring of the Holy Spirit, as she once did for the early Church."[876] Through this gift, there can be the new evangelization and a revitalized catechesis in which Christ's disciples of this new millennium can be his powerful witnesses "in Jerusalem, throughout Judea and Samaria, and to the ends of the earth."[877]

---

876   EA, no. 11.
877   Acts 1:8.

Index

A

Abortion, 25, 39, 144, 160-61, 171, 176

Absolution, 133

Adolescents, Catechesis for, 6, 11, 142, 199-202, 211, 230, 254, 264-65; *Catechism of the Catholic Church*, 201; challenges regarding, 15-17; instructional materials, 283; lack of, 13, 13n25; language suited to, 87. *See also* Children; Young Adults

Adoration, 173; of the Blessed Sacrament, 52, 150; prayer of, 112-13; sacred art and, 148

Adultery, 177-78

Adults, Catechesis for, 187-93, 257-58; *Catechism of the Catholic Church*, 190; goals, 188-89; tasks, 189-90. *See also specific topics*

Advent, 146

Angels, 113, 149

Annulment, 145

Anointing of the Sick, Catechesis for, 113, 132, 136-38

Apostles, 195-96; bishop as local apostle, 218, 248; catechesis, as model for, 66; catechists and, 217; Church founded on, 44, 60, 210; emissaries of Jesus, 3-6, 18, 40-41, 44, 66, 68, 80, 187, 245; as forgiving sins, 132; initial creedal statements, 69; Jesus as Teacher of, 19, 92; Jesus' friendship with, 92; John Paul II, Pope, on, 195-96; lives of, commemorating, 146-47; and Sacred Scripture, 70, 74, 280; and Successors of, 44-45, 53-54, 140-41; teaching of, 156; Word of God, echoing, 41. *See also* Apostles' Creed; Disciples

Apostles' Creed, 69, 72, 84, 86, 102-3, 110, 115; *Catechism*, four pillars of, 293; sacred music, 151

Apostolic Succession, 44, 210. *See also* Bishops

Architecture, 149-50, 291

Art, 115, 130, 148-49, 154, 291

Artificial Insemination, 177

Autonomy, Personal. *See* Individualism

Avarice, 180

B

Baptism, 84, 113, 157, 164, 167, 228; children and, 120-21, 197, 235; of Christ, 147, 299; Church as priestly people through, 139-40; and Church's apostolic mission, 5; and Church unity, 27, 31, 80, 298; early creedal statements and, 69; Easter, renewing baptismal promises on, 147; evangelizing the baptized and non-baptized, 47, 51; faith and, 217; Lent, renewing baptismal commitment at, 147; marrying an unbaptized person, 143; parents and, 203, 235; sacramentals and, 152; and vocation to holiness, 139. *See also* Christian Initiation; Sacraments

Baptism, Catechesis for, 120-22, 265-66; adolescents and, 199; the baptismal catechumenate, 10, 75, 115-18, 221, 265-66; and baptismal responsibilities, 104-5, 170, 190, 191, 199, 276; baptismal spirituality, fostering, 188; initiatory catechesis, 57, 75, 118-22; instructional materials, 283-86; before or after baptism, 57-58, 187-88; parents and, 197; post-baptismal, 47, 50-51, 68, 186, 187, 254

Baptismal Catechumenate, 10, 75, 115-18, 221, 251, 256, 265-66; catechetical materials, 283, 285-86

Beatitudes, 78, 85-86, 103, 158, 163, 172, 182-83, 191, 224

Bereavement, 193

Biotechnology, 25

Birth control, 144

Bishops; Episcopate, 123; apostolic succession, 44; catechetical responsibilities of, 218-20, 248-50, 266, 295; Catholic social teaching, seven key themes, 171; conferences, 122, 282; and diocesan catechetical office, 250-53; liturgy, regulation of, 129; the Magisterium, 14, 43-44; USCCB Catechetical Office, 9, 12, 247, 275, 294-95. *See also* Holy Orders; *specific topics*

Body: education of, 262; and soul, 14; suffering of, 136-38, 194

Body of Christ, Church as, 19, 52, 81, 100, 109, 124-25, 130-31, 150, 210, 298; building, 6, 29, 57, 245, 276. *See also* Church

C

Call. *See* Vocation

Calumny (Slander), 182

Campus Ministry, 197, 227-28, 271-72

Capital Punishment, 161

Catechesis, 3-7, 54-63, 67-68; apostles as model for, 66; Body of Christ, building, 56-57; contemporary challenges to, 12-17; evangelization, as central to, 67-68; goal of, 56-57; God's plan of salvation, 3-4; initiatory, 57-58; John Paul II, Pope, on, 6-7, 219, 224; methodology, 89-107, 94-97, 107, 191-93, 237, 241, 282, 284; ministry of, 53; object of, 55-56; ongoing, 58-59; organizing, 246-47; outside the parish, 267, 273-74; primary objective of, 96; renewal of, 7-8; Scripture and, 53-54, 59, 60; six fundamental tasks of, 60-62; source and sources of, 53-54; in special situations, 209-10; subject of, 56; vitality in, 8-12. *See also specific topics and areas of catechetical focus*, e.g.: Adults; Baptism; Penance

Catechetical Materials: approval process, 292-96; textbooks, requirements, 283-86

Catechism of the Catholic Church, 9, 12, 69, 70-75, 251, 281-83; adolescent catechesis, 201; adult catechesis, 190; catechetical leaders and, 225; Catholic schools, 232; formation of catechists, ongoing, 240, 242; four golden threads of, 72; four pillars of, 293; John Paul II, Pope, on, 71-72; other catechetical materials and, 286, 292, 294; youth ministry, 11. *See also specific topics*

Catechisms: local, 282-83

Catechists; Catechetical Leaders, 40, 217-18, 228-30, 234-36, 241; *Catechism of the Catholic Church*, 225; formation of, 235-43; parish leaders, 224-26. *See also specific topics*, e.g. Christian witness: of catechists

Catechumenate, 7, 118, 221, 234; children and, 119; marriage preparation as similar to, 197. *See also* Baptismal Catechumenate; *specific topics*

Catholic Colleges and Universities, 9, 225, 242, 247, 251-52, 269-72, 290

Catholic Schools, 10, 11, 13n25, 35, 230-33, 253; catechetical materials, 295-96; catechetical responsibilities of, 17, 204, 217, 231-33, 260, 262-63, 267; *Catechism of the Catholic Church*, 232; office, and diocesan catechetical office, 253; principals, 217, 231, 251, 295; teachers, 193, 232-33

Celibacy: and ordained ministry, 141. *See also* Chastity

Charity, 210, 216; Acts of Faith, Hope, and Charity, 103; "bond of perfection," 164; catechists and, 229; Catholic schools and, 11; the Christian life and, 10, 104, 156, 254; conversion and, 48; the Eucharist and, 125; initiatory catechesis and, 50; instructional materials, 284; of Jesus Christ, 182; popular piety and, 155; post-baptismal catechesis, 117-18; as theological virtue, 158, 164; twofold commandment of, 158; of the Virgin Mary, 301; vs. what is due in justice, 80; works of, encouraging, 181, 188-89. *See also* Love; Poverty

Chastity, 141, 177-78

Children, 99; autonomy at earlier ages, 39; baptism of, and evangelization of parents, 197; with cognitive disabilities, 99; dignity of, 205; evangelization, 49-50; the Fourth Commandment, 175; the Internet, 290-91; legitimacy in cases of annulment, 145; in modern society, 15-16; openness to having, 144, 177; parents, honoring, 175; parents' responsibilities to, 144, 175; television and, 286. *See also* Adolescents; Families; Parents; *specific topics*

Children, Catechesis for, 203-6, 220, 234-35, 254, 259-64; and catechetical formation, 99, 113, 119-20, 260-62; and Christian initiation, 119-20; and Eucharistic liturgy, 129-30; First Communion, 126-28; First Penance and Reconciliation, 135-36; instructional materials, 283, 285; language suited to, 87; public schools and, 261-62. *See also* Catholic Schools

Chrismation, 122-23. *See also* Confirmation

Christ. *See* Jesus Christ

Christian Faith, the, 98. *See also specific topics*

Christian Initiation, 57-58, 114-15, 117-31, 134, 147, 188; the bishop and, 266; children and young people, 119-20, 205, 254; godparents and, 265-66; the parish and,